Hello! IOS Development

Hello! IOS Development

Lou Franco
Eitan Mendelowitz

MANNING

SHELTER ISLAND

For online information and ordering of this and other Manning books, please visit
www.manning.com. The publisher offers discounts on this book when ordered in
quantity. For more information, please contact:

Special Sales Department
Manning Publications Co.
20 Baldwin Road
PO Box 261
Shelter Island, NY 11964
Email: orders@manning.com

Manning Publications Co.   Development editors: Scott Stirling, Susanna Kline
20 Baldwin Road   Technical proofreader: James Hatheway
PO Box 261   Copyeditor: Tiffany Taylor
Shelter Island, NY 11964   Typesetter: Marija Tudor
                                            Cover designer: Leslie Haimes

ISBN: 9781935182986

Printed in the United States of America
1 2 3 4 5 6 7 8 9 10 – MAL – 18 17 16 15 14 13

To my mother, Josephine,
who taught me what was truly important

—L.F.

To my love Elanit, and to Amalya,
who wants me to create a game about pirates

—E.M.

Brief contents

Contents

Preface

We came to iOS development from two different paths. Lou is a commercial software developer with a traditional CS background and degree, and Eitan has a mixed design and technology background and a career in academia. Lou is from NYC, and Eitan is from LA. We both decided to settle in a small town in Western Massachusetts, and although we live less than a mile from each other, we never met.

Troy Mott, a development editor at Manning, contacted Lou, an iOS developer and blogger, about Manning's *Hello* series. The whimsical take on programming education and Troy's persuasion convinced Lou that it would be a worthwhile project. After Lou got started, though, he became convinced he needed a coauthor, and he set out to find one.

Late last year, a chance mention of this coauthor search to a mutual friend led to an introduction to Eitan. An hour or so after sharing a coffee at a local cafe, we knew we wanted to write this book together.

So, a coauthor search that began over the web and with global reach via social networking ended the old-fashioned way—over brunch and face-to-face networking. And, in a time where virtual collaboration is the norm, we were lucky to be able to meet when we needed to.

We hope you find that our different backgrounds each bring something to this book. Between us, we have decades of programming, designing, writing, and teaching experience, and we needed it all to fit the vast domain of iOS development into something a little gentler than most other books—and, we hope, a lot more fun.

Acknowledgments

We would like to acknowledge all the folks at Manning who expertly guided us through the development and production processes: Troy Mott, Sebastian Stirling, Susanna Kline, Tiffany Taylor, Toma Mulligan, Mary Piergies, Marija Tudor, and Janet Vail, and many others who worked on our book and whose names we do not know.

Special thanks to our technical proofreader, James Hatheway, who made sure the technical content in our manuscript was up to par and who checked the code examples shortly before the book went into production.

And we would like to acknowledge our peer reviewers, who took the time to read our manuscript at various stages of its development and who provided invaluable feedback: Al Scherer, Christopher Haupt, Craig Smith, David Barkol, David Strong, Frank Ableson, Lester Lobo, Nikolaos Kaintantzis, Paul Stusiak, Peter Friese, Premkumar Rajendran, Ray Booysen, Robert McGovern, Sanchet Dighe, Santosh Shanbhag, and Sarah Forst

Finally, thanks to J.D. "Illiad" Fraser of *User Friendly* for letting Manning use the *User Friendly* cartoons in the *Hello!* series and for allowing us to put our own words in the characters' mouths in this book.

LOU FRANCO

I would like to thank my wife, Jennifer Rippel, whose seriousness and self-motivation are daily inspirations to me. Thanks also to my mom, who did so much to help me find my life's work, from touch-typing lessons to getting me the TRS-80 color computer I learned to program on. Also, thanks to my extended family for their warmth and lifelong support. Thanks to my colleagues at Atalasoft and the rest of Kofax, who make my work day rewarding and productive. And finally, a very grateful thanks to Dominique Thiebaut for introducing me to Eitan, without whom this book would not exist.

EITAN MENDELOWITZ

I would like to thank my colleagues at Smith College who encouraged me to work on this project; and my Mobile Computing students, who were both patient and helpful as I was developing material for this book. Most of all, I am grateful for the fantastic iOS developer community, whose creativity and experimentation are a continual source of inspiration.

About this book

How this book is organized

Part 1 of this book is your introduction to the world of iOS development. By the end of this section, you'll know your way around Xcode, its GUI building tools, and enough of Objective-C and object-oriented development to build an app:

- Chapter 1 introduces Xcode, the main tool you'll be using to develop iOS apps. We show you how to write Hello World!, the first app that programmers generally learn to write.

- Chapter 2 explains the model-view-controller pattern used to organize iOS apps.

- Chapter 3 introduces Objective-C so you can add interactivity to your apps. We'll take Hello World! and show you how to connect up buttons, labels, and text fields to make it more useful.

Part 2 takes you through the main features of iOS as you build three apps. Each chapter will show you all the steps, from sketching a GUI, through object-oriented design, and, finally, how to code the final result:

- Chapter 4 starts with a simple flashcard app that teaches US state capitals. By the end of the chapter, you'll know how to use outlets and actions to react to the user and simple navigation to get from screen to screen. You can adapt this app for any subject.

- Chapter 5 shows how to polish the look of your app with imagery, custom buttons, and animations.

- Chapter 6 takes the flashcard app and adds a local database using iOS's Core Data framework. You'll also learn how to show database information in table views.

- Chapter 7 starts with a new app, Disguisey, that lets you put mustaches, hats, wigs, and other disguise elements onto any photo. In this chapter, we'll cover tabbed interfaces and accessing the device's camera or photo album.

- Chapter 8 adds gesture recognition to Disguisey. You'll learn how to recognize long press, pinch, and pan gestures to interact with your face photo and disguise elements.

- Chapter 9 explores iOS's location and mapping frameworks in a new app, Parkinator. You'll learn how to show a map and put a new pin on it to remember where you parked your car.

- Chapter 10 adds networking capabilities to Parkinator. You'll learn how to show web pages and how to search and post to Twitter.

Part 3 shows you that once you've built an app, there's a lot more to learn. This part guides you around some of the tools that make sure your app doesn't have bugs and explains how to get the app into the App Store:

- Chapter 11 examines Xcode's debugger and instruments. You'll purposely add problems to your completed app and then find them using Xcode's tools.

- Chapter 12 shows you everything you need to know to get your app into the App Store.

Finally, the appendix provides a list of external resources that will help you make a great app.

What you'll need

In order to follow along with this book, you'll need to have access to a Mac with the latest Xcode on it (we'll show you how to get Xcode). This means you must have at least Lion. Most of what we do works on slightly older versions, but the screenshots may not match exactly.

If you want to put any of these apps on your iOS device, you'll need an iOS developer account, which costs $99 per year. None of the apps in this book require that—you can run all the code in the Simulator. There are parts, like taking a picture with the camera, that we show you how to fake if you aren't running on a device. If you want to make a real app, you'll need to join the developer program.

Code conventions and downloads

This book contains all the source code for three iOS apps, built up over a few chapters each. Code samples are annotated so you can easily follow along. Code in listings and in text is set in a monospaced font `like this` to distinguish it from ordinary text.

If you want to download the source, it's available on GitHub at http://github.com/loufranco/hello-ios-source. The code uses the MIT open source license so you can grab whatever you need for your projects or use any of the example apps as a starting point for your own app. You can also download a zip file with the source code for this book from the publisher's website at www.manning.com/HelloiOSDevelopment.

Author Online

Purchase of *Hello! IOS Development* includes free access to a private web forum run by Manning Publications where you can make comments about the book, ask technical questions, and receive help from the authors and from other users. To access the forum and subscribe to it, point your web browser to www.manning.com/HelloiOSDevelopment This page provides information on how to get on the forum once you're registered, what kind of help is available, and the rules of conduct on the forum.

Manning's commitment to our readers is to provide a venue where a meaningful dialogue between individual readers and between readers and the authors can take place. It's not a commitment to any specific amount of participation on the part of the authors whose contribution to the book's forum remains voluntary (and unpaid). We suggest you try asking the authors some challenging questions, lest their interest stray!

The Author Online forum and the archives of previous discussions will be accessible from the publisher's website as long as the book is in print.

About the authors

LOU FRANCO runs Atalasoft imaging and PDF toolkit development for Kofax and has been a mobile app developer for over a decade. He lives in Northampton, MA.

EITAN MENDELOWITZ is an assistant professor of computing and the arts at Smith College, where he teaches courses situated at the intersection of computer science and media art. These include "Seminar on Mobile and Locative Computing," which uses iOS as its development platform. Eitan is currently developing mobile platforms to enable citizen science.

About *Hello!* books

At Manning, we think it should be just as much fun to learn new tools as it is to use them. And we know that fun learning gets better results. Our *Hello!* Series demonstrates how to learn a new technology without getting bogged down in too many details. In each book, *User Friendly* cartoon characters offer commentary and humorous asides, as the books moves quickly from Hello World! into practical techniques. Along the way, readers build a unique hands-on application that leverages the skills learned in the book.

Our *Hello!* books offer short, lighthearted introductions to new topics, with the authors and cartoon characters acting as your guides.

Part 1

Hello! iPhone

This part of the book will help you get started being an iPhone application developer. By the time you're finished with this part, you'll have done the following:

- Seen the Apple Developer website and tools
- Set up your machine for development
- Learned about the basic concepts required to create applications
- Created two simple applications

Chapter 1 is focused on getting your machine ready for development. You'll learn to navigate the Apple Developer website, download and install the Apple tools that you need to create apps, and take a tour through the two most important tools, Xcode and Interface Builder. At the end of the chapter, you'll have created a Hello World! application.

Chapter 2 will help you start thinking about iPhone apps like a developer. You'll begin by learning the basics of the model-view-controller model of GUI development and object-oriented design. Then we'll move on to the topic of object lifetime, and you'll apply what you've learned.

Then, in chapter 3, we'll move on to the syntax of Objective-C, the programming language you use to write apps. We'll end by showing you how to use these new concepts in Xcode and Interface Builder to create a slightly more complex application.

Hello! iPhone

This chapter covers

- *The Apple Developer website*
- *Installing the iPhone SDK*
- *Introduction to Xcode and Interface Builder*
- *Hello, World!*

The iPhone is a fun and powerful phone, and no matter how many apps there are in the App Store, everyone has an idea for another one. It's great that there's finally a combination of a large market, a distribution model, and a way to get paid that makes it easy for hobbyist program-mers to make a little money (or in some cases, a lot of money) with sim-ple apps.

Look at iSteam. It's an app that lets you steam up your phone with your breath and that squeaks when you run your finger across it, and it was written in seven days by first-time iPhone programmers. It made $100,000 in its first three months in the App Store.

(*BREATH* *BREATH* *BREATH*)

The last new platform that caused this much excitement was the web. Today, we have so many tools that can help us make websites without knowing any HTML that it's hard to remember we used to have to know how to pro-gram to create even the simplest site.

I USED TO GET HTML SNIPPETS FROM WEBMONKEY.

But HTML is a nearly ideal way to get started with programming. Its structure looks like what you see in the browser, and you can create simple websites know-ing just a few tags and using Notepad and a browser. And if you see a page you like, you can view its source and learn how it was done. This combination of simple coding, an easy on-ramp, cheap tools, and lots of avail-able examples makes it possible for many people to learn to program in HTML.

iPhone programming, unfortunately, isn't as easy. iPhone apps aren't just text you can create in any editor, so you need to use the tools that Apple provides to help you create your app. And although lots of code samples are available on the web, there aren't many complete examples to learn from.

We wrote this book to solve these problems by offering simple expla-nations of the concepts used by Apple's tools and step-by-step instruc-tions for complete applications. Let's get started.

Turning your Mac into an iPhone app factory

Apple does a lot to make sure Macs are useful for a wide variety of things right out of the box. Your Mac can organize digital photos, play music, make DVDs, and edit videos, and it evens supports a bunch of programming language environments like Java, Python, and Ruby. But if you want to make iPhone apps, you need to set it up.

To start, visit https://developer.apple.com/devcenter/ios, and register for a developer account. The Apple developer site has everything you need to create iPhone apps. The most important thing you need is the developer tools, but you can also find the full SDK documentation, sample code, and video tutorials. After reading this book, you'll understand a lot of the standard documentation much better.

With the release of Xcode 4.2, you now get Xcode from the Mac App Store, so it's easy for everyone to get started. You could start programming without the developer account, but it's free, so you should go ahead and sign up.

If you want to sell apps in the App Store, you'll need to pay to join the iOS Developer Program. You'll also need to join to test your app on your own devices. Apple charges $99 per year to join its developer program. But hey, it's not that much for a hobby, especially one that might make you

99 DOLLARS! ...
A YEAR!

money, and you can have as many apps as you like without paying any more.

Don't worry: for almost all the code samples in this book, just being a registered developer will be fine. Apple provides an iPhone simulator that works on your Mac, so you don't need to have your apps on your device to learn how to make them. Of course, some features of the iPhone aren't in the simulator (don't shake your laptop!). If you want to use those features in your app, you'll need to join the iOS Developer Program so you can put your app on your phone. When we get to one of those features, it will be clearly marked.

I WILL WHITELIST YOU FOR NOW, BUT DON'T MAKE ME ADD YOU TO MY KILL FILE.

Register as a developer on the iOS Dev Center home page. Registering begins with filling out a simple multistep form that consists mostly of contact information, and ends with an email verification form. Once you've completed the process, Apple will send you an email with instructions for activating your account (you might need to add Apple to your whitelist or check your spam folder).

After you've received the email and followed its directions, you're ready to log in to the iOS Dev Center and look at what you can access. Now you're ready to go get Xcode.

Installing the iPhone SDK

Nearly every great iPhone application was written with the same tools you're going to use. You might not be as good at using them yet, but it's not like you're trying to match Clapton on a toy ukelele. You have a long way to go, but you won't be held back by inferior equipment.

To get these tools, open the Mac App Store and search for Xcode. When you find it, click the Install button and give your credentials.

A large file will begin to download. When it's done, the installation will start.

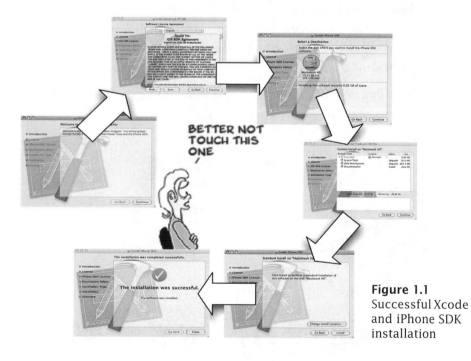

Figure 1.1
Successful Xcode and iPhone SDK installation

The installer will guide you through the process. When you get to the Installation Type page, you should choose the default settings for now and let the installer proceed with a standard installation. Once you're done with accepting the licenses and other setup, the installer will install Xcode and all the other tools you need. It's a long installation and could take half an hour to complete.

When it's done, let's look at what you have. If you've installed anything else on your Mac, you know you can find the installed application in your Applications folder. Xcode is no exception: you can find it in /Applications.

When you install Xcode and the iOS SDK, you get all the tools you need to create Mac, iPhone, and iPad applications. The same tools and

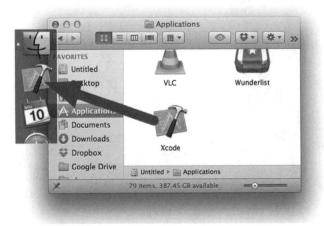

Figure 1.2
Location of Xcode on your Mac

concepts you learn can be applied to these other platforms. In the developer applications folder, you'll see a lot of applications; you'll be spending the most time with Xcode. It's so important, that it's a good idea to put it in your Dock right now. You can do this by dragging it from the Finder window onto your Dock.

WE USED TO CALL THAT "MAKING AN ALIAS."

Running Xcode for the first time

DOES LOGO COUNT?

With Xcode on your Mac, you need to learn a little about it before you make your first app. If you've ever used another programming environment, some of this will feel familiar. If you haven't, Xcode is about as complex as Photoshop, AutoCAD, Final Cut Pro, or any professional software used to create complex things. Even software like Access or Excel is a good starting point if you've created macros or added forms to make simple apps.

Xcode is an *Integrated Development Environment* (IDE for short). It has

* *An editor*—For writing your code
* *A GUI editor*—For drawing your application's screens
* *A compiler*—To build applications from your code
* *A debugger*—To probe your running applications
* *A profiler*—To collect data on how your applications perform

Over the course of this book, you'll learn about all those parts, but for your first app you just need to know a little about Xcode's file organization and a little more about drawing a user interface. Each app you write will introduce a little more.

Using application templates

Your entire project is managed by Xcode, and it's a lot bigger than you might expect. Even the simple app you're going to create has nine files. Luckily, Xcode will do some of the work for you.

Start Xcode by clicking the icon in your Dock. When it starts, it shows a welcome screen. Choose Create a New Xcode Project. When you do, you'll see these templates.

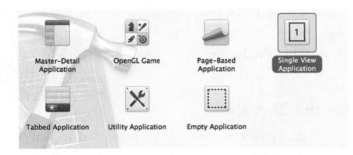

Figure 1.3
The New Project dialog in Xcode

To make your life easier, Xcode comes with application *templates*. A template is a set of files that has all the code to get you started with some common application types. It's like a less annoying version of the way Clippy makes a letter for you in Word.

These are the most important templates:

Figure 1.4 Single View Application

A single-view application starts with one view and has no built-in navigation. It's a good starting point if your application doesn't use one of the common navigation styles. This would be the template to use to make the Calculator app that's on your phone.

A tabbed application is good for any application that uses a tab bar as its main navigation. The iPod, App Store, and iTunes applications on your phone are examples of this style.

Figure 1.5 Tabbed Application

A page-based application lets you build apps that look like books and have built-in page turning animation and navigation.

Figure 1.6 Page-Based Application

A utility application has two views: a main one with your app and another for the app's settings that is meant to be on the back of the main view. An info button is put on the main view to flip it over. You can see this style used in the Weather and Stocks apps.

Figure 1.7 Utility Application

An empty application starts with nothing except the bare bones of an application. If you don't even want the code that a single-view application has, this is the one to use.

Figure 1.8 Empty Application

The easiest to understand and use is the single-view application. Click it, and then click the Next button. Xcode will prompt you for a product name, an organization name, and a company identifier. For the product name, use Hello. Enter your full name for the organization name. Add a domain name you own as the basis for your identifier. If you don't have

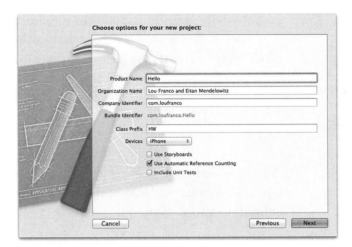

Figure 1.9
Saving your project

a domain name, use anything you think will be unique. Put in HW as your class prefix (which is short for "Hello World"), and choose the iPhone as your device. Check Use Automatic Reference Counting, uncheck Use Storyboards and Include Unit Tests, and click Next.

When you click Next, you'll be prompted for a location to save and source-control parameters, which you can turn off if you don't want to save your project in a local source-control repository right now. If you don't use source control (or know what it is), uncheck the box.

The Use Automatic Reference Counting option tells Xcode to automatically manage memory allocation and deallocation. Storyboards are a fantastic tool for creating and organizing complicated projects, but they're a bit much for smaller apps. You'll begin using them in chapter 7; but in the meantime, its important to learn how to create projects without them. Unit tests are a software engineering tool that is beyond the scope of this book.

Learning Xcode's user interface

Xcode's main window will now come up. Xcode can be overwhelming at first, even for the simplest of projects. As you use it, it will feel increasingly natural. You'll learn more and more about Xcode's features as you need them. This figure shows you what you need to know right now.

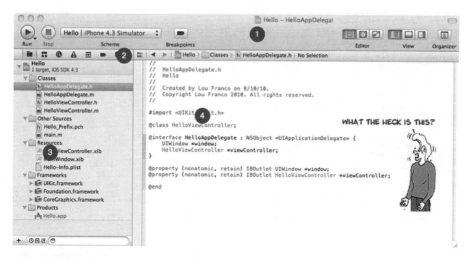

Figure 1.10 Xcode's main window

❶ *Toolbar* — The most common tools you'll need.

❷ *Navigator tools* — Used to change how you navigate your project. The default, and most common view, is the Project Navigator.

❸ *Project Navigator* — Listing of all source, outputs, and other information about the project. It's used to navigate to the various parts of the project.

❹ *Editor* — The place where you'll type in code. It shows the file currently selected in either of the two file-navigation controls. In the figure, the editor is shown after we selected HWAppDelegate.h.

To help you be productive in Xcode, we'll go over the menus, hotkeys, and views that let you edit a project.

Looking at Xcode's menus

Xcode's menus control various aspects of creating applications. The File, Edit, View, Window, and Help menus are similar to what you'd find in most Mac applications. The main things you do in Xcode are manage your project, build your application, and test it. To do that, you'll use the Navigate, Editor, and Product menus.

Figure 1.11 Navigate menu

The Navigate menu has items that let you get around your project efficiently. The best way to use this menu is to learn the hotkeys for each action.

Figure 1.12 Editor menu

The Editor menu is useful when you're writing code and gives you ways to get extra help while editing.

Figure 1.13 Product menu

You use the Product menu to build and run your projects.

Running Xcode's iPhone simulator

You haven't really done anything yet, but the Single View Application template created a fully working application for you. It's just a blank gray window, but let's build and run it to see how it works. To build the app, press Cmd-B (or choose Product > Build). The message *Build Hello: Succeeded* should appear at the top of Xcode, like this.

Figure 1.14 Build results in Xcode

There are a lot of ways to run the application. To get you used to the one that's the most useful during development, press Cmd-R (or choose Product > Run).

The iPhone simulator will come up with a blank gray screen. Now is a good time to look at the simulator. To simulate turning the iPhone into landscape mode, press Cmd-Left (or choose Hardware > Rotate Left);

and to put it back, press Cmd-Right (or choose Hardware > Rotate Right). You can also click the Home button at the bottom of the phone and see an iPhone home screen with a few apps, including Safari, installed.

Play around with the simulator to get a feel for how it works. When you're done, quit the simulator so you learn how to do more with this app.

Figure 1.15   The iPhone simulator running the Single View Application template

Introducing Interface Builder

CAN'T WAIT UNTIL CODINK.

CODE CODE DEBUG

Interface Builder is the part of Xcode that lets you draw your application. Well, not really. You'll still have to write code to make your apps do anything, but for a lot of your screens, you'll be able to use Interface Builder to make them.

To start Interface Builder, go to the Project Navigator tree in Xcode, and click HWViewController.xib. The file will open in Interface Builder, and you'll see this:

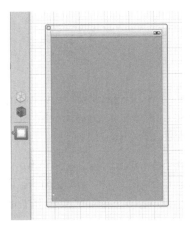

Figure 1.16
Interface Builder
main editor

This is Interface Builder's main editor, and it lets you navigate through the parts of the user interface. The left side is the dock, and the editor shows the actual UI you're building. There are inspector panes to show you more detail. You get to them by showing the utilities pane with this toolbar or pressing Opt-Cmd-0.

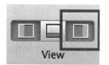

Figure 1.17
Xcode's Show Utilities toolbar

Figure 1.18
The Attributes Inspector

That will give you access to all the inspectors. The fourth one, the Attributes Inspector, can be used to change how the view looks.

You use inspectors to change the selected part of the view. The easiest thing to change is the background color. Do it by clicking the gray rectangle to the right of the word Background in the inspector. The Colors dialog will come up, and you can change the color in a variety of ways. Choose a new color, and then run the new application by pressing Cmd-R.

Figure 1.19 Interface Builder Colors dialog

The last utility to take a quick look at is the Object Library. It should have come up automatically, but you can open it with Ctrl-Opt-Cmd-3 (or by choosing View > Utilities > Show Object Library). The Library is a way of browsing all the available controls you can add to your view. The objects in the Library are what you'll add to your view in order to define your user interface.

There's a lot more to Interface Builder. You probably noticed that every utility we looked at had multiple tabs. We'll discuss those when you need them, but you now know enough to make your first app, Hello, World! —so let's make it.

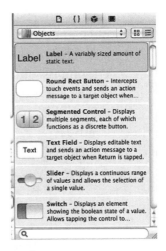

Figure 1.20
Interface Builder's Object Library Dialog

Making Hello, World!

You're going to make a lot of apps in this book, each one building on the ideas you've learned. The first of these apps is called Hello, World!, and it's the simplest app you can make that does something. It may not seem like much, but there are apps in the App Store that are just a variation on it. One of the most famous was the I Am Rich app, which was just a picture of a ruby and which sold a couple of times for $1,000 each before Apple removed it.

Even though this app is simple, we suggest that you build it the same way you'll build all apps, and begin with a drawing and a simple description of what the app does. It would be a good idea to get some graph paper for sketching your apps. The ratio of a pre-iPhone 5 screen is 320 wide by 460 high, so try to keep that ratio in your drawings (the iPhone 5's ratio is 320 by 568). Here's a sketch of Hello, World!:

Figure 1.21
A sketch of Hello, World!

After you sketch the views, the next thing to do is list the behaviors, transitions, data, and external resources that the app has or uses. Your app is non-interactive, has no other views, stores no data, and accesses no other resources, so that's easy to specify.

Let's build the app. In Interface Builder, follow these steps:

1 Drag Label from the Object Library onto the view.

2 Double-click the label, and type `Hello, World!`.

3 With the label selected, bring up the Attributes Inspector (Opt-Cmd-4).

4 Change the font or color to your preference.

5 Save.

It should look like this:

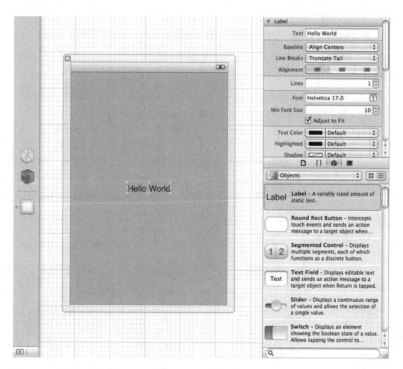

Figure 1.22 Hello, World! in Interface Builder

Press Cmd-R to build and run the application. The iPhone simulator will open with your app.

Hello, World! is now complete. You might want to take a second to do a little celebratory dance before we move on. Go ahead. No one's looking.

Figure 1.23
Hello, World! in the iPhone simulator

Editing, building, and running

You've now seen most of the major pieces of iPhone development and have used Xcode and Interface Builder to draw, build, and run your first application. Making apps is a constant iteration of this edit-build-run cycle. You'll be doing it over and over, and eventually you'll have completed apps. Each time through the cycle, you'll learn a little more about how to use the tools.

The one thing you haven't seen is how to code in Objective-C, which is the way you can get your application to react to touches, change views, use data, and access the resources and features of the iPhone. In the next two chapters, you'll learn the underlying concepts of object-oriented programming, how they work in the iPhone, and how to write code in Objective-C.

Thinking like an iPhone developer

This chapter covers

- *Model-view-controller*
- *Object-oriented programming*
- *Object lifetime*

There's only so much you can do with Xcode and Interface Builder without code, but before we get to Objective-C, you need to know more about

how iPhone apps are structured. Once you understand that, it will be easier to understand how to code your app. Think of this as the part of *The Karate Kid* where Miyagi has Daniel painting fences and waxing floors. Or when Yoda makes Luke carry him through the swamps of Dagobah. Or maybe you're more of a *Sound of Music* fan. If so, let's start at the very beginning.

21

Using model-view-controller to dissect apps

When Maria danced through the streets of Salzburg with the von
Trapp children, she taught them how to sing using the song "Do-Re-
Mi." Similarly, iPhone development can best be understood with the
letters *M-V-C*. MVC, or model-view-controller, is a common way of
thinking about apps and is used by web programmers, Windows and
Mac programmers, and mobile app programmers (like us). It's useful
for any application that has a user interface.

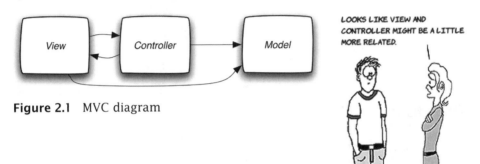

Figure 2.1   MVC diagram

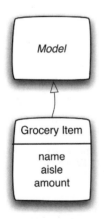

Figure 2.2
Model diagram

A *model* is anything in your app that isn't related to the user
interface. In applications that store data, models are used to
represent the things that you store. For example, imagine a
grocery list application where you keep track of everything
that you want to buy, where it is in the store, and how much
of it you need. A model can be used to represent the items
you want to buy. Each item has a name (such as "Bananas"),
the aisle (such as "Produce"), and the amount you want to
buy (such as "One bunch").

A *view* is what you see on the screen and interact with. When you draw sketches of iPhone apps or use Interface Builder, you're drawing the view. To make things easier later, you keep each part of the user interface in a separate view. That means each button you click, text box you fill in, or check box you check is its own view. Views do more than just show the user what is going on—they're also responsible for letting the rest of your application know they're being touched. On that grocery list, the list you see is the view. Each item is in its own view, and when you touch the item to cross it off the list, its view is the part of the app that is first to know.

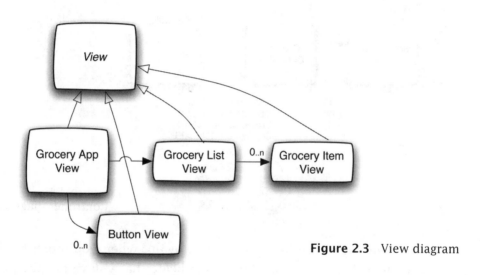

Figure 2.3   View diagram

A *controller* is where you coordinate everything. Your controller decides what to do when a button is clicked, when to show a different view, and what models should be changed. If you were to draw a flowchart of how your app works, a lot of that would be represented in your controllers.

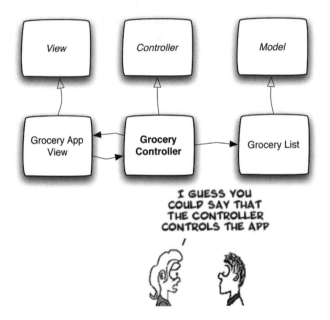

I GUESS YOU
COULD SAY THAT
THE CONTROLLER
CONTROLS THE APP

Figure 2.4
Controller diagram

So, using a grocery list app example again, when you touch the Grocery Item View on your phone to indicate that you've put the item in your shopping cart, the view tells the Grocery Item View Controller that it's been touched. The controller tells the model to remember that it's been taken, and then it tells the view to show it crossed out.

TALK OF GROCERIES IS
MAKINK ME HUNGRY.

The best way to learn MVC is to open apps on your phone and start seeing their features as models, views, and controllers. Every app on your phone can be broken down into these parts. You don't have to do it this way, and your app will still work if you put something in the wrong place, but it's much easier to understand and work on your application if you keep the components straight.

Thinking about apps as models, views, and controllers

Maria told us that once we knew the notes to sing, we could sing most anything. That applies to MVC and iPhone development too. Now that you know MVC, you know something about how every app is made. Again, they might not be made this way, but let's not let that stop us.

Let's look at one of the built-in apps on your iPhone. The easiest to understand is Calculator. Play with the app a little, and think about the kinds of things that are happening in it.

The app starts by displaying a grid of buttons that have numbers and symbols on them. It also has a result area that starts with the number 0 in it. Let's call the whole area of the screen the *calculator view*. It uses *button views* to draw buttons and a *result view* to show the result. Each view—the calculator view, button views, and result views—have to be able to draw themselves on the screen. To do that, they all need to know their position and size.

Figure 2.5
The Calculator app

Button views also need to know what text to show and what color they are. Position, size, content (such as text), and color are common things that views need to know.

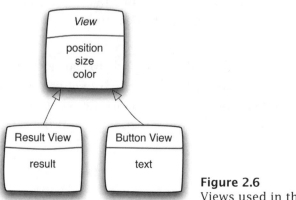

Figure 2.6
Views used in the Calculator app

Once you're running the app, several buttons are created, each with a location, a size, content, and a color. For example, the 7 button is near the left and about halfway down. It's black. It has the number seven drawn on it in white, and it's about the size of the tip of your finger. The Calculator app creates 22 button views on itself when it starts.

Now, click the 7 button. The result view displays 7. Click 3, and the result view now shows 73. Using what you know about MVC, here's how it works.

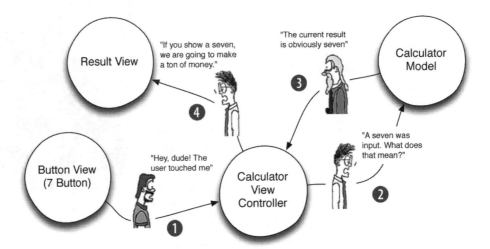

Figure 2.7   How MVC works in the Calculator app

This continues as you push buttons. The model creates the numbers from the button presses and does the arithmetic, the view shows the answers and detects the touches, and the controller figures out what happens next.

This might seem complicated, but by doing this for larger projects, you can keep related code together. Also, by keeping views separate from logic in the models and controllers, you can change what the app looks like by replacing the views and keep the rest of the app the same.

Think that's far-fetched? Turn your iPhone 90 degrees.

Turned 90 degrees, the app is still a calculator. There's no reason why the models and controllers you created can't be reused. By making sure the view of the app is separate, you can create an alternate view to use in landscape. Separation allows you to vary each part independently.

Figure 2.8
The Calculator app in landscape

A lot of apps come with the phone, so take a look at them. If you're bored, download a game and goof off for an hour (we mean, figure out how MVC is used in it). When you're done, take the test in the next section.

Test yourself on models, views, and controllers

These are some of the things the various apps that come with your iPhone do. Would the code for the feature be in the model, the view, or the controller?

Table 2.1   Test yourself

App feature	Model, view, or controller
1. In the Clock app, the current time is found in a …	
2. In the Photos app, when you resize a photo by pinching it, your pinch is detected by a …	
3. In the Photos app, when you swipe a photo, the app interprets that to mean to go to the next photo. The code for that is in a …	
4. To unlock your phone, you need to slide a …	
5. In the Contacts app, your best friend's name and phone number are stored in a …	
6. In the Calendar app, the current date is drawn in blue by the …	
7. In the Calendar app, when you touch the right arrow, the … decides to go to the next month.	
8. In the Phone app, when you click a contact, the … dials the phone for you.	
9. In the iPod app, the titles of the albums are found in a …	
10. In the Weather app, the sun and rain icons are shown in a …	

1-M, 2-V, 3-C, 4-V, 5-M, 6-V, 7-C, 8-C, 9-M, 10-V

NO PEEKINK!

If you've done well on this pop quiz, you're ready to learn more about a broader concept called *object-oriented pro-gramming*. If not, it might be a good idea to reread this section, because under-standing MVC is essential to understand-ing how iPhone apps are organized. When you're ready, go get a snack. You deserve it.

Breaking down your applications to models, views, and controllers is a start, but there are two more concepts that will help get you from there to an iPhone app. The first is understanding how the various parts of your apps communicate with each other, and the second is understanding how to take each part (whether it's a model, a view, or a controller) and break it down further. To do that, you need to learn about object-oriented design and message passing. Let's get started.

Designing apps with objects

When Steve Jobs was between his two Apple stints, he headed a company called NeXT. Apple acquired NeXT and used its software as a basis for Mac OS X, Xcode, Objective-C, and much of what makes up the system software for Apple's products. In 1994, while still at NeXT, Jobs did an interview with *Rolling Stone* where he extolled the virtues of object-oriented programming, a style of programming he saw at Xerox on the same day he first saw the graphical user interface. Here is an excerpt from that interview.

OBJECTS ARE MAGICAL AND REVOLUTIONARY, AND WE'VE GOT THEM FOR AN UNBELIEVABLE PRICE!

Would you explain, in simple terms, exactly what object-oriented software is?

Objects are like people. They're living, breathing things that have knowledge inside them about how to do things and have memory inside them so they can remember things. And rather than interacting with them at a very low level, you interact with them at a very high level of abstraction, like we're doing right here.

Here's an example: If I'm your laundry object, you can give me your dirty clothes and send me a message that says, "Can you get my clothes laundered, please." I happen to know where the best laundry place in San Francisco is. And I speak English, and I have dollars in my pockets. So I go out and hail a taxicab and tell the driver to take me to this place in San Francisco. I go get your clothes laundered, I jump back in the cab, I get back here. I give you your clean clothes and say' "Here are your clean clothes."

You have no idea how I did that. You have no knowledge of the laundry place. Maybe you speak French, and you can't even hail a taxi. You can't pay for one, you don't have dollars in your pocket. Yet I knew how to do all of that. And you didn't have to know any of it. All that complexity was hidden inside of me, and we were able to interact at a very high level of abstraction. That's what objects are. They encapsulate complexity, and the interfaces to that complexity are high level.

When your app is running, each piece, whether it's a model, a view, or a controller, is an *object*. As Steve Jobs described, each has memory inside it and a list of messages it understands. To use an object, you need to have access to it and to send it a message. It will do the work associated with the message and provide a result. Most messages need you to provide something along with them. In the laundry example, your dirty clothes are what you provide to the message, and the result of the message is the bag of clean clothes. The things you provide are called *arguments* or *parameters*, and the result is called the *return value*.

To describe what an object can remember and what messages it understands, you create a *class* in Xcode. It can be confusing to remember the difference between classes and objects. Just remember that classes are what you write in Xcode. They're the blueprints. Xcode takes those blueprints and creates an app. When you run the app, it creates the objects that are the "living, breathing things" that make the app do something. Multiple objects can be made from the same class. For example, most of the button objects you see in an app are made from one class.

To help keep things straight, in diagrams in this book, classes will be in rectangles and objects will be in circles. Here are the parts of a class.

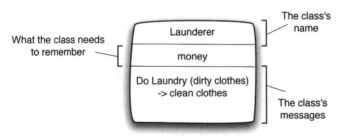

Figure 2.9 Classes

You create classes in Xcode to describe the objects that will do what you want your app to do. In your class, you define the messages that each object will be able to understand and what it needs to remember.

But objects need to collaborate in order to get their work done. To do that, you need to connect them.

Establishing class relationships

If objects are living and breathing, they're going to want to get into relationships with each other. This is an important part of object-oriented programming, because without knowing another object, you can't send a message to it. Our job, as programmers, is to make introductions, help the objects make small talk, convince them to form long-term relationships, and then, eventually, help them break up.

The weakest relationship is the *uses-a* relationship. All this means is that in some way, one class uses another class. Usually, one of its messages takes a class as an argument or returns a class. Or it could be that while doing the message, a class needs temporary access to an object of the other class. If that's the only way two objects are related, we show that with a dashed arrow, like so:

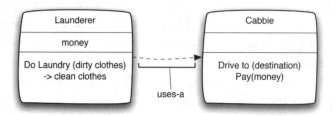

Figure 2.10
uses-a relationship

The next type of relationship is *has-a*, which we represent with a closed arrowhead. Sometimes it's important to see other details, like how many of another object each object has and what that object calls the other object it has. If you don't see a number by the arrowhead, you can assume the object has only one of the other object.

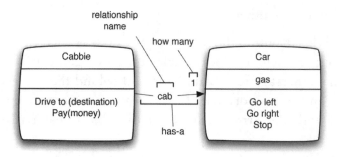

Figure 2.11
has-a relationship

The has-a relationship means the class could be considered an integral part of the one that has it. For example, a person has eyes, or a car has wheels. Or it could be that one class just has to keep track of another, like the way a person has a car. In the latter case, the has-a relationship can be mutual—the person has a car, and the car has an owner.

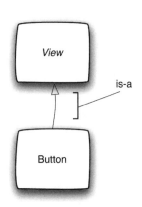

Figure 2.12
is-a relationship

The most intimate relationship is *is-a*. This is a special relationship that means one class can perform every message that another one can, plus more. In addition, the class can choose to change the messages so that each message can do more. This is allowed as long as the changed messages do everything that the original message promised it would do. We represent this relationship with an open arrowhead. We won't use it as much as the other relationships, but the iPhone SDK uses it all the time. You saw this type of relationship with views earlier.

Buttons, tables, and labels are all views, so they remember everything that views remember and handle all messages that views handle. This relationship is also called *inheritance*, and the class is said to *inherit* its parent's or *superclass's* messages. If the message is changed in the child, or *subclass*, that is called *overriding* the message.

These diagrams show you how classes are related, which tells you which messages they can send. What's more interesting is to know which messages they *do* send. This is something that happens when the app is running, so it involves the objects, not the classes. We can use a diagram like the one on the next page to show the objects and the messages they send to each other.

To understand this diagram, the first thing to notice is what the objects are that are represented by individual circles. To get your laundry done, you send a message to a Launderer, and behind the scenes, they use a Cabbie and a Laundromat. Each arrow represents a message being passed, with the arrow starting at the object that passes the

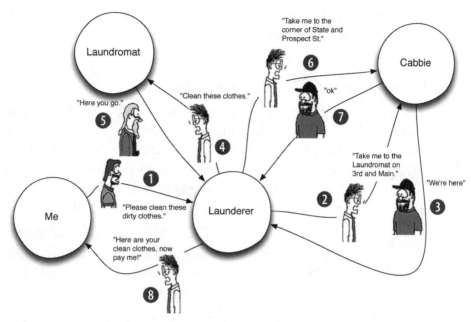

Figure 2.13 Object interaction diagram for doing laundry

message and pointing to the object that receives the message. The numbers determine the order of the messages:

❶ You ask the Launderer to do your laundry. You provide dirty clothes as a parameter.

❷ The Launderer hails a taxi and asks the Cabbie to go to the Laundromat.

❸ The Cabbie drives to the destination and lets you know when you're there.

❹ The Launderer asks the Laundromat to clean the dirty clothes.

❺ The Laundromat returns clean clothes.

❻ The Launderer hails a taxi to get back.

❼ The Cabbie drives the Launderer back.

❽ The Launderer returns your cleans clothes to you.

Eventually, once you've worked out your class and object structures, you need to put them in Xcode. If you poked around the Hello World! project in chapter 1, then you've seen some files that were automatically generated, and by now, some of their names, like HWViewController.h, are starting to make a little more sense. You know enough to understand them better.

Organizing classes in headers and modules

In Xcode, each class has two parts: a *header* and a *module*. The header is like a table of contents. It contains a list of everything that objects of this class can do, but no details about how they do it. To use one of a class's objects, you only need to know what's in the header. If you poke around Xcode's Project Navigator, you'll find headers stored in .h files. The content of the header file is called the *interface* of the class.

The modules (which are put in .m files) are the actual details of how to do the tasks indicated in a message. The content of a module is called the *implementation* of the class.

Many times, in the implementation, you send messages to other objects. For example, in the Launderer class's module, inside the "do my laundry" message, you'd find that it sends messages like "hail a taxicab" and "talk to the driver." As you have seen, the messages for the driver would be in another class, and the cab's messages would be in yet another. For example, the driver understands "take me to the laundromat," and the car understands "go left," "go right," and "stop."

One nice thing about all this is that it makes it possible for you to get some of your classes from other people. Maybe you're working on a team, and you're great at writing code for a car, and your teammate is great at writing cabbie code. They don't need to know how the car does anything, and you don't need to know the directions to the laundromat. You each work on the modules you understand, and the classes will work together just fine.

PHONE! WHAT STATE
AM I IN?

CONFUSION

And the best part is that all the features of the phone are available for you to use this way. You send the Camera object a "take a picture" message and the GPS object a "Where am I?" message. You can concentrate on the parts that make your app unique.

Objects can be in a lot of relationships. But every relationship story has a beginning and an end. How do these objects meet? How do they break up? How are they born, and when do they die? These questions are some of the most important of object-oriented programming, and we'll get to them in the next section. In the meantime, now might be a good time to strengthen your own relationships. Call an old friend, say hi, catch up.

Avoiding crashes by understanding object lifetime

In this chapter, so far, everything has been a guideline. If you don't get it right, your app will probably still work. You don't have to use MVC, and you can put all your code in one giant class. It will be hard to make improvements, but the iPhone doesn't care about that. The same isn't true for this section. If you don't get object lifetime right, your app will eventually crash.

Before you can send a message to an object, the object needs to be created. If you never intend to send another message to it, it should be destroyed. This is because each object uses system memory while it's alive. Your iPhone has a lot less memory than a desktop or laptop, so if the iPhone senses that you aren't letting your objects die, it will kill your app. If you destroy an object and then another object sends it a message, the iPhone will kill your app because it's talking to dead objects. There are other reasons why iPhone apps crash, but these are the most common. Luckily, with Automated Reference Counting (ARC), which we'll always use in this book, you don't have to do this yourself; but it's good to understand what's going on in case you run into problems, which is still possible.

1, 2, 3, 4, C'MON BABY
RETAIN THAT OBJECT
5, 6, 7 TIMES
(TUNE OF "123" BY GLORIA ESTEFAN)

The first thing to know is that Objective-C gives every object a count for you to use to keep track of how many objects are in a relationship with it. ARC is responsible for increasing this count whenever an object enters a relationship and decreasing it when the object relationship breaks up. The count is called the *retain count*. ARC increases it by sending a *retain* message and decreases it by sending a *release* message.

Creating an object is called *allocating* it (as in, "allocating memory for it") and destroying it is called *deallocating* it. When an object is allocated, it's assumed that the object will immediately enter into a relationship, so its retain count starts at one. When an object has a retain count of zero, it's sent a deallocate message to free the memory associated with it.

As a result of the deallocate message being called, ARC knows that the objects it has are no longer being referenced, and it sends them a release message to indicate that the has-a relationship is about to end (because the containing object won't exist). If no other object is using the object, its retain count becomes zero as well, causing a deallocate, and so on.

BORN WITH RETAIN COUNT ONE
I WAS BORN WITH RETAIN COUNT ONE
("BORN IN THE USA" BY SPRINGSTEEN)

The object-lifetime diagram on the next page shows how the Launderer example might work. Objects start to exist after they're allocated, and they live until they're sent a release message that brings their retain count to zero. In this case, you have a simple, balanced allocate and release, remembering that the allocate created the object with a retain count of

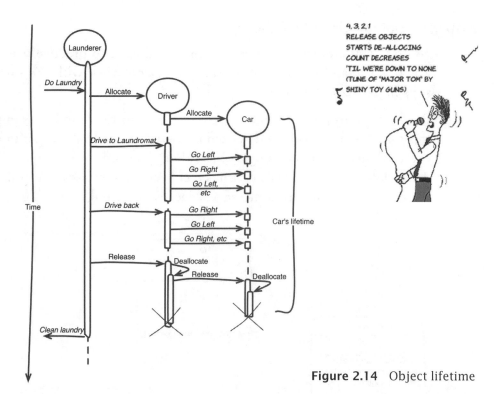

Figure 2.14 Object lifetime

one. The final release causes a deallocate message to be sent to the object, which triggers releases to any objects it has. In this case, the release to Cabbie causes it to deallocate and release its Car (causing it to deallocate as well). The reason you never send a deallocate yourself is that you can never be sure that some other object isn't also using it. The retain counting makes sure you don't need to know if the object is still in use.

Object lifetime is an important topic, and one that you need to understand well to make sure your apps don't crash. ARC helps by sending all the release and retain messages for you; but you may still run into a crash now and then, so it's a good idea to know what's happening under the hood.

Applying object-oriented design

To understand object-oriented design, you'll have to practice using it. You'll get lots of chances to do this when you work with the sample apps in part 2 of this book.

But let's try to put together the concepts using the laundry example. Imagine the object-oriented system inside the Laundromat. Until now, you've thought of it as a single object that you send the message "clean these clothes." But in reality, it has a collection of classes that it needs in order to implement its messages. Here's a partial class diagram to start with:

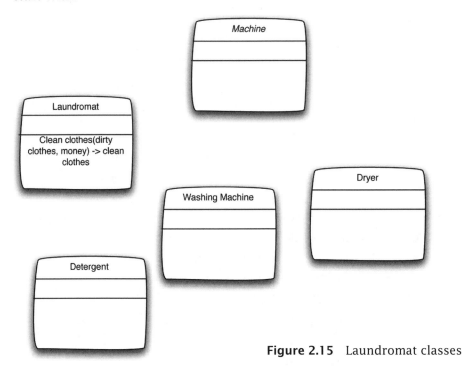

Figure 2.15 Laundromat classes

Fill in the following information:

- Washing Machine and Dryer are Machines.
- All Machines need to remember how much time is left.
- Laundromat has one or more Washing Machines and one or more Dryers.

- Washing Machine uses Detergent.
- A Machine needs messages like "load clothes," "put in money," and "start." Both Dryers and Washing Machines inherit these messages from Machine.
- Washing Machine needs an additional message: "put in detergent."
- Dryer needs an additional message: "set heat level."

When you're done, the diagram should look something like this, but don't worry if it's not exact.

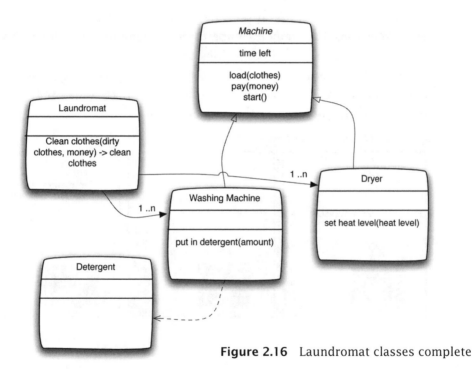

Figure 2.16 Laundromat classes complete

How did you do? Did you remember the three types of relationships you learned? Did you know where to put the messages? Did you understand how inheritance was represented? This is something we're going to revisit, so you'll have plenty of chances to see working examples.

Preparing to code object-oriented designs

You now have all the tools to start learning Objective-C. The diagrams you've seen are meant to help you organize your ideas enough that you can begin to code them. You'll find that as you code, your diagrams will be wrong, and you'll learn more about what you need to do as you do it. Maintaining the diagram to some extent will help, because looking at one diagram will help you understand things that can only be seen across many code files. Remember that each class consists of two files, and even very small apps may have half a dozen or more classes.

In the next chapter, you'll see how each rectangle, circle, line, arrow, and other diagram element maps to code elements. You'll see how to create the header and module files that describe a class, fill the class with messages, and handle the messages. Along the way, you'll learn about conditionals, loops, variables, and the other things that are necessary to code the functionality of your apps.

Coding in Objective-C

This chapter covers

- *Creating classes to match your designs*
- *Declaring and implementing messages and properties*
- *Connecting code to views in Interface Builder*

In the last chapter, you learned how to go from ideas to object-oriented designs. In this chapter, you'll learn how to code those designs. By iteratively applying the concepts of sketching, designing, and coding, you'll eventually have an app.

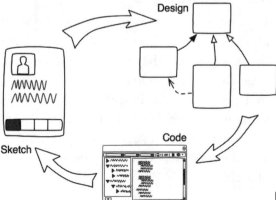

Figure 3.1 Sketch, design, code

CODING ISN'T HARDER THAN
SKETCHING OR DESIGNING.
JUST DIFFERENT

To finish an app, you'll go through this loop many times, refining it on each pass. You already know how to create designs by sending messages to classes that are organized into models, views, and controllers, so you're halfway there.

Representing those designs as code is the most exacting of the three skills you need to create an app. Your notebook won't complain if it doesn't like your sketch or design, but Xcode will put up error after error if you don't get the syntax exactly right. In reading this chapter, pay attention to every detail about creating classes, messages, and properties.

Creating classes to match your designs

HEADERS HAVE AN OVERVIEW OF THE CLASS,
AND MODULES HAVE THE COMPLETE
DETAILS.

HEADERS SEEM LIKE A GOOD WAY
TO QUICKLY LEARN A CLASS.

In your designs, you spent a lot of time thinking about what the classes should be, what properties they should have, and what messages they need to respond to and send. You've also learned that classes can be in different kinds of relationships with each other. In Objective-C, you'll see each piece of the class in two places, the header and the module, which together define the parts of a class.

You can start learning how to code each part by looking at the classes Xcode generated for you in the "Hello World" app. Open Xcode, and click HWViewController.h. It looks like this:

```
#import <UIKit/UIKit.h>

@interface HWViewController : UIViewController {

}

@end
```

The #import statement indicates a relationship, in this case to the iPhone UI classes. In your diagrams, wherever you've drawn an arrow from one class to another, you'll need to use an import to let Xcode know that one class relies on the information in another.

THE PARTS OF THE HEADER REMIND ME OF CLASS DIAGRAMS.

The @interface line is where you put the name of the class and list any is-a relationships you're in. In iPhone programming, all view-controller classes need to inherit from UIView-Controller. So, your class will automatically respond to all of the messages in a UIViewController, which means you can concentrate on how yours is different.

The interface of the class is defined between the @interface and @end statements. You put the class's properties (which include the other classes this one *has*) between the curly braces, and you put the messages after the closing curly brace and before the @end. Remember, the interface is like a table of contents. You just need to list the messages here, not say how they work.

Declaring a message

Before you can fill out the header, you need to learn how to code messages. Objective-C, like most programming languages, requires that you get each character you type in exactly right. Before you fully understand the syntax, it may seem like a random collection of letters and punctuation, but you need to make sure you copy it into Xcode exactly as you see it.

I HAVE THOUSANDS OF TYPES, BUT YOU'RE NOT ONE OF THEM.

When you list a message in the header, that's called *declaring* it. To declare a message, you need to know its name, its parameters, the types of the parameters, and the type it returns. Many types are available. To start with, each class you make can be used as a type, and the iPhone comes with thousands of classes you can use; there are also built-in types for simple things like numbers and yes/no values. Some of the most common are shown in this table.

Table 3.1 Common classes and built-in types

Type	Description
NSString*	Text values like @"Hello" and @"Good–bye"
NSDate*	Dates like July 4, 1776
int	Positive and negative integer numbers, like -1, 0, and 5
bool	YES or NO
double	Positive and negative decimal numbers like 3.14159, 0.0, and -123.45
void	Message return values that indicate there isn't a return value
NSMutableArray*	A collection of any number of other objects, such as a list of strings or dates
UIButton*	A button on a view
UILabel*	A label, like the one you used in the Hello World! app

Here are some ways a message can look in your header. The simplest is a message without any parameters or a return. You use it to tell an object to do something it knows how to do without any more information, and you don't want anything back from the message.

void means no
  return type

-(void) msgWithNoParamsOrReturn;

message
name

Figure 3.2
Message with no parameters or return

Here's an example of a message that returns an int (an integer number).

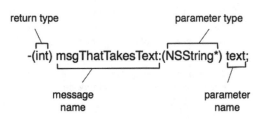

I COULD USE THIS TO MAKE A MESSAGE TO CALCULATE THE NUMBER OF TIMES I TOLD STEF TO GO AWAY.

return type

-(int) msgThatReturnsInt;

message
name

Figure 3.3
Message with no parameters and
an int return

Here's an example of a message that returns an int and takes a text parameter using the type NSString*. Anything of type NSString* is called a *string*.

I WOULD USE THIS TO MAKE A MESSAGE THAT REPORTS HOW MANY FAVORS EACH TECH OWES ME.

return type   parameter type

-(int) msgThatTakesText:(NSString*) text;

message   parameter
name   name

Figure 3.4 Message with a string parameter

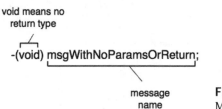
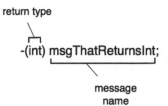

MESSAGES LOOK LIKE
SENTENCES WITH
PARAMETERS THAT ARE
SUBCLAUSES.

Finally, you can have a multiple-parameter message. In this case, the name of the message is split up so that parts of it can be associated with the role of the parameter within the message. Here's what it looks like:

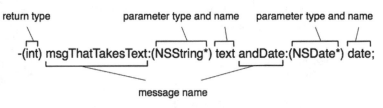

Figure 3.5 Message with multiple parameters

Your actual messages will have more descriptive names for both the message and its parameters. Let's try some examples. Think of a name for the message, what it should return, and any parameters it takes. For types, let's use `int` or `double` for numbers, `bool` for yes/no values, `NSString*` for text strings, `NSDate*` for dates, `NSMutableArray*` for lists, and `void` if you don't need a return value.

Table 3.2   Declare these messages

Message description	Declaration
1. A message that returns the first name of a person object as a string	
2. A message that returns how old someone is, given a birth date	
3. A message that takes the name of a parent and returns a list of their children	
4. A message that takes a string and returns the number of letters in it	
5. A message that takes a number and returns whether it's positive or not	
6. A message that takes two yes/no values and returns yes only if the values match each other, and no otherwise	

Table 3.2   Declare these messages *(continued)*

Message description	Declaration
7. A message that takes a number and returns the date that is that number of days in the future	
8. A message that takes two strings a state, and a capital, and returns yes if the capital is the capital of that state	
9. A message that takes a first name and a last name and returns a string with them separated by a space	
10. A message that takes a string and shows an alert containing the string	

At this point, you should be working on getting the syntax of the message declaration correct. You don't need to match these choices of names exactly or care whether you used an int or double if the choice was arbitrary. Here's a possible set of correct answers:

I'VE GOT A MESSAGE FOR YOU THIS IS FLIPPING AWESOME.

```
1  -(NSString*) getFirstName;
2  -(double) getAge: (NSDate*)birthdate;
3  -(NSMutableArray*)    getChildrenOfParent:
   (NSString*)parent;
4  -(int) getNumLetters: (NSString*)string;
5  -(bool) isPositive: (int)number;
6  -(bool) doesBool: (bool)a matchBool:(bool)b;
7  -(NSDate*) getFutureDate: (int)days;
8  -(bool) isCapital:(NSString*)capital ofState:(NSString*)state;
9  -(NSString*) getFullNameFromFirstName: (NSString*)firstName lastName:
   (NSString*)lastName;
10 -(void) showAlert:(NSString*) text;
```

Although the names and exact types might be arbitrary, the minus signs, stars, parentheses, and semicolons aren't. If you get this wrong, Xcode will let you know with fairly cryptic error messages. You have to get good at writing the syntax exactly or noticing when it's not right.

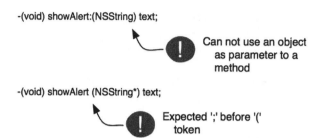

```
-(void) showAlert:(NSString) text;
```

Can not use an object as parameter to a method

```
-(void) showAlert (NSString*) text;
```

Expected ';' before '(' token

```
void showAlert: (NSString*) text;
```

Expected '=', ',', ';', 'asm' or '__attribute__' before ':' token

Figure 3.6   What errors you'll get for each change

Now that you've had practice with declaring messages, it's just a small jump from here to writing messages for view controllers that Interface Builder can attach to views. We'll cover that next.

Declaring a view-controller message for your views to send

As you saw in the previous chapter, in model-view-controller (MVC) applications, views need to send messages to controllers whenever the user does something with the app. In iPhone programming, because you you use Interface Builder to draw views and don't write any code, there isn't a place to put the code to send a message. Instead, you create special messages in the view controller called *actions*, and Interface Builder lets you attach them to views.

Actions must take one parameter called sender with type id, which represents the view that caused the message to be sent. Actions don't return anything, but Interface Builder want us to use IBAction as the return type instead of void. Here's what an action message declaration looks like:

OH. ACTIONS MUST BE HOW BUTTONS SEND TOUCHES TO THE CONTROLLER.

```
-(IBAction) actionMessage: (id)sender;
```

Messages are the main building block of classes. In your apps, you'll be spending a lot of time defining them, sending them, and processing their results. But they aren't enough. Next, you'll see how objects remember things between messages.

Using properties to save data in objects

So far, we've concentrated on messages, but objects also need to carry around data with them to keep track of where you are in your app. Additionally, all those has-a relationships we talked about must be remembered, and you can use properties for those as well.

A property consists of a type, a name, and two messages to get and set its value. This combination is so common that Objective-C provides some shortcuts to help you make them quickly. The first step is to declare the field in your header file to set the type and name of the property. This is put between the two curly braces:

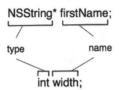

Figure 3.7 Syntax for a field (instance variable)

To have Objective-C create the two messages for you, you need to use @property. It's used in the messages section of the header, and it looks a lot like the field declaration you just saw:

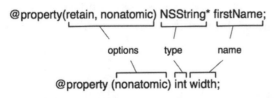

Figure 3.8 Syntax for a property

MY FIRST NAME IS MIRANDA AND
MY WIDTH IS NONE OF YOUR
BUSINESS.

You're only going to use two options. The first one is either strong (which is the same as retain) or weak. These terms let Objective-C's Automated Reference Counting (ARC) know how it should manage memory for you. You only need to use the strong option if you create the property manually and the property is using a class for its type (using a class name and star). If the propriety is automatically created by Xcode, then the option will most likely be weak. The second option, nonatomic, says that you aren't accessing this property from multiple threads (which you aren't, because you don't know how).

I THINK I'D BETTER REVIEW MEMORY MANAGEMENT.

If you want to use a piece of a view in a view controller, you use an *outlet* property. To declare the outlet, you use this:

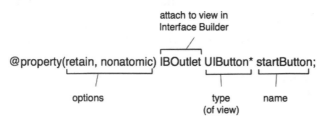

Figure 3.9   Syntax for an IBOutlet

So far, you've broken down apps into classes; organized classes into models, views, and controllers; and learned that classes are made up of properties and messages. The next steps are to learn how to define the messages to say what they do and to get the various objects to communicate with each other. The easiest connections are between the views and view controllers, because if you use outlets and actions, Interface Builder can help us connect them with a GUI. You'll see how to do that in the next section.

Connecting code to views in Interface Builder

You draw views in Interface Builder and write code in the text editor. As you've seen, there are special messages called actions and special properties called outlets that connect views and controllers. Views send actions to controllers when they're touched, and controllers can access and change views through their outlet properties.

To see this better, let's make the Hello World! app a little more interactive. Instead of saying hello to the entire world, let's have it ask for your name and then say hello to just you. It will look like this:

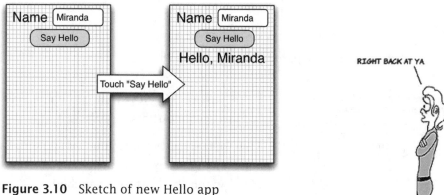

Figure 3.10   Sketch of new Hello app

The first thing to do is identify all the parts of the view:

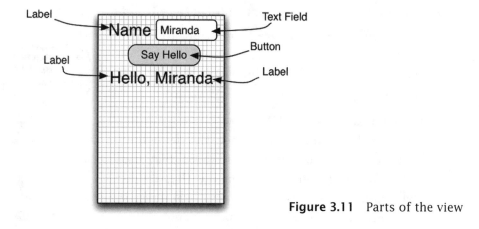

Figure 3.11   Parts of the view

Next, you need to figure out which parts of the view will be changed or accessed by the controller. These are your outlets:

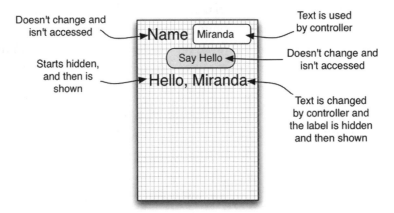

Figure 3.12   The parts of the view that change

Each part of the view that can change will use a GUI to create outlets.

The last step before you code is to list any actions. In this example, the only action is to Say Hello when the button is touched.

Using the Connections Inspector in Interface Builder

Now you're ready to draw the view to match your sketch. You already labeled each part, so it will be easy to go into Interface Builder and draw what you need.

To get started, click HWViewController.xib in Xcode to bring up the Interface Builder editor. In chapter 1, you put a label there that said Hello, World!; you should change that to just Hello and resize it so the text fits exactly in it. You need another label that says Name, a text field next to it, a button that says Say Hello, and a label that says User Name (until you change it). You can find these pieces in the Object Library. When you're done, the view will look like this:

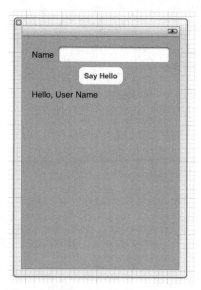

Figure 3.13 Say Hello view

Remember that you change the text of a label or button by double-clicking it and typing a new value. You can click and drag the parts of the view to position them and use the grab handles at their corners to resize them. You want the Hello and User Name labels to start out hidden, so click each one and then check the Hidden field in the Attributes Inspector. Interface Builder will show these labels grayed out rather than hidden so they're easy to work with. When you run the app, they will be hidden.

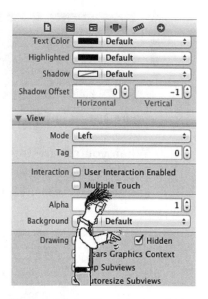

Figure 3.14 Check box to hide views at start

Creating outlets and actions using the assistant

Xcode provides an assistant that allows you to create outlets and actions using the Interface Builder GUI. It's nowhere near as helpful as Alfred the butler, but the Xcode assistant does save a lot of typing. To display the assistant, click the button in the toolbar that looks like a butler's tuxedo.

Figure 3.15
Xcode's assistant

When you're viewing a .xib file, the assistant will display the associated header file. So, because you're viewing HWViewController.xib, the assistant is displaying HWViewController.h. To create an outlet for the User Name text field, Control-click the text field and drag the mouse into the assistant between the beginning and end of the interface declaration:

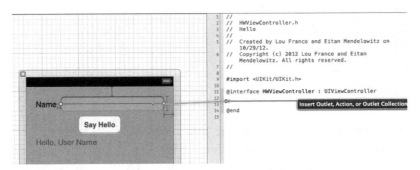

Figure 3.16   Control-click and drag to create outlet

When you release the mouse button, a dialog will pop up with settings for the outlet. Leave the default settings, but set the outlet name to userNameTextField and then click Connect.

Figure 3.17   Name the outlet

Presto, Xcode declares a properly typed IBOutlet property and automatically connects it to the text field. Repeat the process for the User

Name label and the Hello label, and name the outlets `helloLabel` and `userNameLabel`. When you're done, you should have the following three definitions after `@interface` but before `@end`:

```
@property (weak, nonatomic) IBOutlet UITextField *userNameTextField;
@property (weak, nonatomic) IBOutlet UILabel *userNameLabel;
@property (weak, nonatomic) IBOutlet UILabel *helloLabel;
```

And because you're using ARC, you don't have to do anything special to release them.

OK I REALLY NEED TO GO REVIEW MEMORY MANAGEMENT NOW.

Finally, you need to declare and define the `sayHello` action. Remember, actions always return `IBAction` and take a parameter of type `id` called `sender`. You can create `IBActions` the same way you created your `IBOutlets` using the assistant. Control-click the Say Hello button, and drag the mouse over to `HWViewController`'s interface declaration:

Figure 3.18 Control-click and drag to create action

This time you need to change the connection type from Outlet to Action. Name the action `sayHello`:

Figure 3.19
Set the connection type and name

Xcode will insert the following message declaration in your header:

```
-(IBAction) sayHello: (id)sender;
```

And in your module, the assistant automagically adds this empty message body, which you'll fill in later:

```
-(IBAction) sayHello: (id)sender
{
}
```

NOTHING IS HAPPENINK. THINK OUTLETS MUST NOT BEINK CONNECTED.

TAP
TAP
TIP
TAP

Your project can now be built, so press Cmd-B or use the Product > Build menu to build. You should have zero errors and zero warnings.

If you've made a mistake, you can always delete a property or action. If you delete an action, be sure to delete both the declaration in the header and the definition in the module.

With your connections in place, it's time to save and start coding. The only thing holding back your app from saying hello to you is that you never filled in the sayHello message in your module. You'll do that next.

Defining the action message

Coding messages can get complex. As you see more of them, you'll learn the tools that you need to make them. This message is simple, but it gives you a chance to see how to access outlets and their properties.

You want the sayHello message to do three things:

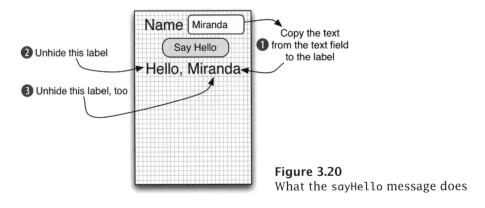

Figure 3.20
What the sayHello message does

To do that, you need to

❶ Set the `text` property of the User Name label to the `text` property of the text field.

❷ Set the `hidden` property of the Hello label to `NO`.

❸ Set the `hidden` property of the User Name label to `NO`.

All you're doing is accessing and changing some properties. The syntax for accessing a property of an object is

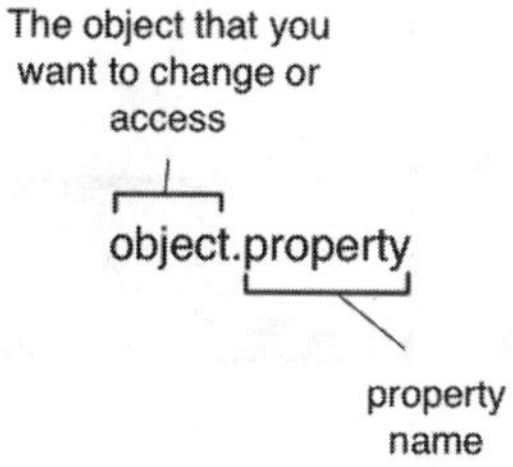

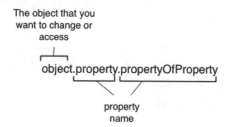

The object that you want to change or access

object.property

property name

Figure 3.21   Property syntax

And because properties themselves are often objects with properties, you can chain together the dots and access the property of a property like this:

The object that you want to change or access

object.property.propertyOfProperty

property name

Figure 3.22   Syntax for accessing a property of a property

You change a property by using an equals sign and providing an object of the correct type, and you access an object's own properties by using a special predefined object name called `self`. To see all this in action, here's the final code for the `sayHello` message.

```
-(IBAction) sayHello: (id)sender
{
    self.userNameLabel.text = self.userNameTextField.text;
    self.helloLabel.hidden = NO;
    self.userNameLabel.hidden = NO;
}
```

Replace the code in HWViewController.m with this code, and you're done! To see the app, build and run the final result in the simulator with Cmd-R. When you type your name in the text field and touch the button, the app should say hello to you.

Of course, real apps need to do a lot more than copy properties around or set them to constant values. You need to take the values in outlets, send them to models, and get back results that you then use to change the view in various ways. In those messages, you might need to make decisions, do calculations, or access databases or the web. The bulk of iPhone app writing is defining these messages.

Over the course of the next part of the book, you'll build a few real-world apps that use different features of the iPhone. Each message will not only help you get the app done, but will also show you a new feature of Objective-C or iOS.

Soon you'll be seeing a full MVC application. You'll implement it, enhance it, and modify it with your own data. In the end, you'll have a unique app that you can put in the App Store.

iPhone applications: step by step

This part of the book will teach you how to use the various features of the iPhone in real applications. In each chapter, you'll learn first how a feature works and then how to use it. Each application includes the full source code and is available on the App Store for you to try. When you're finished with this part, you'll have seen all of the code for the following:

- A simple game that uses touch and animations
- An application that uses multitouch and the camera and accesses your photos
- An application that has a database, uses table views, and accesses contacts and the calendar
- An application that uses locations and maps

In chapter 4, you'll start with a few drawings of a simple FlashCards game, learn how to identify its views, and draw them in Interface Builder. Then, you'll implement the models and controllers that make the game work. In chapter 5, you'll add some polish to the app with icons and startup images. You'll learn how to make custom buttons that stretch, and you'll use animation to make the app come alive. In chapter 6, you'll finish the FlashCards app by adding Core Data to store results and view them later in navigation and table views.

In chapter 7, you'll start a new app, Disguisey, which will teach you how to make a tab-based application, access the Photos app, and get touch locations for images. You'll add a little animation to Disguisey in chapter 8 and then learn how to use gestures to get multitouch events. Finally, you'll learn how to composite images and save them to the Photos app.

Chapter 9 discusses how to use maps in views, insert pins into those maps, and figure out your current location. Then, in chapter 10, you'll learn how to access the internet via your app: displaying web pages in your UI, posting to Twitter, and using information that comes from the web.

Writing an app with multiple views

This chapter covers

- *Designing classes to match your sketches*
- *Defining your models, views, and controllers*
- *Changing views based on user interaction*

In the last chapter, you learned the syntax for messages and properties and how you can make them into actions and outlets so that Interface Builder can connect views to them. In this chapter, you're going to take the sketches for a real application and see how to create all of the various pieces. By the time you're done, you'll have made an application to show flashcards, which you can customize with your own content.

Designing a flashcard application

For the content of your flashcards, you'll use U.S. state capitals. Do you know Juneau from Topeka without peeking? If not, this app will help.

This app is more complex than the ones you've seen so far, so it's even more important that you plan it out a little before starting. So, let's make some sketches of what you want it to look like. The opening screen is shown at right.

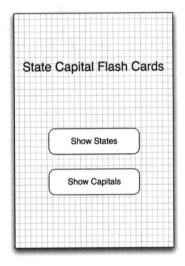

Figure 4.1   Sketch of flashcard start screen

Once you choose which way you want to practice, you'll see a sequence like this:

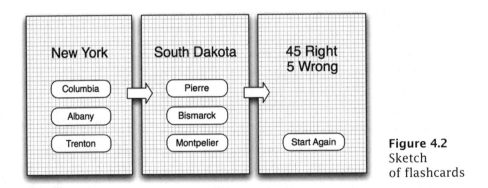

Figure 4.2
Sketch
of flashcards

The sketches show that you need three different views: one for the opening screen, another that shows text and has three buttons for answers, and another with the final score and a restart button.

Let's look at how this app flows:

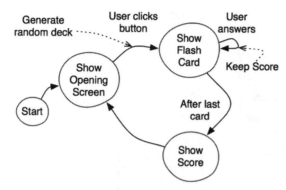

Figure 4.3   Behavior of flashcards

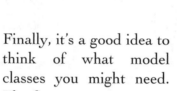

Finally, it's a good idea to think of what model classes you might need. The first one, FCCard, represents a flashcard and can handle a recordAnswer message.

Figure 4.4   FCCard model class

To hold the state of the game, you'll use a FCGame class. It has cards, gives you access to them, and tells you when you're done.

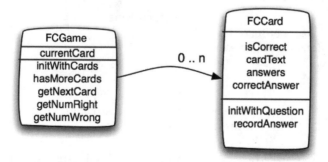

Figure 4.5   FCGame and FCCard model classes

To configure a game, you'll use a class called FCAnswerKey that can generate a deck of cards, each with one right answer and two wrong ones.

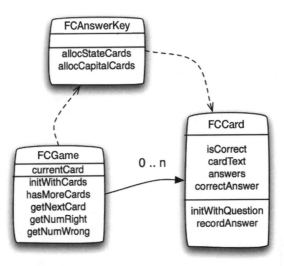

Figure 4.6
FCGame, FCCard, and
FCAnswerKey model
classes

These three classes hold all the information that each of the views might need. For example, to show a card, the card controller will ask the card for its card text and answers and then use them on the card view.

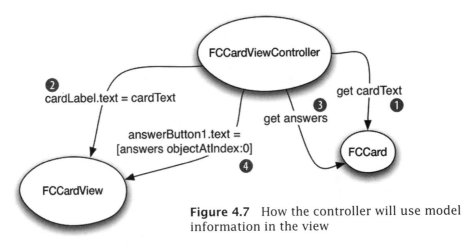

Figure 4.7 How the controller will use model information in the view

To show the final score, the result controller will ask the game for the number of right and wrong answers.

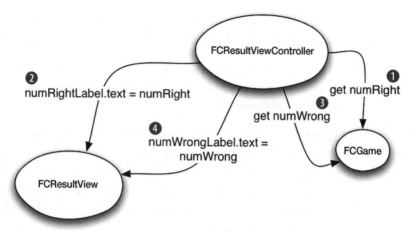

Figure 4.8 How the result controller uses game properties in the view

Here's how the whole class diagram looks.

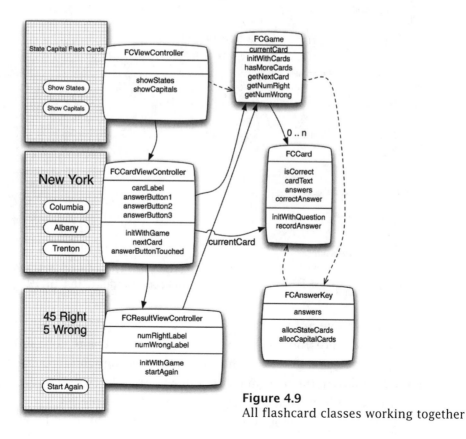

Figure 4.9
All flashcard classes working together

Each different view needs a controller, and, as you saw, the controllers use the models to figure out which view to show and what to show on it.

> **INIT** This is the first message that should be sent to an object after allocating it. There are variants that take arguments if they're needed. You should only call one init per object.

Another thing to notice is that some classes have a special init message. Every class automatically gets an init message to set it up right after it's been allocated. If you would like to send parameters to the init, then you need to make special ones, and you name them starting with *init*. For example, you'll want to give the view controllers the Game object that you create at the beginning.

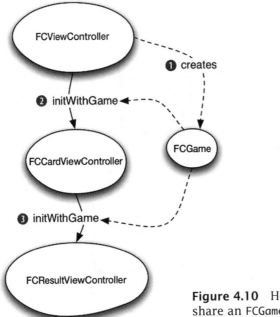

Figure 4.10 How the controllers will share an FCGame model using initWithGame

Now that you've got the basic structure in place, you can learn how to code it. The more you do up front, the easier it will be to concentrate on coding one piece at a time. When you start coding, you'll find that you made mistakes in the diagram. And once your code is running, you'll get better ideas of how your app should work. Still, a little planning is good practice until you're more comfortable jumping right in and coding.

Creating classes to match your designs

You did a lot of work to get to the point that you can code. This is typical, because once you write code, the app becomes a little harder to change. The sketches will help you keep yourself organized while you're coding, and they're also a great way to explain the code to someone else. Sometimes that "someone else" is you in the future when you come back to the project after being away, so do a good job, and remember to thank yourself later.

With your design and specification reasonably fleshed out, you're ready to begin trying to make this app. In chapter 3, you created your view first and then used the Assistant Editor to create actions and properties. In some cases it's easy to define your controllers and models first and then create the view. This is especially true when your project is well planned. This is what you'll do in this chapter. First you'll go through the view controllers and add the messages the view will need. Then you'll code the models. Finally, you'll draw the views and finish the controllers.

To start, open Xcode and create a new project called *FlashCards* using the Single View Application template. This is exactly the same way you started your Hello World! project:

1 Choose File > New > New Project.

2 Click Single View Application, and click Next.

3   Type in FlashCards as the product name, fill in your company identifier (using your domain or anything unique), use FC as the prefix, uncheck Storyboard, use ARC, and click Next.

4   Pick a folder in which to save the project.

To organize your files a little better, create a Classes group and a Resources group. To create each group, choose File > New > New Project. You're also going to create folders in the Finder that mirror your project's group structure. For each group, open a file dialog by selecting the group and then clicking the small square under the Path drop-down in the Utilities tray, which is located on the right side of the Xcode window.

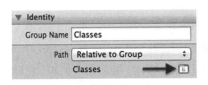

Figure 4.11
For each group, open the file dialog to create a folder.

When the file dialog opens, click the New Folder button, name the folder Classes (or Resources), click Create, and then click Choose. Move the headers and modules to Classes and the XIB files to Resources.

Open the Classes group, and click FCViewController.h. It looks like this.

Listing 4.1   FCViewController.h overview

```
                                                    ❶ NEEDED FOR
                                                       RELATIONSHIP
#import <UIKit/UIKit.h>

                                                                ❷ COLON
                                                                   FOR IS-A
@interface FCViewController : UIViewController

                                                    ❸ DATA
                                                       DECLARATIONS
                                    MESSAGE
@end                            ❹ DECLARATIONS
```

As you saw in the last chapter, the parts of your diagram map onto the class definition like this:

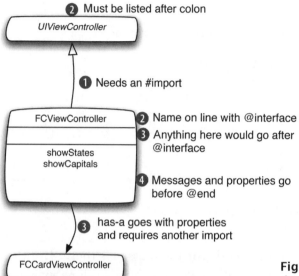

2 Must be listed after colon

UIViewController

1 Needs an #import

FCViewController

showStates
showCapitals

2 Name on line with @interface

3 Anything here would go after @interface

4 Messages and properties go before @end

3 has-a goes with properties and requires another import

FCCardViewController

Figure 4.12 How the class diagram maps to the header

The Xcode template helps structure your files, so you just need to put each part in the correct place. Unfortunately, it only knows about Objective-C source files. To add structure to the rest of the things in your life, you're on your own.

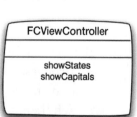

I NEED A TEMPLATE TO ORGANIZE MY EXPENSE REPORTS.

Declaring a view-controller message for your views to send

Xcode creates your first view and controller for you when you use the view-based template. Because you have that one already, let's start with it. It's easy to use because it only has actions.

In the diagram, FCViewController looked as shown here.

FCViewController

showStates
showCapitals

Figure 4.13 FCViewController class diagram

The class diagram lists two messages, showStates and showCapitals, that will be called by the view, depending on what button is clicked. These are actions, so they need to return IBAction and take a sender. Here's the code for the header:

```
@interface FCViewController : UIViewController

-(IBAction) showStates:(id)sender;
-(IBAction) showCapitals:(id)sender;

@end
```

And here's how you define the messages in the FCViewController.m file:

```
-(IBAction)showStates:(id)sender {
}

-(IBAction)showCapitals:(id)sender {
}
```

Eventually, you'll put the code for the messages there. But the application can now be built, so let's make sure you've done everything right by pressing Cmd-B. Xcode should say *Build Succeeded*. If you get any errors, check all of the code carefully against the listings.

Now that you've written most of this controller and declared and defined its messages, you're ready to create the rest of your views and controllers. Controllers define the flow of your application, and as you saw, if the actions and outlets are done, Interface Builder will let you attach them to your views.

Creating your other views and controllers

The design has three view/view-controller pairs. The one you made will be the startup screen, but you also need to be able to show a flashcard and the final results. Let's do that.

In Xcode, chose File > New > File, and then choose Cocoa Touch in the list at the left and Objective-C Class in the template list. The window should look like this:

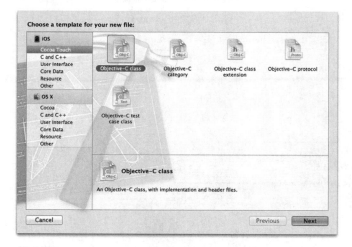

Figure 4.14
Creating a view-controller class

Click Next. In the next window, name the class FCCardViewController, and choose the subclass UIViewController (this makes your class a UIViewController). Make sure to create a XIB.

Figure 4.15
Choosing the base class and target

SUBCLASS In an is-a relationship, where class A is-a class B, A is called the base or *superclass*, and B is called the *subclass*. You can also say that B *inherits from* A.

Click the Next button, and in the next dialog, make sure the location is set to the Classes subfolder and group of your project.

Figure 4.16
Saving the view-controller class

Click the Finish button. Xcode will create three files: FCCardViewController.m, FCCardViewController.h, and FCCardViewController.xib. Drag the .xib file to your Resources group with the other files. Repeat these steps for `FCResultViewController`.

Your `FCCardViewController` class now looks like this.

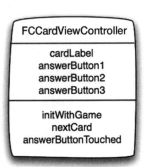

Figure 4.17 `FCCardViewController` class diagram

The code for the messages and outlet properties looks like this in the header:

```
@interface FCCardViewController : UIViewController

@property (nonatomic, strong) IBOutlet UILabel* cardLabel;
@property (nonatomic, strong) IBOutlet UIButton* answer1Button;
@property (nonatomic, strong) IBOutlet UIButton* answer2Button;
@property (nonatomic, strong) IBOutlet UIButton* answer3Button;

-(void) nextCard;
-(IBAction)answerButtonTouched:(id)sender;
```

And here's the module (you'll create `initWithGame` when you make the `FCGame` class):

```
-(void) nextCard {
}


-(IBAction)answerButtonTouched:(id)sender {
}
```

MAKING EMPTY MESSAGES
FOR NOW LETS US CHECK
THAT WE CAN STILL BUILD.

Check your work by pressing Cmd-B to build.

Now you can work on `FCResultViewController`. It looks like this:

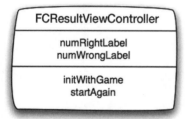

Figure 4.18
`FCResultViewController` class diagram

Add these messages after the closing curly brace and before the `@end`:

```
@interface FCResultViewController : UIViewController {
    UILabel* numRightLabel;
    UILabel* numWrongLabel;
}
```

```
@property(nonatomic, strong) IBOutlet UILabel* numRightLabel;
@property(nonatomic, strong) IBOutlet UILabel* numWrongLabel;

-(IBAction)startAgain:(id)sender;
```

And add this code in the module file:

```
-(IBAction)startAgain:(id)sender {
}
```

Check your work with Cmd-B. If you have any errors, look carefully at each part of the syntax. Xcode will usually put you on the line it's having problems with, so check that one against these listings. If they match, make sure you entered the code in the correct place.

Creating the model classes

In previous chapters, the apps you built didn't do much with user input, and they certainly didn't need to store anything for later. Now you're going to see what to do when your apps get complex enough to need models.

The model classes, FCGame, FCCard, and FCAnswerKey, have all the information about the app. They work together to set up the game and keep track of what card you're on, when you're done, and how many right and wrong answers you have.

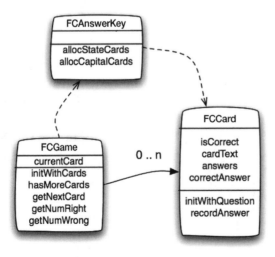

Figure 4.19
The model classes

Let's start with FCCard. To create it, in Xcode, right-click the Classes group, and then choose New File from the menu. In the following dialog, choose to create an Objective-C class; and in the next dialog, call it FCCard and make it a subclass of NSObject (all classes have a parent, so use this if you don't need a different one).

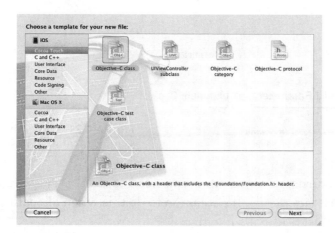

Figure 4.20
Creating a class

In the next dialog, put the class in the Classes folder.

Click FCCard.h in your Project Navigator. Here you need to declare its four properties and two messages. It looks like this.

Listing 4.2 Adding properties and messages to FCCard.h

```
@interface FCCard : NSObject

@property(nonatomic) bool isCorrect;
@property(nonatomic, strong) NSString* cardText;                    PROPERTIES
@property(nonatomic, strong) NSMutableArray* answers;
@property(nonatomic) int correctAnswer;

-(id) initWithQuestion:(NSString*)question
               answer:(NSString*)answer
          wrongAnswer1:(NSString*)wrongAnswer1                      MESSAGES
          wrongAnswer2:(NSString*)wrongAnswer2;

-(void) recordAnswer:(int)answerNum;

@end
```

Now you need to define your class in the module. In it, you'll create objects, store them in properties, and send messages to them.

The first thing to do is define the `initWithQuestion:` `answer:` `wrongAnswer1:` `wrongAnswer2:` message. To do that, you'll need to send messages for the first time. The syntax for that is as follows:

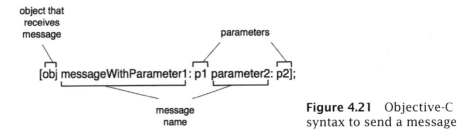

Figure 4.21   Objective-C syntax to send a message

If a message returns an object, and you need to send a message to it, you can nest message sends. It's common to do this when allocating and initializing an object. It looks like this:

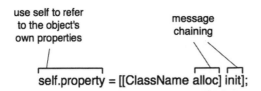

Figure 4.22   Objective-C syntax to set a property to a new object

Here's the code for the message.

Listing 4.3 FCCard.m **init** message

```
-(id) initWithQuestion:(NSString*)question
              answer:(NSString*)answer
        wrongAnswer1:(NSString*)wrongAnswer1
        wrongAnswer2:(NSString*)wrongAnswer2
{
    if (self = [super init]) {
        self.cardText = question;

        self.answers = [[NSMutableArray alloc]
                                    init];                    ❶ CREATE ANSWERS ARRAY

        [self.answers addObject:answer];                      ❷ ADD ANSWERS
        [self.answers addObject:wrongAnswer1];
        [self.answers addObject:wrongAnswer2];

        int randomAnswerSlot = arc4random() % 3;              ❸ RANDOMLY MOVE CORRECT ONE
        [self.answers exchangeObjectAtIndex:0
                        withObjectAtIndex:randomAnswerSlot];
        self.correctAnswer = randomAnswerSlot;                ❹ REMEMBER CORRECT ANSWER
    }
    return self;
}
```

In the init, you build up an array of answers by allocating it ❶, adding your answers to it ❷, randomly swapping the correct answer with a wrong one ❸, and then making sure you remember where the right answer is ❹.

The built-in function arc4random() returns a random integer. Then you use the modulo operator,

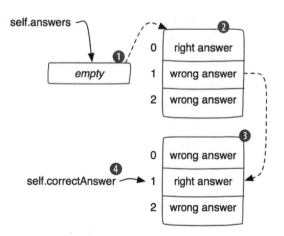

Figure 4.23 How answers are stored in a Card object

%, to find the remainder when you divide by three. This leaves you with a random number between zero and two, which means the right answer can end up in any spot with equal probability.

> **MODULO** An operator that returns the remainder after dividing. The result is always between zero and the right-hand operand minus one.

In recordAnswer, you need to remember if the answer matches the correct one:

```
-(void) recordAnswer:(int)answerNum
{
    self.isCorrect = (answerNum == self.correctAnswer);
}
```

This class is done, so build the project to make sure you've done everything right. You started with FCCard because it didn't depend on any other class. The next class we'll look at, FCAnswerKey, creates the cards that make up the game and only depends on the FCCard class, which is already finished.

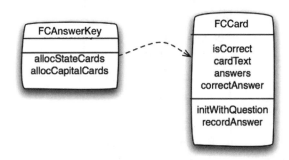

Implementing FCAnswerKey

So far, most of the classes you've seen don't know anything about states or capitals and could easily be reused in any flashcard application. FCAnswerKey is different. If you were to adapt this app to a different topic, this class is where you'd put the information that is used on the cards.

The purpose of the FCAnswerKey class is to create the deck of cards that is used to play the game. It has two messages to allocate the two kinds of decks you'll use in the game.

Create the class files by choosing File > New > File. Then choose the

Figure 4.24 FCAnswerKey and FCCard class diagram

Objective-C class template, and enter the class name FCAnswerKey. FCAnswerKey should be a subclass of NSObject. Here's the header:

```
#import "FCCard.h"

@interface FCAnswerKey : NSObject

-(NSMutableArray*) allocStateCards;
-(NSMutableArray*) allocCapitalCards;

@end
```

The only thing to note here is that there is a convention of starting a message with alloc if its main purpose is to create an object. Here is the FCAnswerKey module.

Listing 4.4   FCAnswerKey.m

```
#import "FCAnswerKey.h"

@implementation FCAnswerKey

-(NSMutableArray*) allocStateCards
{
    NSMutableArray *cards = [[NSMutableArray alloc] initWithObjects:
    [[FCCard alloc]
     initWithQuestion:@"Alabama"        answer: @"Montgomery"
     wrongAnswer1:@"Birmingham"         wrongAnswer2:@"Mobile"],
    [[FCCard alloc]
     initWithQuestion:@"New York"       answer: @"Albany"
     wrongAnswer1:@"New York City"      wrongAnswer2:@"Buffalo"],
    [[FCCard alloc]
     initWithQuestion:@"New Jersey"     answer: @"Trenton"
     wrongAnswer1:@"Camden"             wrongAnswer2:@"Newark"],
    [[FCCard alloc]
     initWithQuestion:@"Oklahoma"       answer: @"Oklahoma City"
     wrongAnswer1:@"Tulsa"              wrongAnswer2:@"Muskogee"],
     nil ];

    return cards;
}

-(NSMutableArray*) allocCapitalCards
{
```

CREATE CARDS AND ADD TO ARRAY ❶

RETURN LIST ❷

```
NSMutableArray *cards = [[NSMutableArray alloc] initWithObjects:
[[FCCard alloc]
 initWithQuestion:@"Montgomery"  answer: @"Alabama"
 wrongAnswer1:@"Mississippi"     wrongAnswer2:@"Tennessee"],
[[FCCard alloc]
 initWithQuestion:@"Albany"      answer: @"New York"
 wrongAnswer1:@"New Jersey"      wrongAnswer2:@"Pennsylvania"],
[[FCCard alloc]
 initWithQuestion:@"Trenton"     answer: @"New Jersey"
 wrongAnswer1:@"New York"        wrongAnswer2:@"Connecticut"],
[[FCCard alloc]
 initWithQuestion:@"Oklahoma City"    answer: @"Oklahoma"
 wrongAnswer1:@"Tennessee"            wrongAnswer2:@"New Jersey"],
nil ];

    return cards;
}

@end
```

The first message allocates an array ❶ and then fills it with cards, and returns it ❷. You make a similar one for state capitals.

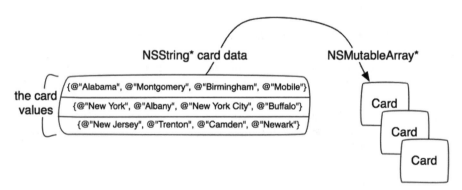

I CAN'T BELIEVE
EVERYTHING BUILT ON
ONLY MY EIGHTH TRY!

Figure 4.25   Creating cards from the String data on them

Build the project to make sure everything is OK. Next you'll write the last model class, FCGame, which uses FCAnswerKey to create cards and then keeps track of them and lets you know when the game is over.

The FCGame class

The FCGame class has a lot of methods, but each is pretty simple. Here's how it fits in your overall structure:

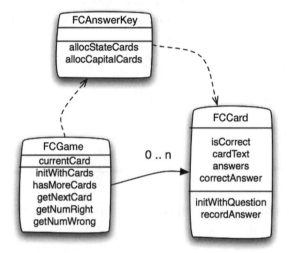

Figure 4.26 FCGame, FCCard, and FCAnswerKey class diagrams

Create FCGame as a subclass of NSObject, and fill in the header.

Listing 4.5   FCGame.h interface to the FCGame class

```
#import <Foundation/Foundation.h>
#import "FCCard.h"
#import "FCAnswerKey.h"


@interface FCGame : NSObject

@property (nonatomic, strong) NSMutableArray* cards;
@property (nonatomic) int currentCard;

-(id) initWithCards:(NSMutableArray*)c;
-(bool) hasMoreCards;
-(FCCard*) getNextCard;
-(int) getNumRight;
-(int) getNumWrong;

@end
```

① REMEMBER TO MAKE PROPERTIES STRONG

The header is straightforward. Remember that you use strong properties ❶ so ARC will deal with memory for you.

Let's go through the module piece by piece. First is initWithCards,
which takes a list of cards and assigns it to a property. Because you're
going to provide the list items one by one, you set the current card to
the beginning:

```
-(id)initWithCards:(NSMutableArray*)c
{
    if (self = [super init]) {
        self.cards = c;
        self.currentCard = 0;
    }
    return self;
}
```

The next two messages let you know if there are any more cards, and if
so, a way to get the next one:

```
-(bool) hasMoreCards
{
    return self.currentCard < [self.cards count];
}

-(FCCard*) getNextCard
{
    FCCard* card = [self.cards objectAtIndex:self.currentCard];
    self.currentCard++;
    return card;
}
```

To get the final score, you call the next two messages.

Listing 4.6   FCGame.m num right/wrong

```
-(int) getNumRight
{
    int numRight = 0;
    for (int i = 0; i < [self.cards count]; ++i) {          COUNT
        FCCard* c = [self.cards objectAtIndex:i];        ❶ CORRECT CARDS
        if (c.isCorrect) {
            numRight++;
```

```
        }
    }
    return numRight;
}

-(int) getNumWrong
{
    return [self.cards count] - [self getNumRight];
}
```

❷ WRONG IS
TOTAL - RIGHT

To keep it simple, you'll just loop through the cards and count the number of correct ones ❶. The number of wrong cards is the number of cards minus the number of correct ones ❷.

Build the project, and fix any errors.

The last part of the app draws the views, hooks them up to the view controllers, and then has the view controllers use the models to play the game. You've already laid out the outlet and actions in the view controllers, so they're ready to be connected to the views. You also have fully functional model classes, so each action in the controller can be fully implemented as well. You'll finish it in the next section.

Connecting code to Interface Builder

You're ready to draw your views and hook them up. In chapter 3, you Ctrl-dragged from Interface Builder into the Assistant Editor and let the Assistant Editor create your properties and actions. This time, you're going Ctrl-drag from Interface Builder into the Assistant Editor to connect your view to code you already wrote. The process is so similar to what you've already done that you've probably got your mouse hovering over the .xib, ready to click. Go ahead, do it, it's OK.

Let's begin with the starting screen, which is shown here.

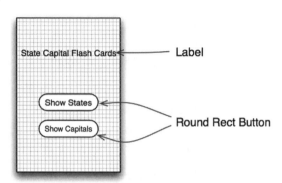

Figure 4.27 Sketch of the FlashCards main screen

Here's how you build it:

1 Select FCViewController.xib in the Resources group.

2 Drag a Label from the Library to the View dialog (as in the Hello World! example).

3 Double-click the label, and type State Capital Flash Cards.

4 Drag two Round Rect Buttons from the Library to the View dialog.

5 Double-click the top one and type Show States. Then double-click the other one and type Show Capitals.

6 Show the Assistant Editor by clicking the button on the toolbar that looks like a tuxedo. FCCardViewController.h should appear in the Assistant Editor.

7 Ctrl-drag from the Show States button in Interface Builder to the showStatesIBAction in FCCardViewController.h. When you're over the action, it will become highlighted, and you'll see a tooltip that says Connect Action.

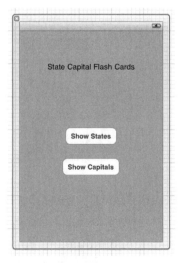

Figure 4.28 The FCViewController view

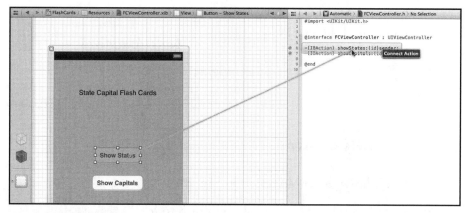

Figure 4.29   Connecting to an action

8 Repeat the process for the Show Capitals button, Ctrl-dragging from the button to the action.

You may have noticed little filled-in circles adjacent to your actions. These represent connections between the view and the file's owner. You can also inspect, create, or delete connections using the Connections Inspector. To bring up the Connections Inspector, select an element in your view and press Opt-Cmd-6, or choose View > Utilities > Show Connection Inspector.

YOU CAN SEE CONNECTIONS FROM FILE'S OWNER OR ANY PART OF THE VIEW.

YOU SEE ME HERE. RIGHT?

Go ahead and save. Next you'll draw the card, which uses outlets in addition to actions. If you build and run this application now, it will show the screen you just built. Your action messages are empty, so the buttons don't do anything yet, but you're getting close.

Connecting the FCCardViewController view

The next view to draw is the one for the FCCardViewController, which is shown for each card in the deck. It's different from the last view because it will be customized rather than having the label and buttons preset with text. You want to access these items in code, so you'll need to connect them to the outlets you created.

Here's what you want the view to look like.

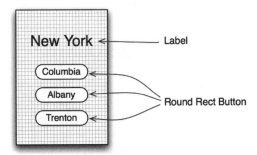

Figure 4.30   Sketch of a card

Here's how you build it:

1   Select FCCardViewController.xib in Xcode.

2   Drag a Label and three buttons onto the view. Make sure they're wide enough to display any state or capital name, and set their text as shown at right.

3   Bring up the Assistant Editor, and then Ctrl-drag to connect the first button to the answerButtonTouched action.

4   Repeat with the other two buttons. Notice that it's OK to connect multiple buttons to the same action.

5   Ctrl-drag the label to the cardLabel outlet.

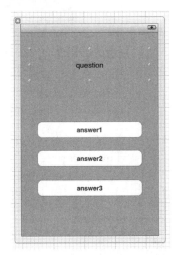

Figure 4.31
Card in Interface Builder

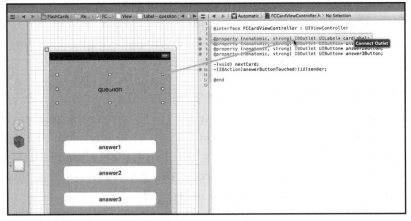

Figure 4.32   Connecting an outlet

Ctrl-drag each button to its respective outlet: answer1button, answer2button, and answer3button.

Save and build again to make sure everything is OK. You're ready for the last view now.

Connecting the FCResultViewController view

Next is the result view. This one needs two labels to show the score and a button to restart the game. The labels are connected to outlets, and the button is connected to an action. Here's what you want it to look like:

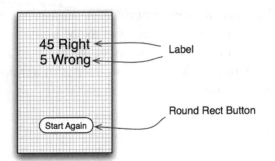

Figure 4.33
Sketch of the result view

Because you've done this twice, you should already know how to do it, but here's a brief guide:

1 Bring up the view in Interface Builder.

2 Put two Labels and a button on the view, and set their Title Text properties.

3 Connect the button's event to the startAgain action.

4 Connect the numRightLabel and numWrongLabel outlets of the file's owner to the corresponding views.

You have completed views and models, and now you need to translate the actions you take in the views to appropriate messages to send to the models. Messages are the way your models determine how the controllers change the views. Controllers have a lot of responsibility. Don't let working on them go to your head.

Orchestrating your app with controllers

As you learned, controllers are where you interpret the various things the user is doing with your app and then respond to the model's results by switching views or updating the current view. In the last section, you used Interface Builder to attach the button events to action messages, so all you have left is to implement those actions.

The first controller you'll write is FCViewController, which is the opening screen of the app. Here's what it needs to do when you click one of its buttons:

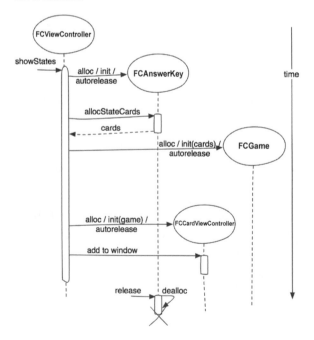

Figure 4.34
FCViewController sequence to show the first card

Because `showStates` and `showCapitals` are similar, you'll create a helper message called `showCards` that's shared. Here's the header code.

Listing 4.7   FCViewController.h

```
#import <UIKit/UIKit.h>                                    ❶ IMPORT
#import "FCGame.h"                                            CLASSES
#import "FCAnswerKey.h"                                       YOU USE
#import "FCCardViewController.h"

@interface FCViewController : UIViewController
@property (nonatomic, strong) FCCardViewController *cardVC;
-(IBAction)showCards:(NSMutableArray*)cards;
-(IBAction) showStates:(id)sender;                         KEEP TRACK OF
-(IBAction) showCapitals:(id)sender;                       OTHER VIEWS ❷

@end
```

You add some imports ❶ for the other classes you communicate with, and you also need to add a property for the `FCCardViewController` ❷ because you'll need to keep it around after the message is complete.

Now, let's go through the model code. Define the helper message, show-Cards:

```
-(IBAction)showCards:(NSMutableArray*)cards {
    FCGame* game = [[FCGame alloc] initWithCards:cards];

    self.cardVC = [[FCCardViewController alloc]
                          initWithGame:game];
    [self.view.window addSubview:self.cardVC.view];
}
```

The `addSubView` message is used to put the card into the main window on top of your start view. Here's how you call the helper message in the two show messages:

```
-(IBAction)showStates:(id)sender {
    FCAnswerKey* key = [[FCAnswerKey alloc] init];
    NSMutableArray *cards = [key allocStateCards];
    [self showCards:cards];
}
```

```
-(IBAction)showCapitals:(id)sender {
    FCAnswerKey* key = [[FCAnswerKey alloc] init];
    NSMutableArray *cards = [key allocCapitalCards];
    [self showCards:cards];
}
```

The last thing each show message does is add a view to the top of the application's window, so after either of the action messages is complete, the view will change to show a card. You'll see the FCCardViewController next.

Handling card events in the FCCardViewController

FCCardViewController goes through each card in the game until you're done. It receives the init message to start, and then the iPhone sends it a viewDidLoad message when it's been attached to the view that was created from the XIB file. FCCardViewController receives a succession of answerButtonTouched messages from the view, which you record; then you proceed to the next card until you're finished. Finally, you need to show the result view.

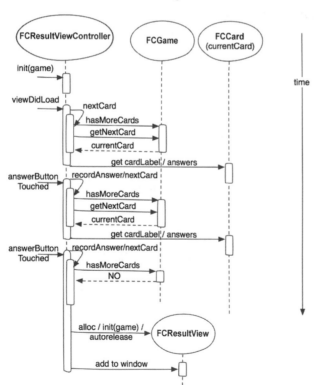

Figure 4.35
FCCardViewController sequence

Let's look at the complete header.

Listing 4.8   *FCCardViewController.h*

```objc
#import <UIKit/UIKit.h>
#import "FCGame.h"
#import "FCCard.h"
#import "FCResultViewController.h"

@interface FCCardViewController : UIViewController

@property (nonatomic, strong) IBOutlet UILabel* cardLabel;
@property (nonatomic, strong) IBOutlet UIButton* answer1Button;
@property (nonatomic, strong) IBOutlet UIButton* answer2Button;
@property (nonatomic, strong) IBOutlet UIButton* answer3Button;

@property (nonatomic, strong) FCResultViewController* resultsVC;

@property (nonatomic, strong) FCGame* game;
@property (nonatomic, strong) FCCard* currentCard;          ← ❶

-(id) initWithGame:(FCGame*)g;
-(void) nextCard;
-(IBAction) answerButtonTouched:(id)sender;

@end
```

❶ REMEMBER CURRENT CARD TO RECORD ANSWER

This is pretty similar to what you've seen so far. One thing to notice is that you need to keep track of the current card ❶ because you get it from the game in `nextCard`, but you need to record an answer later when an answer button is touched.

The module is also similar to what you've seen. Here are the `initWith-Game` and `viewDidLoad` messages.

Listing 4.9   *FCCardViewController.m* **init** and **viewDidLoad**

```objc
-(id) initWithGame:(FCGame*)g {
    if (self = [self initWithNibName:@"FCCardViewController"     ←
                             bundle:[NSBundle mainBundle]]) {
        self.game = g;
    }                                                 ❶ LOAD VIEW
    return self;                                          FROM XIB
}
```

❶ LOAD VIEW FROM XIB

```
-(void)viewDidLoad {
    [super viewDidLoad];
    [self nextCard];
}
```

❷ CAN CHANGE
   OUTLETS HERE

In your init, you need to connect it to a view created from the XIB file you drew in Interface Builder by calling initWithNibName ❶. The connection is completed when the iPhone sends you the viewDidLoad message, where you can get the next card ❷ and set up the card's label and answer buttons. Until viewDidLoad is sent, you can't access the outlets to update the view. Here's nextCard.

Listing 4.10   FCCardViewController.m nextCard

```
-(void) nextCard {
    if ([self.game hasMoreCards]) {                              CHECK FOR
                                                             ❶  MORE CARDS
        self.currentCard = [self.game getNextCard];

        self.cardLabel.text = self.currentCard.cardText;         UPDATE VIEW
                                                             ❷  FROM CARD
        [self.answer1Button
            setTitle:[self.currentCard.answers objectAtIndex:0]
            forState:UIControlStateNormal];
        [self.answer2Button
            setTitle:[self.currentCard.answers objectAtIndex:1]
            forState:UIControlStateNormal];
        [self.answer3Button
            setTitle:[self.currentCard.answers objectAtIndex:2]
            forState:UIControlStateNormal];

    } else {
        self.resultsVC = [[FCResultViewController alloc]
                            initWithGame:self.game];
        [self.view.window addSubview:self.resultsVC.view];

        [self.view removeFromSuperview];                    REMOVE CARD
    }                                                   ❹  FROM WINDOW
}
```

ADD RESULT
TO WINDOW ❸

The `nextCard` message checks to see if any cards are left in the game ❶. If so, it gets the card and uses it to set up the view ❷. If not, it's time to show results, so `nextCard` creates a result view and adds it to the window ❸. Because you're finished showing cards, the last step is to remove the card view from the window ❹.

Each time an answer button is touched, it calls this message.

Listing 4.11   FCCardViewController.m answerButtonTouched

```
-(IBAction)answerButtonTouched:(id)sender {
    if (sender == self.answer1Button) {          RECORD WHICH
        [self.currentCard recordAnswer:0];       BUTTON WAS
    }                                        ❶  TOUCHED
    else if (sender == self.answer2Button) {
        [self.currentCard recordAnswer:1];
    }
    else if (sender == self.answer3Button) {
        [self.currentCard recordAnswer:2];
    }
    [self nextCard];                   GO TO
}                                   ❷  NEXT CARD
```

All the answer buttons are set to call this message when they're touched. You need to check which one was touched ❶ and record the answer on the `currentCard`. Then, you call `nextCard` ❷.

You're almost there. The last class you have to define is the result view that shows the final score.

Showing the result in the FCResultViewController

The last view of your app shows how many you got right and wrong. If you know the difference between Pierre and Bismarck, then you should be fine. If not, well, at least you got Oklahoma City right.

The result view works like this:

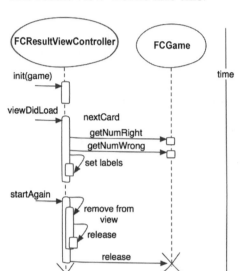

time

Figure 4.36
FCResultViewController sequence

And the code is pretty similar to what you've seen.

Listing 4.12 FCResultViewController.h

```
#import <UIKit/UIKit.h>
#import "FCGame.h"

@interface FCResultViewController : UIViewController

@property(nonatomic, strong) IBOutlet UILabel* numRightLabel;
@property(nonatomic, strong) IBOutlet UILabel* numWrongLabel;
@property(nonatomic, strong) FCGame* game;

-(id) initWithGame:(FCGame*)g;
-(IBAction)startAgain:(id)sender;

@end
```

Listing 4.13 FCResultViewController.m

```
-(id) initWithGame:(FCGame*)g {
    if (self = [self
           initWithNibName:@"FCResultViewController"
```

① LOAD XIB

```
                    bundle:[NSBundle mainBundle]]) {
        self.game = g;
    }
    return self;
}


- (void)viewDidLoad {
    [super viewDidLoad];
    self.numRightLabel.text =
        [NSString stringWithFormat:@"%d Right",
            [self.game getNumRight]];
    self.numWrongLabel.text =
        [NSString stringWithFormat:@"%d Wrong",
            [self.game getNumWrong]];
}

-(IBAction)startAgain:(id)sender {
    [self.view removeFromSuperview];
}
```

2 UPDATE VIEW WITH RESULTS

3 REMOVE RESULT VIEW

The init message needs to load the XIB file **1**. Then, in the viewDidLoad message, you get the score from the game and update the labels **2**. When the startAgain message is sent **3**, all you need to do is remove yourself from the window to reveal the FCViewController's view.

The app is done. You should be able to build and run the application using Cmd-R.

Reflecting on your progress

There you have it: a complete model-view-controller app that you can use to practice your state capitals (once you fill in the other 47 states, of course). More important, by changing how the AnswerKey works and altering a few message names, you can turn this app into a set of flashcards for anything you know about, from Spanish verbs to Lady Gaga song lyrics.

SOY UNA PAPARAZI.

Even a simple app like this one required you to juggle nine different classes, three views, three controllers, and three model classes. As you progress, it will be important to make sure you map out your app and maintain a good overall picture of what is going on. Even though in this case it might seem as though the design was completely developed and then the code progressed from there, it wasn't like that. The design was revised several times as the code was developed, to reflect new choices that were discovered as it was coded. You shouldn't worry about getting the design perfect, but keep it up to date with what you figure out as you code.

5

Polishing your app

This chapter covers

- *Setting your application's icon and start image*
- *Using images for buttons*
- *Customizing built-in views*
- *Animating view transitions*

The flashcards app from the last chapter does what it needs to do, but without any style. Professional iPhone apps need to do better than that.

There are some things that Apple requires you to do, like making an application icon. Other things, such as transition animations, make your app look a lot more polished, and iPhone users will expect and appreciate them.

Pick up your phone right now, and start your favorite app: not necessarily the most useful one, but the one that gives you the best feeling when you use it. What do you notice? Professional iPhone apps have a polished look and professional graphic design and imagery, and they make extensive use of animations.

If you want to see apps from well-known designers, check out anything from Tapbots to Sophiestication. For example, here are two screenshots of Tapbot's Weightbot.

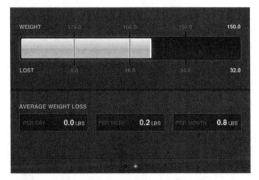

Figure 5.1
Weightbot main screen

Figure 5.2   Weightbot summary

And at right is the main screen of Sophiestication's Groceries app.

The designers of these apps paid careful attention to the details, and the apps are top sellers in their competitive categories because of that work. It's not just the colors and imagery. The designers also use animations to add life to their apps.

But don't be overwhelmed. Each of these apps is built on a foundation of techniques that can be applied step by step. Once you understand how, you'll only be limited by your imagination.

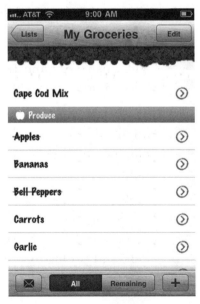

Figure 5.3
Groceries main screen

Setting up your application's images

Every app needs to have an icon and a startup image. Because these are required, Apple made it easy to add them without any code, which should be a relief after the last chapter. Don't worry: some fun chunks of code are coming later in this chapter, but right now you'll get far with a little drag-and-drop.

Replacing the default application icon

The icon is the first thing users will see from your app, so it's worth trying to make a good one. Most professional app icons are made by graphic designers, and if you can afford that or have a friend or co-worker who can help, it will be worth it.

If you're making an icon, keep in mind that you might need it in a lot of sizes, so either use software that lets you create vector images or design your icon at 512 x 512 to make sure you can reduce it to all the necessary sizes. Here's what you'll use for this app; note that the icon doesn't have rounded corners or a glossy effect on it. The iPhone will add those for you.

Figure 5.4
An icon without rounded corners or a glossy effect

For now, you need the icon in two sizes. iPhones before 4.0 use 57 x 57 icons, but the retina display doubled the pixel density of the screen, so you need an icon at 114 x 114 for that. Name the first icon Icon.png and the second Icon@2x.png (the capital *I* is important).

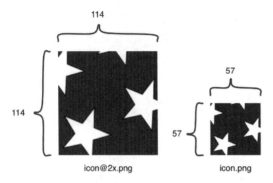

114

114

icon@2x.png

57

57

icon.png

Figure 5.5
Dimensions of an icon

Once you've created the icons, select your project in the Project Navigator and click FlashCards under TARGETS. Then select the Summary tab, if its not already selected, and scroll down to the App Icons section of the Summary page. Right-click the leftmost square that says No Image Specified, and choose Select File.

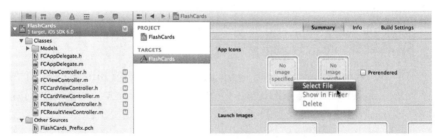

Figure 5.6   Selecting an app icon file

Select your 57 x 57 icon. Next, right-click the square labeled Retina Display, choose Select File, and select your 114 x 114 icon. When you select the icon files, they're automatically copied into the project. If you're a neat freak, move the icons files into the Resources group.

Figure 5.7   Icons in the Resources group

Run the app. When it starts, click the Home button so you can see the simulator's home screen. There you'll see the new icon being used for the app.

Figure 5.8 FlashCards icon on the home screen

YOU DON'T NEED TO ROUND THE CORNERS OR ADD THE GLOSSY EFFECT.

NOW YOU TELL ME.

Good icons are memorable, distinctive, and well-crafted. They're your first impression in the App Store and a constant reminder of your app on the phone once it's installed. It's worth being sure your app has a good one. Many icons have a prominent shape and a dominant color; both those things help them stand out in a crowd.

Having a great icon is just the start of polishing the look and feel of your application. To get the overall feel right, you need to make sure your application starts as quickly as possible. Professional iPhone apps seem to start instantaneously, and because you're not doing much at the beginning of the FlashCards app, it's weird that it seems to take longer. We'll look at fixing that in the next section (hint: it's a trick).

Making your application seem to load faster

You might have noticed that when your app starts up, there's a period of time when the screen looks black. If the app is a black hole simulator or a promotional vehicle for a Metallica, Spinal Tap, or Jay-Z album, then you can skip this section. If you need something different, read on.

THE APP IS STILL COMING UP BLACK. DIDN'T YOU PUT IN A DEFAULT IMAGE?

I DID, BUT IT WAS SOLID BLACK

For the FlashCards app's background, you'll use a style similar to the icon and repeat a lot of small stars. If you're not going to use the built-in iPhone backgrounds, stick to a simple, small repeating pattern or a naturally occurring surface like wood grain or brushed metal.

Figure 5.9 Background image

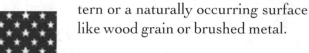

For the older iPhones, you need a 320 x 480 image called Default.png. For the retina display phones, you need one at 640 x 960 called Default@2x.png. And if that weren't enough, for the iPhone 5, you need a 640 x 1136 image called Default-568h@2x.png.

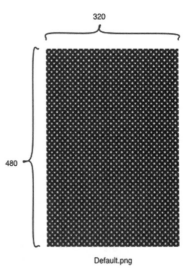

REPEATING PATTERNS LOOK NICE AS BACKGROUND TEXTURES.

Using these is just like using icons. In the Summary tab of FlashCards is a Launch Images section just below App Icons. Right-click each rectangle, and select the appropriate default image. When you're done, move the added images into the Resources group to keep things neat.

Figure 5.10 Default image dimensions

You'll want to incorporate this background into your app's screens as well. To do that, open each XIB in Interface Builder and then add an image view to the view. Using the Attributes Inspector, set the image view's image to Default.png. Size it correctly, and send it behind the other controls by clicking it and choosing Editor > Arrange > Send To Back from the menu.

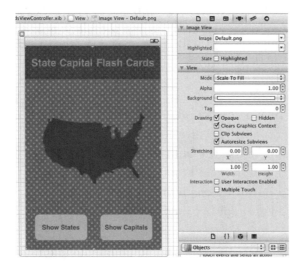

Figure 5.11 Setting the background image in Interface Builder

Figure 5.12 Running the updated app in the simulator

As you can see, we also resized and positioned the title label. To make it semitransparent, we set its Alpha to 0.5 using the Attributes Inspector.

If you run the app, you'll notice that it doesn't start with a blank, black screen. When it comes up, it looks as shown at left.

The middle of the app's start screen is blank and calling out for a graphic. The Default.png image should match whatever you decide to put there, but you still need a version of the image with blank space for the card views.

It's also obvious that the buttons need an upgrade. The default no longer matches the new look. Now would be a good time to take a break and find a matching t-shirt as well.

Using images for buttons

Because your app uses a lot of buttons (six total), the easiest way to spruce it up is to make custom buttons. It would be nice to be able to reuse a background image for all of them, because you want consistency.

I BET STRETCHABLE
IMAGES LOOK GOOD ON
THE RETINA DISPLAY.

The easiest way to use an image for a button is to set its image in the Attributes Inspector. This is fine if you've made the exact button you want and aren't going to change its size. A better way is to prepare a stretchable image and have the iPhone put the text on it for you. If you do that, you only need one image for all your buttons, and it will work no matter what the size or text.

Preparing a stretchable image

A *stretchable* image is an image that has a middle part that can be stretched and end caps that shouldn't be altered when the image changes size. Here's an example that shows how it works:

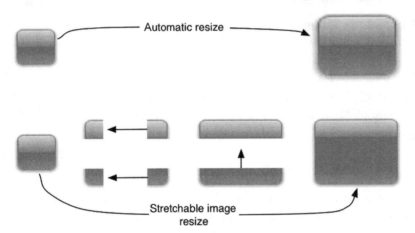

Figure 5.13   How stretchable buttons work

If you resize an image without doing anything, the edges are treated the same as the middle and look pixelated. To make an image stretchable, you need to know the width of the left cap and the height of the top cap.

Create two images with end caps that are the same size, one darker than the other. You'll use the lighter one normally and the darker one when you're touching the button. Name them as shown at right.

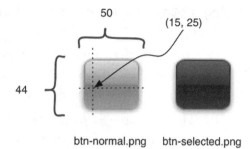

btn-normal.png   btn-selected.png

Figure 5.14 The position of the left and top caps

On the left is a better look at what would happen if you just resized an image to a wide button without doing this. For comparison, our stretchable button is on the right.

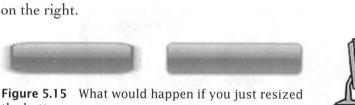

Figure 5.15 What would happen if you just resized the button

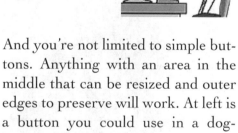

IT ONLY WORKS IF THE MIDDLE IS SOLID.

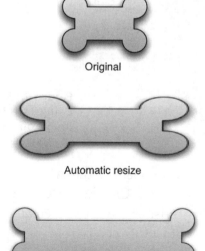

Original

Automatic resize

Stretchable resize

And you're not limited to simple buttons. Anything with an area in the middle that can be resized and outer edges to preserve will work. At left is a button you could use in a dog-training app.

Using those guidelines, you can design images that can be used on every button in your app, no matter the size. They'll also look great on the retina display without needing to alter them.

Figure 5.16 Stretchable resize on a more complex button

Using a stretchable image for a button

Once you have the buttons, you need a little code in order to use them in your app. Unfortunately, Interface Builder doesn't have direct support for stretchable images.

The first step is to tell Interface Builder that you want to use a custom button style. Do this by selecting the buttons and setting their Type to Custom in the Attributes Inspector. Their background will be invisible, but you'll still see them because of their text.

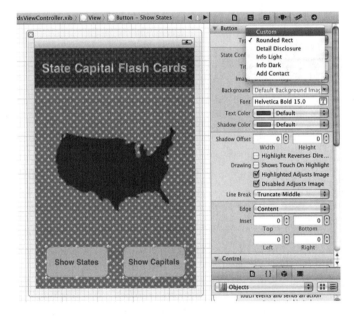

Figure 5.17
Using a stretchable image on a button in Interface Builder

Next, create outlets for the buttons by opening the Assistant Editor and Ctrl-dragging into FCViewController.h. Call the outlets showStates-Button and showCapitalsButton. The Assistant Editor will create properties that look like this:

```
@property (weak, nonatomic) IBOutlet UIButton *showStatesButton;
@property (weak, nonatomic) IBOutlet UIButton *showCapitalsButton;
```

Now that you're finished creating the Show States and Show Capitals buttons, open FCResultViewController.xib and create a Start Again button. Don't forget to create an outlet named startAgainButton for the button, using the Assistant Editor.

Here's how you code the stretchable buttons. Open FCAppDelegate.h, and add these message declarations:

```
- (void)setupButtonAsImage:(UIButton*) btn
              normalImage:(NSString*) normalImage
            selectedImage:(NSString*) selectedImage
                  leftCap:(NSInteger) leftCap
                   topCap:(NSInteger) topCap;
```

MAKING HELPER MESSAGES MEANS WE'LL HAVE LESS CODE.

```
- (void)setupButtonAsImage:(UIButton*) btn
                    image:(NSString*) image
                 forState:(UIControlState) state
                  leftCap:(NSInteger) leftCap
                   topCap:(NSInteger) topCap;
```

Then, open FCAppDelegate.m, and add these messages.

Listing 5.1   FCAppDelegate.m: loading and stretching the images, and using them for the button

```
- (void)setupButtonAsImage:(UIButton*) btn
                    image:(NSString*) image
                 forState:(UIControlState) state
                  leftCap:(NSInteger) leftCap
                   topCap:(NSInteger) topCap
{
    UIImage* originalImage = [UIImage imageNamed:image];        ❶ LOAD IMAGE
    UIImage* stretchImage = [originalImage
            stretchableImageWithLeftCapWidth:leftCap            ❷ STRETCH IT
                               topCapHeight:topCap];
```

```
        [btn setBackgroundImage:stretchImage forState:state];
```
❸ USE IMAGE ON BUTTON

SET TEXT COLOR TO WHITE ❹
```
        [btn setTitleColor:[UIColor whiteColor] forState:state];
    }

    - (void)setupButtonAsImage:(UIButton*) btn
                    normalImage:(NSString*) normalImage
                  selectedImage:(NSString*) selectedImage
                        leftCap:(NSInteger) leftCap
                         topCap:(NSInteger) topCap
    {
```
❺ SET NORMAL STATE
```
        [self setupButtonAsImage:btn image:normalImage
            forState:UIControlStateNormal leftCap:leftCap topCap:topCap];
```
SET SELECTED STATE ❻
```
        [self setupButtonAsImage:btn image:selectedImage

            forState:UIControlStateSelected leftCap:leftCap topCap:topCap]
        ;
    }
```

To use the images, first you need to copy them to your Resources folder. Then you can use the first message to load them ❶ into a UIImage object by calling its imageNamed message. Once you load it, you send it a message ❷ to stretch it based on its left-cap width and top-cap height. Finally, you set the button's background image ❸ and set the text of the button to white ❹.

DESIGN YOUR BUTTONS TO HAVE NON-STRETCHED CAPS. AND MEASURE THEIR SIZE.

Each button needs this done twice—once for the normal state ❺ and once for the selected state ❻—so the next message does that. The second message uses the first and makes it easier for you, so you'll be using it in your views.

In FCViewController.m, add #import "FCAppDelegate.h" to the import statements. Then you can call the new message by adding this code to the viewDidLoad message:

```
FCAppDelegate* delegate = [[UIApplication
                              sharedApplication] delegate];
[delegate setupButtonAsImage:self.showStatesButton
          normalImage:@"btn-normal.png"
        selectedImage:@"btn-selected.png"
          leftCap:15 topCap:25];
[delegate setupButtonAsImage:self.showCapitalsButton
          normalImage:@"btn-normal.png"
        selectedImage:@"btn-selected.png"
          leftCap:15 topCap:25];
```

You can use similar code in all of your view-controller viewDidLoad messages. Run the app to see how it looks.

Isn't that better? Well, it's only as nice as your design, so be creative. We've emulated the Mac OS X aqua gel button look, but you're free to make buttons with as radical a look as you want.

Icons, background images, color schemes, and buttons are a start, but to make your app stand out, you need to use animation. Without it, your app won't seem as professional; with it, the app will appear to come to life.

Figure 5.18 The app with stretchable buttons in the simulator

Adding animation

If you play around with the built-in iPhone apps, you'll notice that new views never snap into place. There's always a little transition animation. It could be a slide, a flip, a page curl, or, with some apps, something even more fun. Good use of transition animations will make your app look more at home on the iPhone.

Sliding views instead of instantly switching

Probably the most common animation used on the iPhone has the next view slide into place. As you'll see later, this animation is built into the navigation-based application template, but nearly every app with multiple views uses it somewhere.

Here's what the FlashCards app will look with a push transition on the second view.

Figure 5.19
A push transition

To do this, add #import <QuartzCore/QuartzCore.h> and these message declarations to FCAppDelegate.h:

```
-(void) pushView;
```

And add this code to the module file (pro tip: you can use Ctrl-Cmd-up arrow to switch between .h and .m files).

Listing 5.2   FCAppDelegate.m: creating a push animation

```
-(void) pushView
{
    CATransition* animation = [CATransition animation];
    [animation setDelegate:self];

    [animation setType:kCATransitionPush];
    [animation setSubtype:kCATransitionFromRight];          ❶ ANIMATION TYPE

    [animation setDuration: 0.5];          ❷ DURATION IN SECONDS

    [animation setTimingFunction:
     [CAMediaTimingFunction          ❸ ANIMATION CURVE
       functionWithName:kCAMediaTimingFunctionEaseInEaseOut]];

    [[self.window layer] addAnimation:animation forKey:@"push"];
}
```

The CATransition class makes it easy to set up animations, and it's used to animate an entire window. To use it, pick its type ❶ and subtype. Then set the duration in seconds ❷. Finally, choose an animation curve to use as a timing function ❸. That last part needs a little more explanation.

An animation sets up a background timing function that makes the changes to the window for you automatically. But it doesn't need to apply an equal change at each point of the animation. In the code, you're using an ease-in/ease-out animation, which will start slowly, speed up, and then slow down.

TECH SUPPORT. GREG SPEAKING.

HOW DO YOU GET THE APP DELEGATE FROM A VIEW?

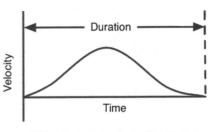

Figure 5.20
An ease-in/ease-out animation over time

UIViewAnimationCurveEaseInOut

You could also have chosen to just ease in. Then it would look like this:

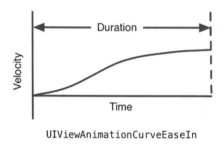

UIViewAnimationCurveEaseIn

Figure 5.21   An ease-in animation over time

And, of course, you could reverse that or have no easing whatsoever by using different curves.

You use this animation by adding the following code to the end of the showCards message in FCViewController.m:

```
FCAppDelegate* delegate = [[UIApplication sharedApplication] delegate];
[delegate pushView];
```

Slide animations are all over the iPhone. You're using a push, which means one view pushes the other out of the way. There are also reveals and move-ins, which you can see by changing the type of the transition to kCATransitionReveal or kCATransitionMoveIn.

The push animation is part of the QuartzCore framework; that's why you had to import QuartzCore.h. In order to use the framework, you also have to add it to your project. Select the project in the Project Navigator, and click FlashCards under TARGETS. Make sure the Summary tab is selected, and scroll down to Linked Frameworks and Libraries. Click the plus sign to add the framework, and choose Quartz-Core.Framework.

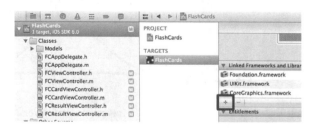

Figure 5.22   Adding the QuartzCore framework

Flipping a view to show its back

Another animation type you see a lot is a flip. Apps that consist of a single screen with settings sometimes use this animation to make it look like the settings are on the back of the view.

Figure 5.23   A flip animation

The code for a flip is similar to that of a push, but because flips can be applied to individual elements as well as the entire screen, you have to use UIView's animation support instead of using CATransition directly. Add this message to FCAppDelegate.h:

```
-(void) flipView;
```

And here's the message implementation for the .m file:

```
-(void) flipView
{
    [UIView beginAnimations:@"flip" context:nil];
    [UIView setAnimationTransition: UIViewAnimationTransitionFlipFromLeft
            forView:self.window cache:YES];

    [UIView setAnimationDuration: 0.5];
    [UIView setAnimationCurve:UIViewAnimationCurveEaseIn];

    [UIView commitAnimations];
}
```

I JUST GOT A NEW ANIMATION WORKING. COME SEE.

IS IT FLIPPING AWESOME?

The messages have the same meaning as their CATransition counterparts, with setAnimationCurve having the same meaning as setTimingFunction.

To call it, use this code in FCCardViewController.m, at the end of answerButtonTouched:

```
FCAppDelegate* delegate =
    [[UIApplication sharedApplication] delegate];
[delegate flipView];
```

Flips work well in this case because the app is emulating cards. It would be even better if you were showing the back of a card in the next view, because then the animation would be closer to the real-life version.

Using custom animations

The only other things that don't animate are the controls that appear when the app starts. This is more complex because you aren't transitioning an entire view at once. Each part needs its own animation.

To use a custom animation, you use the UIView animation support; but instead of setting a type and a subtype, you start an animation, change the view, and then commit the animation. The iPhone will know to make the change using the animation. For example, if you wanted the Show States button to start offscreen (at y-position 460) and move to its final location at y-position 380, you'd use the steps shown at right.

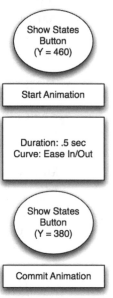

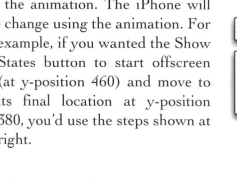

DON'T START ANYTHING IF YOU AREN'T READY TO COMMIT.

WHAT ARE WE TALKING ABOUT?

Figure 5.24
The steps for animating a property of a subview

If you choose an ease-in/ease-out curve, it will look like this:

ANIMATIONS CHANGE A NUMERIC PROPERTY OVER TIME.

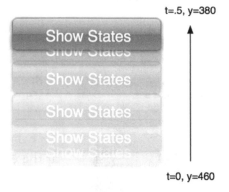

t=.5, y=380

t=0, y=460

Figure 5.25 What the button animation will look like

To do that, add this message to FCViewController.m, above viewDid-Load.

Listing 5.3   FCViewController.m: creating a custom animation

```
-(void) animateViewEntrance:(UIView*)v
   startY:(int)startY delay:(NSTimeInterval)delay
{
    CGRect frame = v.frame;                          ❶ ORIGINAL
    CGFloat endY = frame.origin.y;                      LOCATION

    frame.origin.y = startY;                            STARTING
    v.frame = frame;                                 ❷ POSITION

    [UIView animateWithDuration:0.25 delay:delay
        options:UIViewAnimationCurveEaseInOut
        animations:^{
            v.frame = CGRectMake(                    ❸ FINAL
                frame.origin.x, endY,                   POSITION
                frame.size.width, frame.size.height
            );
        } completion:nil];
}
```

You'll use this code for the title and buttons. It remembers the passed-in view's position as set in Interface Builder ❶. Then it sets a new starting position ❷ and starts an animation. In the animation, the code sets the original position ❸ as the final position so it looks like it does in Interface Builder at the end.

You can already call animateViewEntrance on the buttons because you have outlets. Before adding the next message, open FCViewController.nib and make an outlet for the title label called titleLabel by Ctrl-dragging into the Assistant Editor.

DON'T FORGET TO UNSET THE NEW OUTLET IN DEALLOC.

After you add the outlet, this code will compile:

```
-(void) animateViewLoad
{
    [self animateViewEntrance:self.showStatesButton
        startY:self.view.frame.size.height delay:0];
```

```
[self animateViewEntrance:self.showCapitalsButton
    startY:self.view.frame.size.height  delay:0];
[self animateViewEntrance:self.titleLabel
    startY:-self.titleLabel.frame.size.height delay:0];
}
```

You call `animateViewLoad` in `viewDidLoad` by adding this code to the end of it:

```
[self animateViewLoad];
```

If you create and commit multiple animations, the iPhone runs them simultaneously:

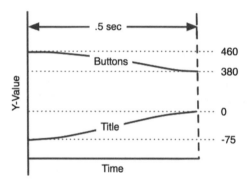

Figure 5.26
Simultaneous animations

It looks like this when you run it.

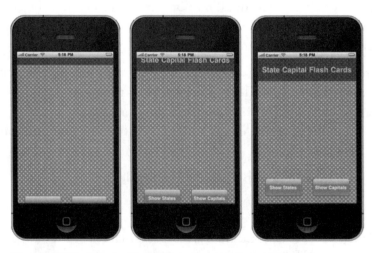

Figure 5.27 The button animation in the simulator

In `animateViewLoad`, you can see that you always use a delay of 0 seconds. If you want to delay the button's appearance until after the title, set the delay to 0.5 for the buttons. It will use a timeline like this:

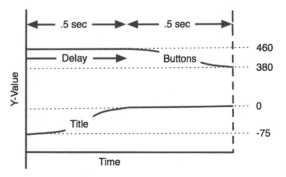

Figure 5.28 An overlapping animation with delays

With overlapping delays and durations, you can have all kinds of animations. The best part is that you only need to provide starting and ending points, durations, and curves. You don't need to update each in-between state yourself.

Making your apps look professional with graphic design

Your icon, startup, overall look, and use of animations go a long way toward making an app look professional. Of course, it's important that your app work, but no matter what it does, there are likely to be a few apps that do something similar. Professional-looking apps stand out in the crowded App Store, so it's worth working with a graphic artist to get this right.

The last step is to make the app track data between runs. It's likely that your users will want to know how well they have done over time. In the next chapter, you'll learn about the iPhone's support for data storage and presentation.

6

Working with databases and table views

This chapter covers

- *Storing and getting data*
- *Using data in table views*
- *Navigating view hierarchies*
- *Changing data model*

You're nearly done with FlashCards. So far, you have applied model-view-controller (MVC) to design a complex app. Then, you learned how to use Interface Builder to draw views and Xcode to code classes. Finally, you added icons, image buttons, backgrounds, and animations to polish up your app.

Next, you'll learn how to store and fetch data so you can track results. Then your users can see how they have progressed at learning state capitals.

Keeping track of data in the FlashCards app

The purpose of the FlashCards app is to help people remember facts. Whether you're trying to learn college football mascots, celebrity couples, dog breeds, or multiplication tables, it won't matter much if you don't improve. To help your users know how well they're doing, you need to keep track of their results.

Deciding what to store

The best way to figure out what information to store is to think about what users will want to see later. If you're using FlashCards to learn something, you at least want to know how long the game took you and when you played.

game	game date	game length
1	1/21/2011	100 seconds
2	1/22/2011	90 seconds
3	1/28/2011	150 seconds
4	1/31/2011	200 seconds

Figure 6.1 What to store for a game result

You also want to know how you did on each card for a particular game.

card	name	was correct	for game
1	Alabama	YES	1
2	Alaska	NO	1
3	Arizona	YES	1
4	Arkansas	YES	1

Figure 6.2   What to store for a card result

THIS IS CALLED RELATIONAL DATA BECAUSE CARD RESULTS ARE RELATED TO A GAMERESULT.

If you know that, you can sum up the number of cards you got right and figure out a percentage of the total, so there's no need to keep track of that separately. Notice that for cards, you don't need to store the date again, because you're storing which game the card result was associated with.

This is the minimum data you need to keep track of in order to provide some historical information. It's also data that you already know or can get easily. The next step is to figure out how to show it.

Sketching how the app will look

To use this data in your app, you'll need to add more views and ways to navigate to them. In iPhone apps, the normal way is to use a hierarchical navigation through tables. You've seen this in the Contacts app, the Mail app, iTunes, and many other iPhone apps. This is a common iPhone user interface, and as you'd suspect, a lot of it's provided by the iOS SDK.

The first thing your app shows is a couple of buttons that let the user choose to see states or capitals. Let's add a button to show history as well.

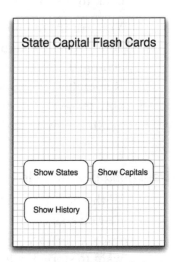

Figure 6.3   Sketch of the new home screen

Once you have that up, you'll show a navigation bar at the top. It will have a title and a Done button. Underneath, you'll put a table with a list of games, the date the user played, and how well they did. You'll put a little arrow to the right of each game to indicate that the user can touch the row to see more information.

Figure 6.4 Sketches of the history screens

And if they touch a row, you'll show the details of each card. On the Card History screen, you'll have a back button to allow the user to go back to the Game History list.

You can try to fancy up that home screen on your own. Perhaps three square buttons arranged horizontally would look nicer. Remember, because you're using stretchable images, you don't have to worry about making new images if you change the button size.

Designing new models

With your screen sketches in place, you now have to think about what new classes you may need and how to update the ones you have. To keep track of historical results, you need classes that can hold the data you want to store. So, let's make GameResult and CardResult classes. You'll add the properties that you identified and link the classes together.

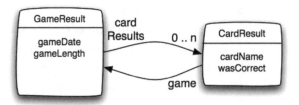

Figure 6.5 GameResult and CardResult classes

Because you're adding a new button, you of course need to add an outlet for it in the FCViewController. If you want the button to do anything, you need an action as well, which you'll call showHistory.

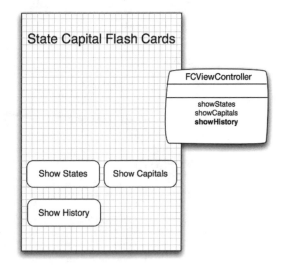

Figure 6.6
FCViewController's
showHistory action

You'll save games as soon as they're finished. The FCResultViewController will take care of that for you by telling the FCGame to save itself.

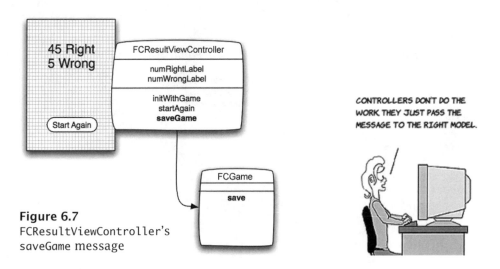

Figure 6.7
FCResultViewController's
saveGame message

CONTROLLERS DON'T DO THE WORK. THEY JUST PASS THE MESSAGE TO THE RIGHT MODEL.

To save its results, a FCGame creates a GameResult object and sets the object's properties. Next, it creates a CardResult object for each card, sets that object's properties, and adds the CardResult to the GameResult. At the end, the FCGame has to send a message to some object to save the GameResult. You don't know how that will work yet, but you will soon.

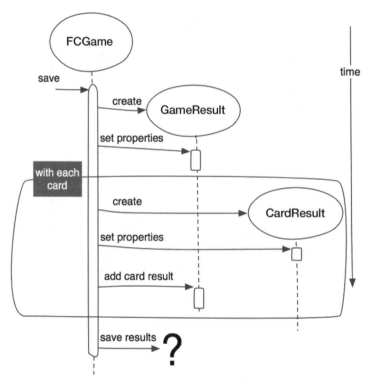

Figure 6.8   The sequence of messages when saving a game

To show the game result data, you're going to use a table. Somehow, you need to load the data and fill the cells. You also need to detect when a row is touched.

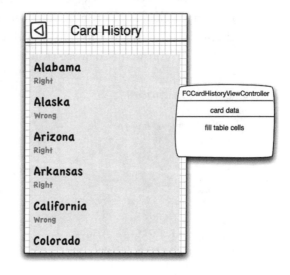

Figure 6.9 FCGameHistory-
ViewController messages

When a row is touched, you'll switch the view to show the related card results. It would be nice to not have to load data again and just pass it from the game-result view to the card-result view, so you'll do that.

Figure 6.10 FCCardHistory-
ViewController messages

It seems like a lot, but you'll see how much the SDK does for you. To help you store and fetch data, Apple provides a framework called Core Data. It makes storing objects easy. Underlying it is a standard SQL database, but don't worry if you don't know anything about those, because Core Data takes care of everything for you. If you know a lot about SQL, it will help you understand how Core Data works.

Introducing Core Data

To help you store and get to objects later, you need to learn about the data-modeling tools built into Xcode. Using them, you can define what you want to store, generate classes automatically instead of coding them, and manage database updates that need to happen if you want to store things differently later.

GENERATE CLASSES AUTOMATICALLY? NOW WE'RE TALKING!

Creating a data model

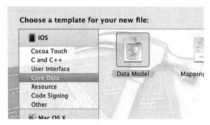

Figure 6.11   Making a Data Model in the New File dialog

To help you define your data, Xcode provides a design tool. You get to it by creating a new data model. Do this by right-clicking the Resources group and choosing New File. In the next dialog, in the iOS section, select Core Data and then choose Data Model.

Name the data model `FlashCards .xcdatamodeld`.

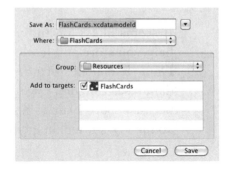

Figure 6.12   Naming the data model

When you do this, Xcode displays a data-modeling interface for your
.xcdatamodel file. Here's where you can design your data.

Figure 6.13   Data model editor

THIS LOOKS LIKE IT'S
GOING TO BE FUN.

Designing data for Core Data is similar to the class
designing you've been doing, so it will feel familiar.
It's so similar that the classes you need in order to
access the data can be automatically generated for
you by Xcode. You'll see how to do that next.

Adding entities and attributes

The first concept to understand in data modeling is the entity. An *entity*
is roughly equivalent to a class in that it defines storage. Unlike a class,
though, you don't define messages for it.

To start, click the Add Entity plus sign at lower left in the editor, and
then name the entity GameResult. Then, add two attributes, gameDate and
gameLength, by clicking the plus sign in the Attribute table. When you're
done, it looks like this.

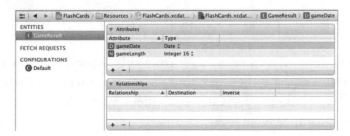

Figure 6.14
Adding attributes

You need to configure each attribute. gameDate is a Date, and gameLength is the number of seconds the game took to play, so it's an Integer. Click each one, and make the Attribute detail pane look like this.

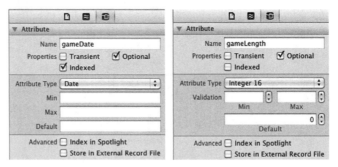

Figure 6.15 Configuring parameters in the Data Model Editor

USE INDEXES WHEN YOU WANT TO SORT OR QUICKLY ACCESS OBJECTS BY THIS ATTRIBUTE.

You've probably already figured out that attributes are like properties when you're designing classes. In the Data Modeler, they're one of the types of data properties, with relationships being the other kind. We'll get to those soon.

Let's create the CardResult entity and its two attributes, cardName (a String), and wasCorrect (a Bool).

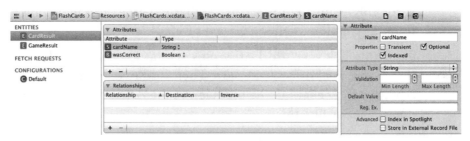

Figure 6.16 Creating a CardResult entity in the editor

You're almost done. If you remember from the beginning of the chapter, you need to associate the cards and games together. For that, Core Data provides relationships. Can you guess what thing from class design a relationship is most like?

Using relationships

When two entities need to be associated with each other, you create a relationship between them. If you're familiar with SQL and relational data, then you understand exactly what this means. If you aren't, think of relationships the sane way you think of has-a in class design. A car has wheels, a game result has card results, and an album has tracks. Like has-a, there can be mutual, part-whole, and ownership relationships; one-to-one and one-to-many; and all the other things you learned about has-a.

I'VE GOT HAS-A DOWN, SO THIS SHOULD BE EASY.

Add a relationship to GameResult called cardResults. In the detail pane, set Destination to CardResult, select the To-Many Relationship check box, and set Delete Rule to Cascade. Then add a gameResults relationship to CardResult. This one isn't to-many, and Destination should be set to GameResult. Now that you've created both, you can say that they're the same relationship by using the Inverse drop-down in one relationship's detail pane to choose the other relationship. When you do so, the editor automatically sets the other relationship's Inverse value for you.

Figure 6.17   Defining a relationship in the Data Model Editor

Your data model is finished. Next you'll let Xcode do the coding for you. You can probably imagine the code you'd need to write to mimic this structure, because it's similar to object-oriented design.

Generating data classes

If you had to write the code yourself, it wouldn't be too hard, but you'd have to remember to keep it up to date every time you made a change. Generating the code not only saves time but also is less prone to errors.

TALKIN' BOUT CODE GENERATION
HOPE I DIE BEFORE I WRITE CODE

(TUNE OF "MY GENERATION"
BY THE WHO)

To do it, you must have the model up in Xcode. Right-click the Classes group, and choose New File. Under Core Data, choose NSManagedObject Subclass, and click Next.

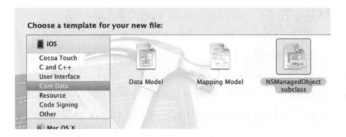

Figure 6.18
Creating a managed object in the New File dialog

In the next dialog, make sure all your entities are selected, and click Next to choose the group they will be stored in.

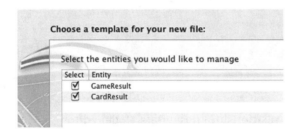

Figure 6.19
Choose the entities to generate code for

That's it! As they used to say in the old iMac ads, "There is no step three."

Go look at the new modules and headers that were generated. It's mostly things you're familiar with, plus a few we haven't covered. If you examine the header, you'll see that you already know a lot about how to use these classes.

Adding Core Data support to your app

KNOWING HOW TO ADD CORE DATA YOURSELF BUILDS CHARACTER.

For every app that needs Core Data, you have to go through a few steps. If you knew you were going to use data, you could have checked a box in the template to set up Core Data for you automatically. It's good to know how to add it later yourself, so you know how.

The first step is to add the Core Data Framework to the Frameworks Group. To do that, click the FlashCards target at the top of the Project Navigator. Then, choose the Build Phases tab and open the Link Binary with Libraries table. Click the plus sign at lower left, and choose to add CoreData.framework.

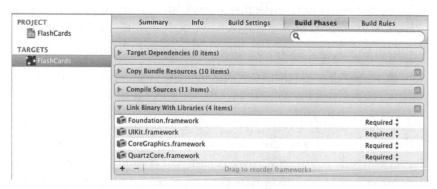

Figure 6.20 Adding the Core Data Framework

To load the model file and use the managed objects in your code, you need to configure Core Data in your app. To better understand how the code works, let's look at some of the major concepts of Core Data and how they work together.

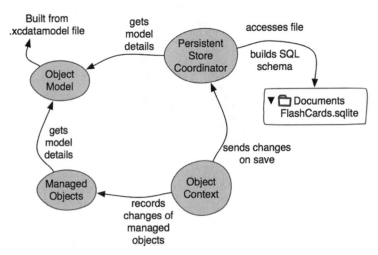

Figure 6.21   The main Core Data concepts and how they work together

The first thing to understand is the *object model*. It's created by Core Data from reading the .xcmodeldata file, and it gives you a way to find out about the entities, attributes, and relationships in your model.

> **OBJECT MODEL**   The object representation of the model data resource file.

The *persistent store coordinator* knows how your model becomes a database. iOS comes with a database called SQLite, and the store coordinator turns all your requests into SQL commands for it.

> **PERSISTENT STORE COORDINATOR**   Manages the actual database file and writes the correct SQL based on your actions.

The *object context* keeps track of all your changes until they're saved to the database. Every time you create a new entity object, it remembers that it needs to insert a row. When you change an attribute, the object context remembers to update the object context's row. The object context also keeps track of objects you fetch from the store. When you're ready to commit your changes, you send the object context a save message, and it tells the store coordinator what was changed.

> **OBJECT CONTEXT** Keeps track of changes until they're saved to the database.

Because you generated `GameResult` and `Card-Result`, you know those are *managed objects*. If you look at their headers, you'll see that they inherit from `NSManagedObject`.

> **MANAGED OBJECTS** The type of objects created by generating classes from your data model

CONTEXTS AND MODELS AND STORES

OH MY!

Let's see how to code the configuration of these objects. In FCAppDelegate.h, add these retained properties:

```
@property (nonatomic, strong) NSPersistentStoreCoordinator *dataStore;
@property (nonatomic, strong) NSManagedObjectModel* dataModel;
@property (nonatomic, strong) NSManagedObjectContext* dataContext;
```

In any file in which you use Core Data, you need to add an import for it, so add this to the top of the header:

```
#import <CoreData/CoreData.h>
```

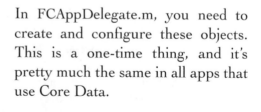

OK, FIRST WE LOAD THE MODEL FROM THE BUNDLE, AND THEN WE CONFIGURE THE STORE WITH THE NAME OF OUR DATABASE FILE AND THE MODEL TO USE. FINALLY, WE MAKE A DATA CONTEXT AND TELL IT WHICH STORE TO SAVE CHANGES TO. THEN WE CAN USE THE CONTEXT TO FETCH AND STORE MANAGED OBJECTS. GOT IT?

YUP!

In FCAppDelegate.m, you need to create and configure these objects. This is a one-time thing, and it's pretty much the same in all apps that use Core Data.

First, add this message to figure out where the Documents folder for this app is on the iPhone. This is where the database file should be stored:

```
-(NSString*)docsDir
{                                                    FIND DOCUMENTS
    NSArray *paths =                                 FOLDER
        NSSearchPathForDirectoriesInDomains(
        NSDocumentDirectory, NSUserDomainMask, YES);
    return [paths objectAtIndex:0];
}
```

Next, add this message to create a persistent store coordinator for a given model. The store coordinator builds the actual database from the entities, attributes, and relationships you defined, so it needs access to the model to do that.

Listing 6.1 **FCAppDelegate.m: creates a persistent store**

```
-(NSPersistentStoreCoordinator*)dataStoreForModel:
        (NSManagedObjectModel*)model
        filename:(NSString*)filename
{                                               ❶ DATABASE
    NSURL* storeLocation =                         LOCATION
        [NSURL fileURLWithPath:
         [[self docsDir]
          stringByAppendingPathComponent:filename]];

    NSPersistentStoreCoordinator* store =
        [[NSPersistentStoreCoordinator alloc]
         initWithManagedObjectModel:model];
                                                ❷ SET OPTIONS
    NSDictionary *options =
        [NSDictionary dictionaryWithObjectsAndKeys:
         [NSNumber numberWithBool:YES],
            NSMigratePersistentStoresAutomaticallyOption,
         [NSNumber numberWithBool:YES],
            NSInferMappingModelAutomaticallyOption, nil];

    NSError* error;                          ❸ CONFIGURE STORE
    if (![store                                 FOR SQLITE
          addPersistentStoreWithType:NSSQLiteStoreType
```

```
            configuration:nil
            URL:storeLocation
            options:options
            error:&error])
    {
        NSLog(@"Error initializing Data Store: %@",
              [error localizedDescription]);
        return nil;
    }
    return store;
}
```

④ REPORT ERRORS

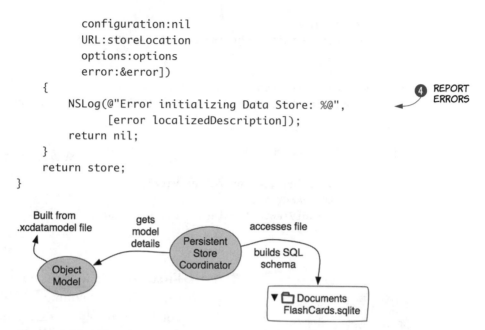

Figure 6.22 The object model and the persistent store coordinator

To create a store, you need to specify a location ❶, options ❷, and the kind of database you want ❸. We'll explain the options we chose in section 6.4. Finally, many things in Core Data can go wrong, so you need to check for errors. In this case, you're logging errors to the console so you can see the problem if you have one ❹.

The next step is to set up properties. Add this configureCoreData message, and make sure to call it.

Listing 6.2   FCAppDelegate.m: configuring Core Data

```
-(void)configureCoreData
{                                                      ❶ CONFIGURE MODEL
    self.dataModel =
        [NSManagedObjectModel mergedModelFromBundles:nil];

    self.dataStore = [self dataStoreForModel:self.dataModel
        filename:@"FlashCards.sqlite"];

    self.dataContext =
        [[NSManagedObjectContext alloc] init];         ❷ CONFIGURE CONTEXT
```

```
    [self.dataContext
        setPersistentStoreCoordinator:self.dataStore];
}


- (BOOL)application:(UIApplication *)application
            didFinishLaunchingWithOptions:(NSDictionary *)launchOption
    s
{
    [self configureCoreData];

    [window addSubview:viewController.view];
    [window makeKeyAndVisible];
    self.window.rootViewController = self.viewController;
    return YES;
}
```

❸ SEND CONFIGURATION MESSAGE

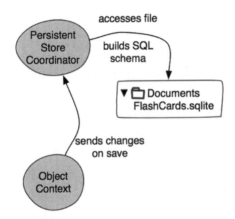

Figure 6.23   Persistent store coordinator and object context

First, you load the model file from the .xcdatamodel file in your bundle ❶. Next, you use the message from earlier to make a store, and then you create a context ❷. Because the context needs to issue changes to the store, you set that up as well. Finally, you configure Core Data when the app launches ❸.

It's a fair bit of code, but you can use it as is in just about any Core Data application. The only change you'd need to make is the name of the SQLite file. With that in place you can finally use your managed objects to create rows in the database.

OK I'LL USE THIS CODE. BUT LATER I'M GOING TO CHECK IT AGAINST A PROJECT TEMPLATE.

Saving your game results

With Core Data configured in your app, you're ready to start using it. A big chunk of the work was done for you when you generated the model objects. And remember that big question mark you had when you were trying to figure out how to save game results? Well, now you know that's going to be done by the data context.

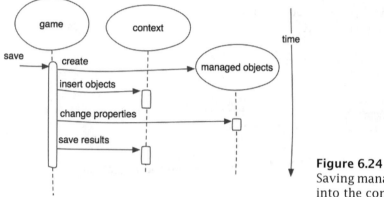

Figure 6.24
Saving managed objects into the context

To do the save, you need to add the code to the FCGame class. It will use Core Data, so add this import to the header:

```
#import <CoreData/CoreData.h>
```

Also declare the save message. You'll have the controller tell you about the context when it requests a save:

```
-(NSError*)save:(NSManagedObjectContext *)context;
```

Finally, here's the implementation for the save. Add #import "Game-Result.h" to the top of the module and then the following message.

Listing 6.3   FCGame.m: saving a game's result

```
-(NSError*)save:(NSManagedObjectContext *)context
{                                                        ❶ INSERT
    GameResult *gameResult;                                 GAMERESULT
    gameResult = [NSEntityDescription
                insertNewObjectForEntityForName:@"GameResult"
                inManagedObjectContext:context];
                                                         ❷ SET ITS
    gameResult.gameDate = self.gameStart;                   ATTRIBUTES
    gameResult.gameLength = [NSNumber numberWithInteger:
                            -[self.gameStart timeIntervalSinceNow]];
```

```
for (FCCard* c in self.cards) {
    [gameResult addCardResultsObject:
     [c cardResultInGame:gameResult withContext:context]];
}

NSError *error;
if ([context save:&error]) {
    return nil;
}
return error;
}
```

③ ADD CARD RESULT
   OBJECTS

④ SAVE CONTEXT

Managed Objects ← records changes of managed objects ← Object Context

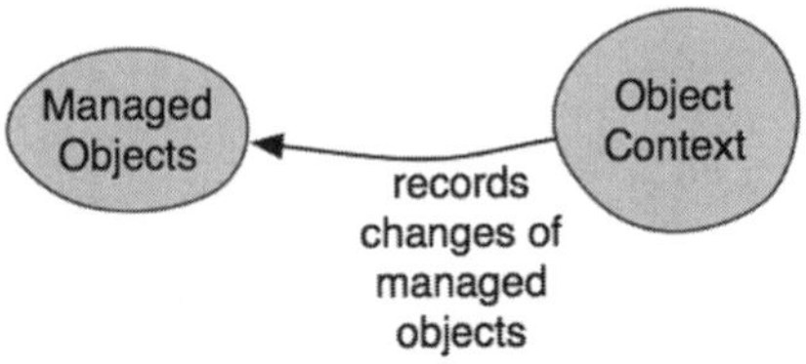

Figure 6.25
Managed objects and the object context

This is typical Core Data code for creating entities. First you create a new GameResult object using its entity description ①. Next, you set the attributes of the GameResult ②. Then you add Card-Result objects that the Card will make for you ③, and finally you save ④ and report any errors you run into.

HOW DO YOU SAY "INSERT INTO TABLE" IN CORE DATA?

"INSERT NEW OBJECT FOR ENTITY FOR NAME"

To get the gameLength, you needed to add another property to FCGame, called game-Start. It's an NSDate*. To initialize it, set it to the current time by assigning it to [NSDate date] in FCGame's init message.

Add this message to Card. You'll also have to remember to declare it in the header and add #import "CardResult.h".

Listing 6.4   FCCard.m: creating a CardResult from a Card object

```
-(CardResult*)cardResultInGame:(GameResult*)gameResult
               withContext:(NSManagedObjectContext*) context
{
    CardResult* cardResult = [NSEntityDescription
               insertNewObjectForEntityForName:@"CardResult"
               inManagedObjectContext:context];
```

```
cardResult.cardName = self.cardText;
cardResult.wasCorrect = [NSNumber numberWithBool: self.isCorrect];

return cardResult;
}
```

This code creates a managed object and configures it. Because you set up an inverse relationship in the model, Core Data will automatically set the CardResult's gameResult property for you when you add it to GameResult.

To call these messages, add this message to FCResultViewController.m.

Listing 6.5   FCResultViewController.m: saving a game

```
-(void)saveGame {
    FCAppDelegate *appDelegate =
        [[UIApplication sharedApplication] delegate];

    NSError* err =
        [self.game save: appDelegate.dataContext];        ← SAVE GAME

    if (err != nil) {                                      ┐ REPORT
        NSLog(@"Error in save: %@",                        ┘ ERRORS
                [err localizedDescription]);
    }
}
```

Also add a [self saveGame]; call to its init method, so the game length is recorded as soon as you're done.

With this code in place, each game will be stored as soon as you're done playing. That's great, but why save the game result if you can't do something with it later? One nice thing to do is to allow the user to navigate around and view their game result history, which you'll learn about next.

Fetching and viewing data

HOW DO I GET TO ALL
THAT DATA I SAVED?

It's no use saving data if you're never going to use it for anything. The easiest thing to do with data is to look at it, and the iPhone provides a nice way to do that with table and navigation views. They're perfect for quickly scrolling through data, choosing rows to get more detail on, and navigating back to the summary. This combination of views is used in a lot of iPhone apps.

Viewing in a table

If you look at the Contacts or Mail app, you're looking at table and navigation views in action. The top bar is the navigation, and the list of data below it is the table. You'll see this basic structure in a lot of apps, sometimes configured a little differently, but fundamentally the same. These views can be used with or without Core Data.

To get started, add a new view controller class to your app.

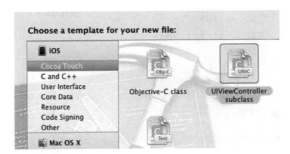

Figure 6.26
Creating a UIViewController

This time, make it a UITableViewController subclass. Name it FCGame-HistoryViewController.m.

Class   FCGameHistoryViewController

Subclass of   UITableViewController

☐ Targeted for iPad
☑ With XIB for user interface

Figure 6.27 Making your view controller a subclass of UITableViewController

When you're done, add another view controller for FCCardHistory-ViewController.m.

Before we look at the code, at right you can see how the tables and Core Data work together.

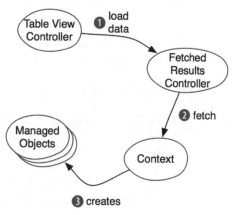

Figure 6.28 The interaction between the table view controller and Core Data objects to fetch data

To start with, your controller will fetch the data into the context using a new class called a NSFetchedResults controller ❶, ❷. This class is designed to help you put data from Core Data into tables. The context takes your request and creates managed objects for you ❸.

Later, the table view will ask for that data like this:

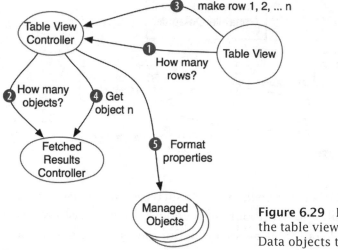

Figure 6.29 Interaction between the table view controller and Core Data objects to show data

First, the table view asks its controller how many rows it should show
❶. To find out, the controller asks the fetched results controller ❷ how
many managed objects it has. Then the table asks for each row in turn
❸, which the controller gets by obtaining managed objects from the
fetched results ❹. The last thing you need to do ❺ is format the properties to look nice in the table. Let's see the code.

Change FCGameHistoryViewController.h to look like this.

Listing 6.6   FCGameHistoryViewController.h: fetched-results property

```
#import <CoreData/CoreData.h>

@interface FCGameHistoryViewController : UITableViewController
    <NSFetchedResultsControllerDelegate>                         FETCHED-RESULTS
                                                              ❶ PROPERTY

@property(strong, nonatomic)
        NSFetchedResultsController *resultsController;            NEED THIS TO
                                                                 USE FETCHED
@end                                                          ❷ RESULTS
```

To use an NSFetchedResultsController, you add a property ❶ and make a
delegate ❷. Let's take a closer look at how the delegate works.

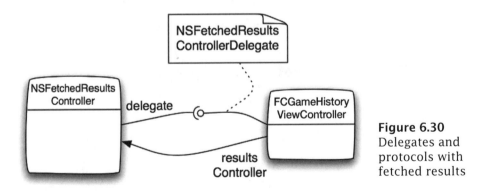

Figure 6.30
Delegates and
protocols with
fetched results

When an SDK class like NSFetchedResultsController needs to use a class
it can't possibly know about (like your FCGameHistoryViewController), it
defines a delegate that acts as a definition of what messages it would

PROTOCOLS ARE LIKE IS-A BUT NONE OF THE MESSAGES ARE IMPLEMENTED YET.

like to send. To receive them, you implement the messages of the delegate. It's a similar concept to inheritance, with the major difference being that there are no default message implementations. In Objective-C, this is called *implementing* a protocol, and we'll diagram that with the ball-and-socket style used earlier.

Let's go to the module file and load data. The first step is to build a request. To make a request, you say what entities you want, which ones, and how to sort them. Here's the code.

Listing 6.7   FCGameHistoryViewController.m: fetching and sorting entity objects

```
-(NSFetchRequest*)requestForGameResults:
    (NSManagedObjectContext*) context
{
    NSEntityDescription* gameResultDesc =
    [NSEntityDescription entityForName:@"GameResult"
                inManagedObjectContext:context];

    NSFetchRequest* request =
        [[NSFetchRequest alloc] init];

    [request setEntity:gameResultDesc];

    NSSortDescriptor *sort = [[NSSortDescriptor alloc]
                                initWithKey:@"gameDate"
                                ascending:NO];
    [request setSortDescriptors:[NSArray arrayWithObject:sort]];

    return request;
}
```

❶ SPECIFY THE ENTITIES YOU WANT ...

❷ ... AND HOW TO SORT THEM

This code makes an NSFetchRequest object that can be used to get NSManagedObjects into your context. First ❶ it builds an NSEntityDescription to say you want Game-Result objects. Next ❷ it builds an NSSort-Descriptor to say it wants them sorted by the attribute gameDate in descending order. You'll use this message in loadData like this.

AND "ORDER BY FIELDNAME" IN CORE DATA IS --?

"SORT DESCRIPTOR INIT WITH KEY FIELDNAME"

Listing 6.8 FCGameHistoryViewController.m: fetching the entity

```
-(void)loadData
{
    FCAppDelegate* delegate =
        [[UIApplication sharedApplication] delegate];        ❶ GET APP
                                                               DELEGATE
    NSManagedObjectContext* context =
        delegate.dataContext;

    NSFetchRequest* request = [self requestForGameResults:context];

    self.resultsController =
        [[NSFetchedResultsController alloc]              ❷ MAKE FETCHED-RESULTS
            initWithFetchRequest:request                   CONTROLLER
            managedObjectContext:context
            sectionNameKeyPath:nil
            cacheName:@"GameResults"];                   ❸ SET ITS
    self.resultsController.delegate = self;                 DELEGATE

                                                 ❹ HANDLE ERRORS
    NSError *error;
    if (![self.resultsController performFetch:&error]) {
        NSLog(@"Fetch failed: %@", [error localizedDescription]);
    }
}
```

loadData uses Core Data, so you need to get the data context from the app delegate ❶ (so you'll need to import FCAppDelegate.h). Next you get the request object and use it to fetch ❷ managed objects into your fetched-results controller, and set its delegate ❸ to the view controller. Finally, you need to handle any errors ❹.

I'LL NEED TO COME UP WITH SOMETHING A LITTLE BETTER TO HANDLE ERRORS.

To get GameResults, you call loadData in viewDidLoad. viewDidLoad also needs to add a Done button to the navigation bar and set up its action, doneWithHistory. Here's how.

Listing 6.9 FCGameHistoryViewController.m: setting up the nav bar with viewDidLoad

```
-(IBAction)doneWithHistory:(id)sender
{
    [self.navigationController.view removeFromSuperview];
```

```
    FCAppDelegate* delegate =
        [[UIApplication sharedApplication] delegate];
    [delegate popView];
}


- (void)viewDidLoad
{
    [super viewDidLoad];

    self.title = @"Game History";
    self.navigationItem.rightBarButtonItem =
        [[UIBarButtonItem alloc]
            initWithBarButtonSystemItem: UIBarButtonSystemItemDone
            target:self action: @selector(doneWithHistory:)];

    [self loadData];
}
```

❶ ANIMATE FROM LEFT

❷ USED BY NAV BAR

The doneWithHistory action needs to remove this view from the window to reveal the home screen. In chapter 5, you made a message pushView to animate views sliding in from the right. Go make another message called popView that moves views in from the left, which you'll call to make the transition smooth ❶.

VIEWDIDLOAD IS THE FIRST PLACE WHERE OUTLETS ARE READY TO USE.

In viewDidLoad, you set the title and Done button ❷ and load the data.

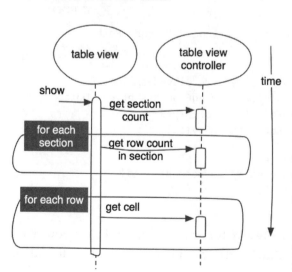

Your view controller has all the data but isn't using it yet. To do that, you need to implement three messages that the table view will send you, as shown here.

Figure 6.31
The sequence of messages for showing data in a table

First the table will ask you how many sections you have. For each section, it will ask you how many rows are in that section. Luckily, NSFetchedResultsController knows this, so you just need to forward that request:

```
- (NSInteger)numberOfSectionsInTableView:(UITableView *)tableView
{
    return [[self.resultsController sections] count];
}


- (NSInteger)tableView:(UITableView *)tableView
     numberOfRowsInSection:(NSInteger)section
{
    return [[[self.resultsController sections] objectAtIndex:section]
          numberOfObjects];
}
```

Once the table view knows how many cells there are, it will begin asking for them. The fetched-results controller has the data you need to make the cell, so the first step is to configure UITableViewCell objects from GameResults (don't forget to add #import "GameResult.h").

Listing 6.10 FCGameHistoryViewController.m: filling a cell

```
-(void)fillCell:(UITableViewCell*)cell
     withResultAtIndex:(NSIndexPath*)indexPath
{                                                          ❶ GET GAMERESULT
                                                              AT INDEXPATH
    GameResult* gr =
      [self.resultsController objectAtIndexPath:indexPath];
                                                          ❷ SET ITS
                                                              PROPERTIES
    cell.textLabel.text =
        [NSString stringWithFormat:@"Game played on %@",
          [NSDateFormatter localizedStringFromDate:gr.gameDate
            dateStyle:NSDateFormatterShortStyle
            timeStyle:NSDateFormatterNoStyle]];

    cell.detailTextLabel.text =
        [NSString stringWithFormat:@"%d seconds long",
          [gr.gameLength intValue]];
}
```

First ❶ you get the right GameResult for the section and row you're in. Then you format the date and length ❷ and use them for the labels inside the cell.

You'll use this message to fill cells when the table view sends you the following message.

Listing 6.11   FCGameHistoryViewController.m: making a cell for the given row

```
- (UITableViewCell *)tableView:(UITableView *)tableView
        cellForRowAtIndexPath:(NSIndexPath *)indexPath
{
    static NSString *CellId = @"Cell";

    UITableViewCell *cell =                               ❶ REUSE CELLS
      [tableView dequeueReusableCellWithIdentifier:CellId];    FOR SPEED
    if (cell == nil) {
        cell = [[UITableViewCell alloc]
                initWithStyle:UITableViewCellStyleSubtitle
                reuseIdentifier:CellId];
        cell.accessoryType =
            UITableViewCellAccessoryDisclosureIndicator;
    }
                                                         ❸ FILL CELL
    [self fillCell:cell withResultAtIndex:indexPath];
    return cell;
}
```

COMMON ATTRIBUTES ❷

YOU NEED TO SAVE THOSE CELLS SO YOU CAN REUSE THEM.

YEAH! IT'S GOOD FOR THE ENVIRONMENT.

This message is supposed to provide cells for your table, and it's called a lot. To make this as fast as possible, the best practice is to share those cell objects. To make that easier, the SDK provides a way to get cells from previous calls ❶, and if it's the first message call, you make a cell with the common attributes. The cells have a title and subtitle and an indicator that more detail is available ❷. Once you have a cell, you need to fill it ❸.

The last step is to add a button to the home screen and make it bring up this view. You know how to do most of this, so follow these steps:

1 Add a button to FCViewController.xib like the ones you have there already.

2 Make an outlet called showHistoryBtn, and connect it.

3 Make an action called showHistory, and connect it.

4 Update `animateViewLoad` with the new button.

5 Update `viewDidLoad` with the new button.

Here's the code to bring up the history inside a navigation controller.

Listing 6.12 FCViewController.m: showing history

```
-(IBAction) showHistory:(id)sender
{
    FCGameHistoryViewController* ghVC =
        [[FCGameHistoryViewController alloc]
            initWithNibName:@"FCGameHistoryViewController" bundle:nil]
    ;

    self.historyVC = [[UINavigationController alloc]
                        initWithRootViewController: ghVC];

    self.historyVC.view.frame = CGRectMake(0, 20, 320, 460);
    [self.view.window addSubview:historyVC.view];

    FCAppDelegate* delegate =
        [[UIApplication sharedApplication] delegate];
        [delegate pushView];
}
```

① USE NAVIGATION CONTROLLER

This is like the code you used to bring up views before, but you need to put the view in a `UINavigationController` **①** to automatically get titles and back buttons for the hierarchical navigation.

Run the game, and go to the history page to see something like this.

Figure 6.32 Game result history in the simulator

The disclosure indicators you added mean that if you touch the row, you should see some detail. But if you touch a row, nothing happens. You'll add that next.

Navigating to related data

Once you know how to connect data to a table view, it's pretty easy to do it again. You could go back to Core Data and this time get CardResult objects, but you don't need to. Your model set up a relationship between GameResults and CardResults. This means that when you fetch a GameResult, the CardResults associated with it come along for the ride. Look at GameResult.h, and you'll see that a property to access them has already been generated for you.

THE RESULTS ARE IN AN NSSET THAT ISN'T ORDERED. TO SORT AND ACCESS THEM, WE NEED TO STORE THEM IN AN NSARRAY.

To use it, add a results property to FCCardHistoryViewController.h:

```
@property(strong, nonatomic) NSArray *results;
```

Now, implement the two section- and row-count messages:

```
- (NSInteger)numberOfSectionsInTableView:(UITableView *)tableView
{
    return 1;
}

- (NSInteger)tableView:(UITableView *)tableView
        numberOfRowsInSection:(NSInteger)section
```

```
{
    return [self.results count];
}
```

You only have one section with as many rows as are in the array.

Filling a cell works pretty much as it does for a GameResult. This time you'll use color to make wrong answers stand out more.

Listing 6.13   FCCardHistoryViewController.m: filling a cell

```
-(void) fillCell:(UITableViewCell*)cell
    withResultAtIndexPath:(NSIndexPath*)indexPath
{
    CardResult* cr = [self.results objectAtIndex:indexPath.row];
    cell.textLabel.text = cr.cardName;
                                                    COLOR CELL BASED
                                                    ON VALUE
    if ([cr.wasCorrect boolValue]) {
        cell.detailTextLabel.text = @"Right";
        cell.detailTextLabel.textColor = [UIColor blackColor];
    } else {
        cell.detailTextLabel.text = @"Wrong";
        cell.detailTextLabel.textColor = [UIColor redColor];
    }
}
```

And you send this message whenever you're asked to provide a cell.

Listing 6.14   FCCardHistoryViewController.m: getting a cell for this row

```
- (UITableViewCell *)tableView:(UITableView *)tableView
        cellForRowAtIndexPath:(NSIndexPath *)indexPath
{
    static NSString *CellId = @"Cell";
    UITableViewCell *cell =
        [tableView dequeueReusableCellWithIdentifier:CellId];
    if (cell == nil) {
        cell = [[UITableViewCell alloc]
                initWithStyle:UITableViewCellStyleSubtitle
                reuseIdentifier:CellId];
    }
    [self fillCell:cell withResultAtIndexPath: indexPath];
    return cell;
}
```

YOU'RE RIGHT THAT REUSING CELLS IS GOOD FOR THE ENVIRONMENT.

LESS WORK MEANS MORE BATTERY LIFE.

This is also much as it is for GameResults. Again, you try to reuse cell objects to speed up table viewing.

When a GameResult is touched, you navigate to the card history. Add the following message to FCGameHistoryViewController.m.

Listing 6.15   FCGameHistoryViewController.m: navigating to the card history

```
- (void)tableView:(UITableView *)tableView
    didSelectRowAtIndexPath:(NSIndexPath *)indexPath
{
    FCCardHistoryViewController* vc =                              ① LOAD CARD
        [[FCCardHistoryViewController alloc]                         HISTORY VIEW
            initWithNibName:@"FCCardHistoryViewController" bundle:nil]
    ;

    NSSortDescriptor* sort =                            ② SORT BY
        [[NSSortDescriptor alloc] initWithKey:@"cardName" ascending:YES]
    ;

    GameResult* gr =                          ③ GET SORTED
        [self.resultsController objectAtIndexPath:indexPath];
    vc.results = [gr.cardResults sortedArrayUsingDescriptors:
                    [NSArray arrayWithObject:sort]];

    [self.navigationController
        pushViewController:vc animated:YES];         ④ NAVIGATE TO
}                                                      CARD HISTORY
```

First you load the view ① from the XIB file. Next ② you create a sort descriptor to sort the cards by their cardName property and apply it to the GameResult's cardResults ③ to get a sorted array of cards. Finally, ④ you navigate to the card history view by handing FCCardHistoryView-Controller to the navigation controller.

Run the game, go to history, and touch a game result to see the related cards.

Phew. We covered a lot, but now have an app that stores data and fetches it later to show it in navigable table views. This pattern of interaction is common in iPhone apps and can be carried out with a fetched-results controller or arrays (and many other ways). The important thing is that you know how many rows you have and what's in them.

Figure 6.33
Card result history in the simulator

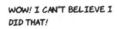
WOW! I CAN'T BELIEVE I DID THAT!

There will come a time, though, when you want to change your data model. If you already have objects stored, then something has to be done to update them, or Core Data won't understand how to read them. We've already covered part of what you need to do, and now you'll learn the rest.

Changing your data model

When you created your data model, you were teaching Core Data how to create a database for you. But you're not likely to get it perfect the first time. Even if you do, you'll probably want to keep adding features to your app, so you'll need more entities, attributes, and relationships.

Versioning your data model

Once you have a stable version of your data model, you should create a version for Core Data to store no matter what changes you make. To do that, choose the data model in Xcode and choose Editor > Add Model Version from the menu. Doing so creates a version of your data model. Then click the parent data model (the .xcdatamodeld file), and set the new version as the current one.

The green check mark shows you the current version.

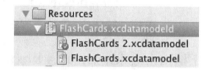

Figure 6.35 Ensuring that the latest version is correct

Figure 6.34 Setting the current data model version

GO CHECK OUT /LIBRARY
/APPLICATION SUPPORT
/IPHONE SIMULATOR
IN YOUR USER FOLDER.

From now on, don't ever change the original .xcdatamodel file. You can change the new one, but if you release it, you need to create a new version.

Now Core Data knows the versions of your model. If you tell it that you want automatic migration, it will make the updates of your database and data for you.

Migrating between versions

Versioning your model is absolutely necessary if you want Core Data to handle migrations for you. It's important that you remember to add a new version after you release any model to the App Store, or your customers won't be able to upgrade. Between released versions, you may want to add versions for convenience if you don't want to delete test data.

You already told Core Data to do the migration for you. Remember this?

```
NSDictionary *options =
    [NSDictionary dictionaryWithObjectsAndKeys:            SET OPTIONS
      [NSNumber numberWithBool:YES],
        NSMigratePersistentStoresAutomaticallyOption,
      [NSNumber numberWithBool:YES],
        NSInferMappingModelAutomaticallyOption, nil];
```

Those options tell Core Data to look at the version in your app's document directory and, if it doesn't match the latest version in the bundle, to automatically add or delete any entities, attributes, or relationships necessary to make the models match.

Planning for what's next

FlashCards now has enough features to launch into the App Store, but if you want to, you can let the user select a CardResult and see their past guesses. To do that, you need to add the attribute to CardResult, regenerate it, copy it from the Card, and then show it in a table view that you push into the navigator.

You've seen a few different ways to transition between views, but there is another popular one called a *tabbed view*. Using it, you can get to various parts of your app quickly without needing a hierarchical navigation. We'll explore a new app that is based on this idea in the next couple of chapters.

7

Creating a photo-based application

This chapter covers

- *Using tab-based navigation*
- *Getting images from the Photos application*
- *Detecting touch positions*

I know that when I (Lou) want to liven up my day, I put on a fake mustache and a rainbow wig. But sometimes, when you need them, they're hard to find. That's where the next app, Disguisey, fits in. Disguisey lets you look through your photo album for a picture of a face and then add a fake mustache, beard, wig, funny hat, or tattoo to it.

You already know a lot about how to make Disguisey. Like every app, it has models, views, and controllers. You'll see a couple of new types, but it's basically the same. You'll still use outlets and actions to connect the view to your code, but you'll also see how to get more information about touches when you need it.

Designing the application

You need to do two basic things in Disguisey. First, you need to be able to grab a picture of a face from your Photos application. Second, you need to be able to pick a mustache, beard, wig, or tattoo from a disguise palette and place it on the face. One way to organize this app is as a group of tabs: one for the face and three for the elements of the disguise. That way, the user has freedom to explore their options.

TABS ARE GREAT WHEN YOU DON'T HAVE A HIERARCHY OR A LINEAR FLOW.

Sketching Disguisey

Let's start with a sketch. For the first time, you're going to use tabs to control your app. As we just said, you'll have one for the face and three for the elements of the disguise. At upper right, you'll have a button to pick a face from your Photos application.

This is what it looks like when you press the Add button and then pick a face.

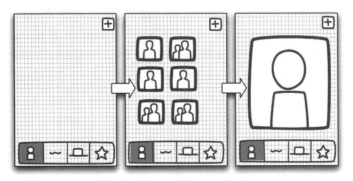

Figure 7.1 Sketch of picking a face

Once you have a face on the first tab, you can pick any other tab and touch a disguise element. When you do, the tab will switch automatically to the face tab, where you can place the element on the face by touching it.

WELL, I KNOW THE
BUTTON NEEDS AN
ACTION BECAUSE EVERY
ONE SO FAR HAS.

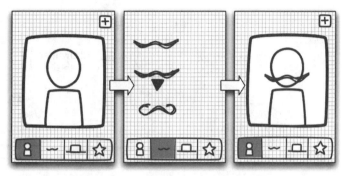

Figure 7.2 Sketch of placing a disguise

As you've seen in previous chapters, these sketches will help you know what views you need when you go into Xcode and Interface Builder. You should already be thinking about the parts of the view that change (and need to be outlets) and the parts of the view that need to have actions tied to them.

Defining the behavior of your application

To go a little further with the sketches, let's draw a diagram of what's happening when you start the app and pick a photo.

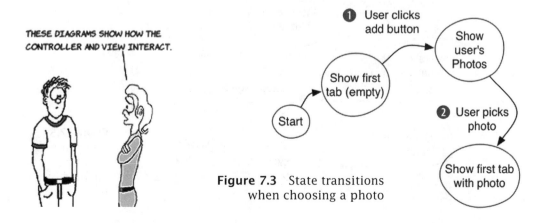

THESE DIAGRAMS SHOW HOW THE
CONTROLLER AND VIEW INTERACT.

① User clicks add button

Show user's Photos

Show first tab (empty)

Start

② User picks photo

Show first tab with photo

Figure 7.3 State transitions when choosing a photo

Generally, arrows indicate the view sending a message to a controller. In response, the controller changes the models and then updates the views based on them.

Here's what happens when you want to put a mustache on the face.

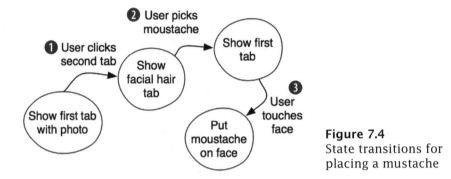

Figure 7.4
State transitions for placing a mustache

So far, that looks pretty simple. Because you're using tabs, the app's behavior is much more complex. At any time, you could go to any tab and pick any disguise element. It's not just a linear flow. Here's a diagram of what the flow could really be like.

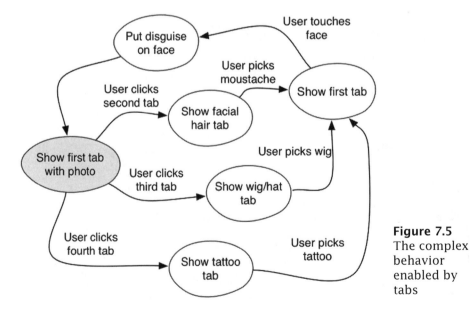

Figure 7.5
The complex behavior enabled by tabs

And that's still simplifying it, which is fine for now.

With these sketches done, you're ready to start designing your app. This app isn't as complex as it seems. The models are a lot simpler than the card game, and the iPhone has built-in controllers to handle the tabs and photo picking. The hardest part will be composing the disguise on the face, but because that's the whole purpose of the app, it's not a big deal.

Designing your application's models, views, and controllers

In every app you've made, you've looked at the sketches and behavior of the app and tried to come up with models, views, and controllers that will implement that behavior. The models you need for this app are the disguise and the elements that make it up. A disguise element consists of an image (for example, of a mustache) and an x-y point to position it. The disguise itself is the list of elements. To manage the elements, you need messages that let the controller alert the disguise when a new element is chosen and when it's been placed on a face.

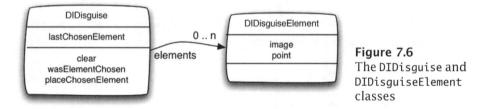

Figure 7.6
The DIDisguise and DIDisguiseElement classes

As you'd expect, disguises have zero or more elements.

Let's look at the face view and controller.

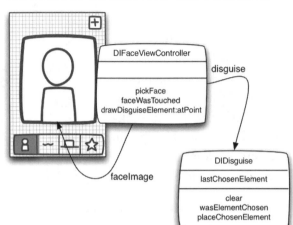

Figure 7.7 The DIFace–
ViewController class
and view

You have messages to add a face to the view, tell when it was touched, add disguise elements, and clear the disguise.

The three other tabs have the exact same behavior, but they have different elements on them. This means you'll have three different views, but they can share the controller. In the past, you've seen a one-to-one correspondence between views and controllers, but if your views are variations of each other, you don't need to have copies of the controller.

This is what the facial hair view looks like. The only message it needs is an action for what happens when you touch one of its elements.

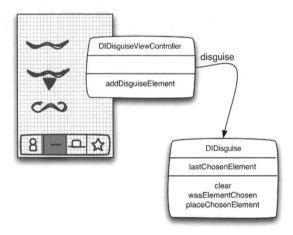

Figure 7.8 The DIDisguise–
ViewController class

You don't have to create messages for the tab at the bottom because tabs are built into the iPhone, and you can drag them and their controllers onto your application. You also don't have views or controllers for picking a photo from the iPhone's Photos app. Like tabs, those are built in.

You now have everything you need to start coding the app. You'll create the views in Interface Builder and then code the controllers and models in Xcode. So far, most of this should feel familiar. Disguisey is just like the other apps you've made, except with a fake mustache and a rainbow wig.

Creating an app with tab-based navigation

Disguisey uses tabs, so you'll begin with the Tabbed Application template. To do that in Xcode, choose File > New Project, and select Tabbed Application.

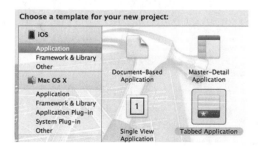

Figure 7.9 The New Project dialog, where you choose the Tabbed Application template

In the next dialog, name the app Disguisey, set the class prefix to DI, and select both the Use Storyboard and Use Automatic Reference Counting check boxes. (That's right, you're finally going to use a storyboard!)

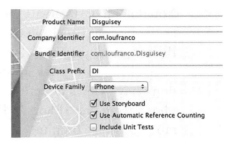

Figure 7.10
Disguisey's project settings

The next step is to rename the default classes generated by the template. It's a pain, but it's a lot quicker than going out to the store to buy Groucho Marx glasses.

Renaming classes with the refactoring tool

If you look at the class names, you'll see two view controllers, `DIFirstViewController` and `DISecond-ViewController`. These names are autogenerated and don't do a good job of describing what you want them to do. In the app design, you named these classes `DIFaceViewController` and `DIDisguiseViewController`. You could rename the files and classes and then hunt down all references to them in Interface Builder, but luckily you don't have to. Xcode has this kind of renaming built in, and it will be sure to do it right.

I JUST SAVED TWO HOURS OF HUNTING DOWN ALL THE PLACES THESE CLASSES WERE USED.

To rename the first class, click DIFirstViewController.h in the Project Navigator. Then, right-click the word `DIFirstViewController` right after the `@interface` keyword. On the menu that comes up, choose Refactor > Rename, and then, in the dialog, rename the class `DIFaceViewController`. You can click through the dialogs that follow, which show you what Xcode will do and offer to keep snapshots of your current code base.

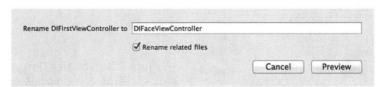

Figure 7.11   Renaming a class

Do the same with `DISecondViewController`. This time, rename it `DIDisguiseViewController`.

The app has four tabs, but remember that three of them use the same controller because they have identical behavior. The next step is to create the views that go along with these classes and connect them. You'll do that using a relatively new feature of Xcode, the storyboard. Storyboards are particularly useful when you're managing a lot of interconnected views.

Storyboarding your app in Interface Builder

With the latest Xcode, it's possible to work with several related views in one canvas by using a storyboard. It makes sense to use this for tabs, and that's why you selected the Use Storyboard check box in the template. Let's look at the storyboard. In Project Navigator, click Main-Storyboard.storyboard.

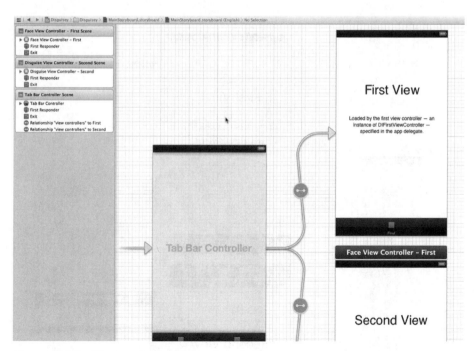

Figure 7.12   The app's storyboard

The template put only two tabs on your app, but it's easy to add more. As you can see, unlike a XIB file, a storyboard holds multiple View-Controller views and even knows that they're related. Because there's a view with tabs already on it and relationships drawn, the tabs know to switch between the views automatically.

To add the others views, drag two more view controllers from the Object Library onto the Storyboard.

Figure 7.13   View controller in the Object Library

You now have a tabbed view controller and four controllers: one for each tab.

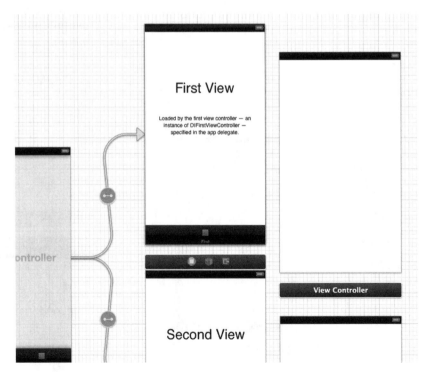

Figure 7.14   The app's five views

Note that only two views are connected. You make relationships by connecting the Relationship connector of the Tab Bar Controller to the individual views. First click Tab Bar Controller in the Dock.

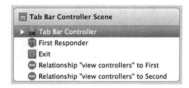

Figure 7.15
The Tab Bar view controller

Go to the Tab Bar Controller's Connections Inspector, and you'll see that its view controller's triggered segues are already connected to the first two views. To connect the other two, drag the little circle on top of each view.

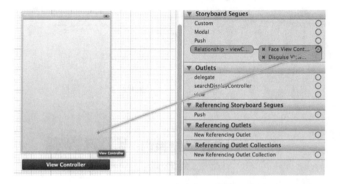

Figure 7.16
Connecting a view to a tab bar

Now the Tab Bar Controller has four tabs.

To finish customizing the template, you need to do a few more things:

Figure 7.17   Tab Bar Controller with four tabs

1   Click the TextView on the Face View Controller, and press Delete to delete it. Do the same with the Label.

2   Also delete DIDisguiseViewController's TextView and Label.

3   Click the tab bar item of the Face View Controller. In the Attributes Inspector, set Title to Face and Image to tab-face.png.

4   Do the same for the next three tabs, setting their titles to Facial Hair, Wigs/Hats, and Tattoos/Scars and their images to tab-facial-hair.png, tab-wig-hat.png, and tab-tattoo.png, respectively.

5 For the two view controllers you added, go to the Identity Inspector and set the class to DIDisguiseViewController.

The storyboard should look like this.

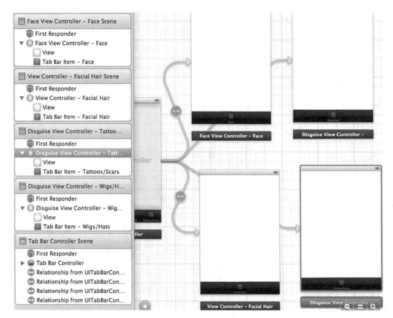

Figure 7.18   The storyboard when it's finished

Your app is now set up. The individual views don't have anything on them, and the tab images haven't been created, so it's not an interesting app yet.

Take a quick break, stretch your legs, and get ready for the next part, where you create the individual views for the tabs. The views on the tabs are no different from other views you've made, so it should feel familiar.

Figure 7.19
The app so far in the simulator

Making images for the tabs

It would be pretty sad if you had question marks as tab images for your app. If you look at any tab-based apps on your iPhone, you'll notice that they usually have nice gradient images that turn bright blue when you touch them. Because every app seems to have this look, you should have guessed that it was built in.

IM LOOKING THROUGH YOU
AND NOW I KNOW
NON-TRANSPARENT
IS WHERE YOU GLOW

(TUNE OF "IM LOOKING THROUGH YOU" BY THE
BEATLES)

All you need to do is create a 32 x 32 pixel PNG image that uses opaque pixels on a transparent background. This image isn't used as is. Instead, it's used as a mask against nice gradients to form the tab's image. Wherever you have opaque pixels, the gradient will show through. Here are our Face and Tattoos/Scars images. The checkerboard pattern shows where the image is transparent.

 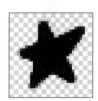

Figure 7.20 Tab mask images

ALWAYS MAKE THE BIGGER
ONE FIRST AND THEN SHRINK
IT TO MAKE THE SMALLER ONE.

Like all images you use on user interfaces, if you make one twice as big and name it with @2x before the extension, it will be used on retina displays. For example, name the 32 x 32 face image tab-face.png and the 64 x 64 image tab-face@2x.png. The other images are named tab-facial-hair.png, tab-wig-hat.png, and tab-tattoo.png.

Once you've created the eight images (two for each tab), add them to the main Disguisey group in Project Navigator. As always, make sure the Copy Items into Destination Group's Folder (If Needed) check box is checked.

If you've done it right, you'll see the images in the tab bar of the Tab Bar Controller in the storyboard. If not, check the names of the files against the Image attribute of each tab bar item.

If you run the application now, you'll see a tab bar with your images, and you can change tabs by touching each one. It's hard to see that the views are changing because they're all the same. You'll fix that in the next section.

Figure 7.21   View with tab titles and images set

Making the face view

When your app comes up, it shows the first tab, the face view. Looking back at the first sketch, you can see that the view has two areas. The top bar has the button that adds a face to the app, and you should probably put the name of the app there too. Most of the view is taken up by the face itself, which is an image. Here's a refined sketch.

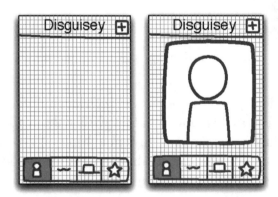

Figure 7.22   Updated sketch of the face view

That standard title bar that you add to the sketch is called a Navigation Bar, and the button you put on it is a Bar Button Item. To add them, click the storyboard in Xcode, and then drag the objects from the Library onto the Face View Controller. One nice thing is that Interface Builder knows that Navigation Bars go on top and what size they are.

If you drag the Navigation Bar near the top, it will snap into position. Similarly, when you drag the Bar Button Item near the right side of the Navigation Bar, Interface Builder will automatically set its size and location. Double-click the title and type Disguisey, and then double-click the button and type Pick Face.

Figure 7.23
Setting the title and item button text

THE TAB BAR IS SIMULATED, SO IT ONLY SHOWS THE TAB FOR THIS VIEW.

Before you add the image into the center, it's worth noting that your view doesn't have the full tab bar on it. That's because DIFaceViewController doesn't know about the other tabs. Interface Builder lets you simulate the tab bar, which helps it show you what views will look like in the real app. Go to the Attributes Inspector of the view (select the fourth tab or press Opt-Cmd-4), and see that the Bottom Bar field is set to Inferred in the Simulated Metrics section. When you place elements in the view, they will know to size and place themselves while taking the tab bar into account.

Now, drag an ImageView from the Library onto the center of the view. It's sized automatically when you drag it to the center, because you have the top and bottom bars in place. While it's still selected, choose Editor > Arrangement > Send to Back so the disguises you drag around stay under the navigation and tab bars.

To finish the view, click the UIImageView and go to its Attribute Inspector. Set Mode to Top Left, and select the User Interaction Enabled check box (because you want to be able to touch the ImageView).

Figure 7.24 The completed face view

Save everything, and then go back to Xcode and build the application and run it.

You'll come back and make outlets and actions later, but think about what you need to send to controllers (with actions) and what they will need to update (with outlets). Keep the sketch, design, and code loop in mind as you do each part so you can flow from one to the next easily.

Making the disguise views

Figure 7.25
The tab-based application in the simulator

TATTOO MY FACE? WHY DO YOU THINK I HAVE THIS GIANT BEARD?

The disguise tabs are the hardest part of this app. First, go grow some facial hair (or call in a favor from your dad), dye your hair rainbow colors, get some cool hats, and tattoo your face.

If this seems like too much work, or if for some reason you don't want a face tattoo, you're still going to have to call in favors. Look through your digital photos for friends and family who have different beard and hair styles, and then use Photoshop or Gimp to extract just the hair from the pictures and paste it onto a transparent background. Here's an example.

Figure 7.26
A mustache on a transparent background

If you can't find what you need in your own photo library, look for royalty-free images online. Check the license carefully if you're planning to use images in a commercial app. The safest thing is to use your own photos and get permission from the models.

Save your images in PNG files that are 150 pixels wide, and name them facial-hair-01.png, facial-hair-02.png, and so on.

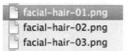

Figure 7.27
The disguise images in the Project Navigator

To put them on the disguise tabs, click the Facial Hair View Controller in the storyboard. Then, drag a Round Rect Button onto its view. Set the button's Type to Custom, and choose the image for it. Do this for each different disguise element (putting them on the correct tab in the storyboard).

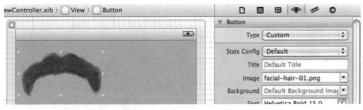

Figure 7.28   Placing disguise buttons on the view

If you save the storyboard and then run the app in Xcode, you'll be able to switch between tabs and see the different disguise elements. But when you touch a mustache, nothing happens. You want the app to switch to the face tab. You know you need actions. Think about which part of the view is sending a message to the controller and what the controller needs to change while you go grab a congratulatory cookie for getting this far.

OK, I ALREADY TOLD YOU I KNOW BUTTONS NEED ACTIONS, SO GIVE ME MY COOKIE.

I'M THE QUEEN OF ACTIONS.

I KNOW, I SAW YOUR TWEET ABOUT IT.

Changing tabs with code

You finally need to add some code. Did you figure out that the disguise button needed an action? That should be obvious by now, because buttons without actions don't do anything when you touch them.

Every button does the same thing, so you need only one action. In DIDisguiseViewController.h, add this code:

```
-(IBAction)disguiseElementChosen:(id)sender;
```

You also need this action, which will change the tab bar to the first tab:

```
-(IBAction)disguiseElementChosen:(id)sender
{
    self.tabBarController.selectedIndex = 0;
}
```

Connect each disguise button's touch event to the action.

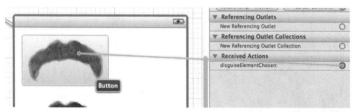

Figure 7.29   Connecting the button's touch event to an action message

Save everything in Xcode, and run the app. Now, when you go to the facial hair tab and touch a mustache, the app automatically switches you to the face tab. If only a face appeared there!

You're getting to the point where you need models to help you finish the code. Because they're simple, you'll do that and then use them to finish the application.

Incorporating models

This app has fairly simple models. You need to be able to create and manage the disguise. It's common to see models when you have a collection of things. The collection and the things are usually classes in the model. In this case, DIDisguise is a collection of DIDisguiseElements.

Coding DIDisguise and DIDisguiseElement

The app's design represents DIDisguise-Element as shown at right.

It's an image and an x-y point on the face. Create a new class called DIDisguiseElement, and edit DIDisguiseElement.h to look like this:

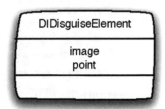

Figure 7.30 The DIDisguiseElement class

```
@interface DIDisguiseElement : NSObject

-(id)initWithImage:(UIImage*)image atPoint:(CGPoint)point;    ◄─── DECLARE
                                                                    PROPERTIES
@property(strong, nonatomic) UIImage *image;          ◄───  CUSTOM
@property(nonatomic) CGPoint point;                         INIT

@end
```

Put the following code in DIDisguiseElement.m.

Listing 7.1 DIDisguiseElement.m: implementation of the DisguiseElement class

```
@implementation DIDisguiseElement
                                              ❶ SYNTHESIZE
@synthesize image = _image;                      PROPERTIES
@synthesize point = _point;
                                              ❷ MAKE CUSTOM
-(id)initWithImage:(UIImage*)img atPoint:(CGPoint)pt  ◄   INIT ...
{
    if (self = [super init]) {
        self.image = img;                    ❸ ... TO INITIALIZE
        self.point = pt;                        THEM
    }
    return self;
}
@end
```

This is the same familiar code you write whenever you have properties. You ❶ synthesize them and ❷ ❸ initialize them. DIDisguiseElement is a simple container of two related properties.

The disguise is a little more complex.

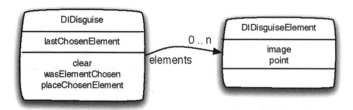

Figure 7.31 The DIDisguise and DIDisguiseElement classes

The disguise is accessed in two different ways. Here's how it works.

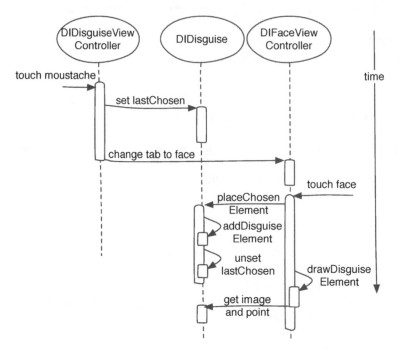

Figure 7.32 Sequence of messages when placing a disguise element

When you're on the facial hair tab and touch a mustache, the disguise keeps track of that as the lastChosenElement. Then, when you're on the face tab and you touch a face, the last chosen element is used to create a new DIDisguiseElement object, which is added to the list of elements.

THE DISGUISE REMEMBERS THE LAST THING YOU TOUCHED...

AND PUTS IT ON THE FACE WHEN YOU TOUCH IT.

To create it, add a class called DIDisguise, and add the following code to DIDisguise.h.

Listing 7.2   DIDisguise.h: the **DIDisguise** class's interface

```
#import <Foundation/Foundation.h>
#import "DIDisguiseElement.h"

@interface DIDisguise : NSObject

-(DIDisguiseElement*)placeChosenElement:(CGPoint)point;
-(void)clear;
-(bool)wasElementChosen;
@property(strong, nonatomic) NSMutableArray* elements;
@property(strong, nonatomic) UIImage* lastChosenImage;

@end
```

CREATE NEW ELEMENT FROM LAST CHOSEN IMAGE

LIST OF ELEMENTS

For the most part, the implementation isn't too bad. Here's everything except placeChosenElement.

Listing 7.3   DIDisguise.m: the **DIDisguise** class's implementation

```
@synthesize elements = _elements;
@synthesize lastChosenImage = _lastChosenImage;

-(id)init
{
    if (self = [super init]) {
        self.elements = [[NSMutableArray alloc] init];
    }
    return self;
}
```

```
-(void)clear
{
    [self.elements removeAllObjects];
}

-(bool)wasElementChosen
{
    return self.lastChosenImage != nil;
}
```

Now, let's take a closer look at placeChosenElement.

Listing 7.4   DIDisguise.m: the placeChosenElement message

```
-(DIDisguiseElement*)placeChosenElement:(CGPoint)point
{
    if ([self wasElementChosen]) {
        DIDisguiseElement* el = [[DIDisguiseElement alloc]
            initWithImage:self.lastChosenImage atPoint:point];
        [self.elements addObject:el];

        self.lastChosenImage = nil;
        return el;
    }
    return nil;
}
```

CREATE NEW ELEMENT FROM LAST CHOSEN IMAGE ❶

❷ CLEAR LAST CHOSEN IMAGE

When the face is touched, you want the disguise element to be centered at that point, so that's what the point you pass in represents.

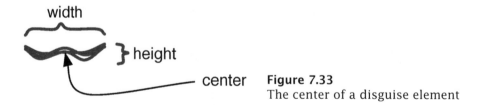

width

height

center

Figure 7.33
The center of a disguise element

Once you create the element ❶, you need to add it to your elements list. And because you don't want to place the last element ever again, you set it to nil ❷.

SETTING IT TO NIL MAKES SURE YOU DON'T KEEP REUSING IT.

With your models in place, you can finish the app. In this case, it was simple to finish the models; but if they're complex, you can make fake versions of them that have the interface you plan to use but a simpler implementation. For example, if you plan to use a database to store data in the real version, use an array early in the project so you can prototype the app.

Working with photos

The next part of your app involves interacting with the Photos app that comes with your phone. Because this is likely to be where the user has pictures of faces, it makes sense to let users pick from among those photos.

Getting images from the Photos application

The iOS SDK not only gives you access to the photos in the user's Library, but also makes the Library easy to integrate because the SDK provides views that control the interaction with the user as well. This isn't just a convenience; it ensures that access to the user's photo Library is under their control and consistent across applications. When you open the photo Library, the iPhone shows a UI like this.

Figure 7.34
The photo picker in the simulator

To do this, you need to create a UIImagePickerController object and handle its events. It will automatically put views on the screen to show albums and then photos, and it even lets the user resize and position the result if you want. At the end of the process, it tells you what happened.

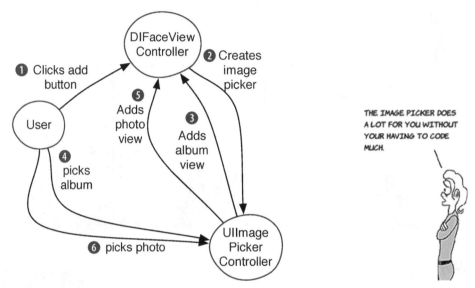

Figure 7.35 The object interactions for picking a photo

To code the image picker, first you need to change the class declaration in DIFaceViewController.h to allow the picker to control your UI. Change it to this:

```
@interface DIFaceViewController : UIViewController
    <UIImagePickerControllerDelegate, UINavigationControllerDelegate>
```

Then add the following messages:

```
-(IBAction)pickFace:(id)sender;
- (void)imagePickerController:(UIImagePickerController *)picker
    didFinishPickingMediaWithInfo:(NSDictionary *)info;
- (void)imagePickerControllerDidCancel:
    (UIImagePickerController *)picker;
```

WHEN I DO THIS. I TELL EVERYONE I'M DOING THE PROPERTY DANCE.

The action `pickFace` is for the button on your view, so attach it to the button's selector action in the storyboard. You also need an outlet for `UIImageView*` that represents the face, so create a property named `faceImage`.

The other two messages are what the image picker will send when the image-picking process is either canceled or completed. To implement these messages, add #import <UIKit/UIKit.h> to DIFaceViewController.h and use the following code in the implementation.

Listing 7.5   DIFaceViewController.m: picking a face from the Photos application

```
-(IBAction)pickFace:(id)sender
{                                                        ❶ CREATE PICKER
    UIImagePickerController* picker =                        AND CONFIGURE IT
      [[UIImagePickerController alloc] init];
    picker.delegate = self;
    picker.allowsEditing = YES;
    picker.sourceType = UIImagePickerControllerSourceTypePhotoLibrary;
    [self presentViewController:picker animated:YES completion:nil];
ADD IT ❷ }

- (void)releasePicker:(UIImagePickerController*)picker
{
    [picker dismissViewControllerAnimated:YES completion:nil];
}
                                                        REMOVE IT
                                                        WHEN DONE ❸
-(UIImage*)resizedFaceImage: (UIImage*)face
{
    CGFloat vw = self.faceImage.frame.size.width;
    CGFloat vh = self.faceImage.frame.size.height;
                                                        ❹ SET IMAGE'S
                                                          FINAL SIZE
    CGSize size = CGSizeMake(vw, vh);
    UIGraphicsBeginImageContext(size);

    CGFloat fw = face.size.width, fh = face.size.height;
    CGFloat ratio = vh / fh;
    CGFloat newW = fw * ratio;                          ❺ FIT HEIGHT
    CGFloat newH = fh * ratio;
                                                  ❻ OFFSET SO
                                                    IT'S CENTERED
    [face drawInRect:
      CGRectMake((vw-(newW))/2, 0, newW, newH)];
```

```
    UIImage *newFace = UIGraphicsGetImageFromCurrentImageContext();
    UIGraphicsEndImageContext();
    return newFace;
}


- (void)imagePickerController:(UIImagePickerController *)picker
didFinishPickingMediaWithInfo:(NSDictionary *)info
{                                                    ❼  USE CHOSEN
    UIImage* face =                                      PHOTO
      [info objectForKey:UIImagePickerControllerEditedImage];
    face = [self resizedFaceImage:face];             ❽  RESIZE FACE
    self.faceImage.image = face;                         TO FIT
    [self releasePicker:picker];
}


- (void)imagePickerControllerDidCancel:(UIImagePickerController *)picker
{
    [self releasePicker:picker];
}
```

Getting a photo starts when the Pick Face button is touched to trigger the pickFace action. In response, you allocate a UIImagePickerController object ❶, configure it, and present it ❷. By setting the picker's delegate property to this controller, it will be able to send messages to the DIFaceViewController. When you're done choosing an image ❸, you remove the picker's controller from the window.

The helper message, resizedFaceImage, makes sure the face fills the whole view. The following figure will help you see how it works.

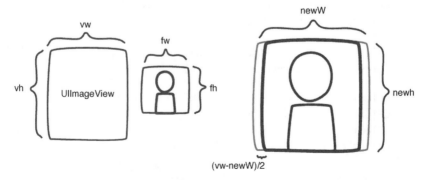

Figure 7.36 Resizing a face to fit the view

First `resizedFaceImage` sets the size of the face image to the size of the view ❹. Then it recalculates a new height and width so the photo fits, but it maintains the same aspect ratio ❺. Finally, it centers the image by offsetting it half the difference in widths between the image and the view ❻. This way, you get the largest possible photo to work with.

When you touch an album, it shows you its photos. Choosing a photo sends it to the controller ❼, which will resize it for you ❽ before you use it. If you cancel the image selection, the picker will send the cancel message. In either case, you need to remove the picker.

If you run the application, the pick face button will now work.

You're down to the final stretch. All that's left is placing the mustache when you touch the face. Unfortunately, you can't use the built-in `UIImage-View`.

SHOULD I EDIT MY
FACE OR NOT?

THIS FEELS LIKE A
TRICK QUESTION.

Adding disguise elements to the photo

The next step is to add a disguise element when you touch the face.

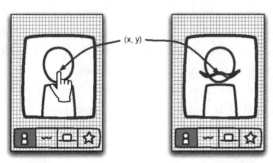

(x, y)

Figure 7.37 Sketch of adding a mustache at a touch point

HMM. SO ACTIONS CAN'T
DO EVERY KIND OF
TOUCH YOU MIGHT NEED.

You might think you just need to wire up an action to `UIImageView` on the face view. Unfortunately, you have two problems. First, `UIImageView` doesn't have touch events. But even if it did, actions don't have x-y coordinates.

When a view is being touched, it gets a series of messages. The one that indicates that a touch started is called touchesBegan: withEvents:. When a button receives this message, it sends out action messages to attached controllers, but images ignore them. You need a way to hook into that message.

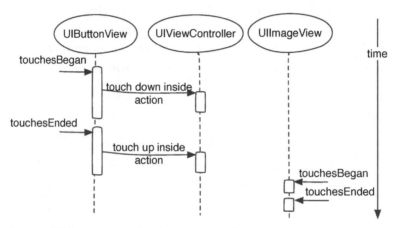

Figure 7.38   UIImageView ignores touches.

To do this, you're going to use a technique you learned about in chapter 2: subclassing, or creating an is-a relationship. If you inherit a new class from UIImageView called DIFaceImageView, you can handle messages that would otherwise be ignored. Because the plan is to send it to the DIFaceViewController, you need to create a has-a relationship with it. In turn, the controller will have-a FaceImageView.

Figure 7.39
Subclass UIImageView
to handle touches.

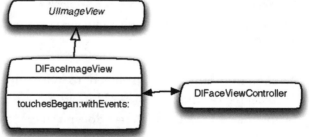

This works as follows.

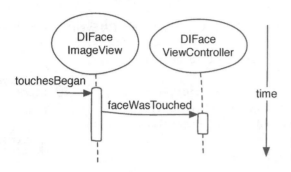

Figure 7.40 `DIFaceImageView` will handle touches.

Create a new class in Xcode called `DIFaceImageView`. You need to inherit from `UIImageView` and override its `touchesBegan: withEvents:` message. Here are the contents of the header:

```
#import <UIKit/UIKit.h>                    ➊ USE A CLASS
@class DIFaceViewController;                   WITHOUT IMPORT


@interface DIFaceImageView : UIImageView
                                           ➋ DON'T RETAIN AN
@property(weak, nonatomic)                     OBJECT REFERENCE
    DIFaceViewController* faceViewController;


-(void)touchesBegan:(NSSet *)touches withEvent:(UIEvent *)event;


@end
```

Whenever two classes use each other, in one of the headers you need to use a `forward` declaration ➊ instead of an `import`, because two files aren't allowed to import each other. Also, although the view controller holds a strong reference to this class, `DIFaceImageView` holds a weak one back to the view controller. ➋. A weak reference doesn't cause a retain and release, which is important because the circular reference would have fooled ARC into thinking these objects were always being used.

In the module, synthesize the controller and handle the touch message:

```
#import "DIFaceImageView.h"
#import "DIFaceViewController.h"
```

```
@implementation DIFaceImageView
@synthesize faceViewController = _faceViewController;

-(void)touchesBegan:(NSSet *)touches withEvent:(UIEvent *)event
{
    NSSet *allTouches = [event allTouches];
    UITouch *touch =
        [[allTouches allObjects] objectAtIndex:0];
    CGPoint p = [touch locationInView:self];
        [self.faceViewController faceWasTouched:p];
}
@end
```

❶ GET FIRST TOUCH

❷ TELL CONTROLLER ABOUT TOUCH

In this code, you get the list of touches and use the first one ❶. If this was multitouch, you'd need to do more. Then, you tell the controller that the face was touched ❷. You haven't written face-WasTouched yet, so this won't build.

SO, I GUESS I'M ON MY OWN HERE. WELL, IT'S ONLY TWO LINES AND A PROPERTY DANCE FOR THE DISGUISE OBJECT.

To finish, you need to connect this new class up with DIFaceViewController. First, change the declaration of the faceImage property from UIImageView* to DIFaceImageView*. Also add a disguise property (of type Disguise*) to the controller.

Then, add #import "DIDisguiseElement.h" and these messages to the controller's header:

```
-(void)faceWasTouched:(CGPoint)point;
-(void)drawDisguiseElement:(DIDisguiseElement*)el
        startingAtPoint:(CGPoint)p;
```

In the module, you need to add the following message implementations.

Listing 7.6   DIFaceViewController.m: making the disguise when you touch the face

```
-(void)faceWasTouched:(CGPoint)point
{
    if ([self.disguise wasElementChosen]) {
        DIDisguiseElement* el =
        [self.disguise placeChosenElement:point];
        [self drawDisguiseElement:el startingAtPoint:point];
    }
}
```

MAKE DISGUISE ELEMENT

```
-(void)drawDisguiseElement:(DIDisguiseElement*)el
        startingAtPoint:(CGPoint)p
{
    UIImageView* imageView =
        [[UIImageView alloc] initWithImage:el.image];

    [self.faceImage addSubview:imageView];
    imageView.bounds = CGRectMake(0,0,
            el.image.size.width, el.image.size.height);
    imageView.center = el.point;
}
```

MAKE DISGUISE
IMAGE

Also add this in `viewDidLoad`:

```
- (void)viewDidLoad {
    [super viewDidLoad];
    self.faceImage.faceViewController = self;
}
```

ATTACH TO
FACE IMAGE

Finally, you need to create a `Disguise` object and give it to each tab. Add a `disguise` property to your app delegate, and make the `init` message in DIAppDelegate.m look like this:

```
-(id)init
{
    if (self = [super init]) {
        self.disguise = [[DIDisguise alloc] init];
    }
    return self;
}
```

Be sure you made a `disguise` property for the two view controllers, and set them like this in the `viewDidLoad` of both view controllers:

```
- (void)viewDidLoad
{
    [super viewDidLoad];
    DIAppDelegate* app = (DIAppDelegate*)
        [[UIApplication sharedApplication] delegate];
    self.disguise = app.disguise;
}
```

Run the app, touch a mustache, and then touch the face.

Well, at least that was better than a face tattoo. To finish this app, you'll want to add more disguise images to the various tabs. Now that you have a framework in place, that should be easy to do. Once you add an image to the appropriate view, connect it to the touch action that makes the tab switch. And if you want to do more, make an icon and a default startup image for the app, too.

Figure 7.41   Placing a disguise in the simulator

Wrapping it up, and what's next

Now you know how to make tab-based applications and work with photos stored on the device. You also learned a little more about touch events, but you'll discover even more about that soon.

In the next chapter, you'll keep playing with this app. You need ways to move, resize, and delete disguises. You can also use a little animation to give the app some life. Disguisey will be App Store ready in no time.

8

Moving, rotating, editing, and animating images

This chapter covers

- *Animating image views*
- *Using gestures to manipulate images*
- *Compositing a new image*

To start out, you kept Disguisey simple, but you can do much more to improve it. Before you can post it to the App Store, you need to polish it. If you've been playing around with it, the first thing you'll notice is that it's hard to position the mustache on the right part of the face. It would be great if you could move it around. Also, disguises don't match all face sizes, so being able to resize the image would be nice, too.

You're going to look at some of these problems and a few others. Spend a minute or so playing with Disguisey and thinking about the features you think it needs. We might not cover all of them here, but you should try to sketch, design, and code them yourself.

Improving Disguisey

Improving any app is similar to writing it in the first place but can be a lot more fun. When you're first building it, it takes a while to get a working app that does anything at all. But a lot of improvements require just small bits of extra code.

Sketching your new ideas

To start with, you learned in chapter 5 that iPhone apps use simple animations to make them come alive. There's a definite feel to well-done apps, and it comes in part from good use of simple animations. Instead of plopping the mustache down on the face, how about you make it grow in place, as shown here.

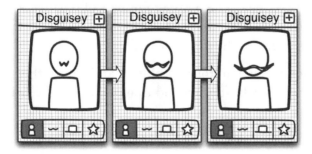

Figure 8.1 Animating the mustache placement

That will look a lot better. You already know exactly how to do this, but we'll go over the code soon.

Another improvement would be to use a touch-and-drag gesture to let the user move the disguises around. That would look as shown at right.

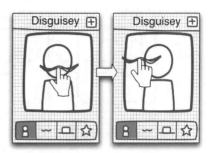

Figure 8.2
Allowing disguises to be moved

In the last chapter, you learned about how to access touch events, but it turns out there is an easy way to recognize common gestures. You'll learn about that technique shortly.

While you're at it, resizing disguises would also be nice. You can use the pinch gesture to do that.

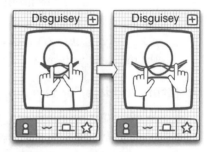

Figure 8.3
Allowing disguises to be resized

Luckily, resizing a disguise is similar to moving it. The first changes the (x, y) position, and the second changes the scale.

And because everyone makes mistakes (or changes their mind), you need a way to delete disguises. The normal way to get a menu of actions is to tap and hold the thing you want to change and then pop up a little menu.

Figure 8.4 Bringing up a Delete menu when the disguise is held

Finally, it would be no fun at all to put mustaches on your friends if you couldn't save the results. Let's use a tap and hold on the face itself to pop up a Save menu, which will put a composited photo in your Photos app.

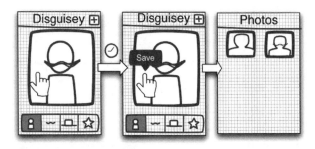

Figure 8.5
Bringing up a Save menu

Did this list cover all your ideas? If not, we may get to them in later chapters. Even if we don't, we're sure you'll figure them out. Sketch them now, and then try to create designs and code them up as you move along.

AND I THOUGHT THIS WAS THE CHAPTER WHERE WE'D FINALLY GET TO FART SOUNDS.

Updating models for the new features

With your sketches in place, you can begin to plan your design. For each of these features, you need to figure out what parts should be handled by the views, the models, and the controllers. You'll have new properties and messages, and you'll also have to design new interactions between them.

Dragging an element has this simple effect on your state.

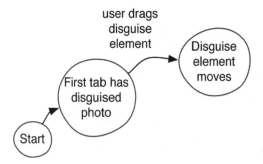

Figure 8.6
Dragging state transition

Similarly, pinching an element is simple to describe in this diagram.

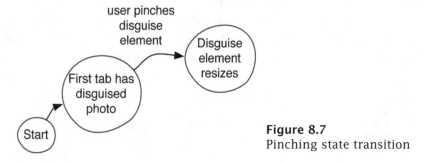

Figure 8.7
Pinching state transition

The interaction and transitions for deleting are a little more complex, but not much.

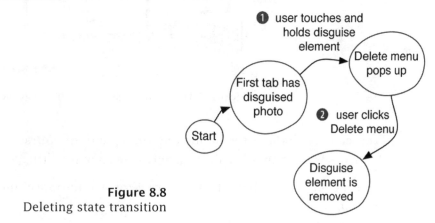

Figure 8.8
Deleting state transition

And saving is pretty much the same as deleting.

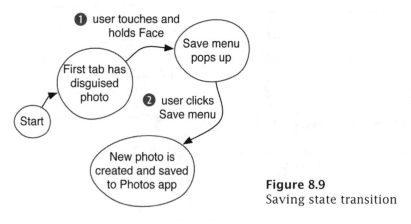

Figure 8.9
Saving state transition

That's what needs to happen, so next you have to figure out which class does what. The Face View Controller is heavily involved, as you might suspect. You know that user interactions are orchestrated by the controller, and you're doing everything on the face view. Here are some of the additional properties and messages you need to add.

MIRANDA TOLD ME THAT STATES ARE CHANGED BY MESSAGES ON CLASSES THAT HOLD THAT STATE. HOPE THAT HELPS.

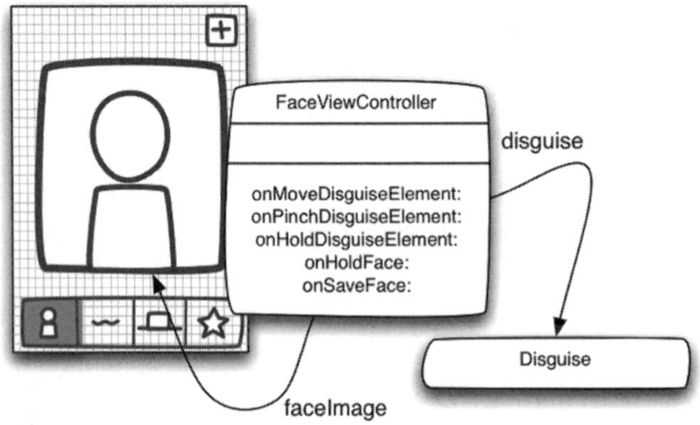

Figure 8.10 New messages in `DIFaceViewController`

You can see that a lot is happening there, and, of course, there will be helper messages that break these messages down a little.

The model classes have to keep track of a little more and need new messages.

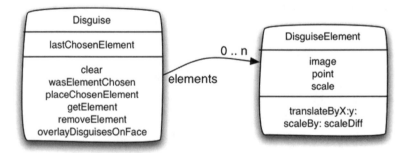

Figure 8.11 New properties and messages in `DIDisguise` and `DIDisguiseElement`

Now that you want to change the disguise, you need ways to get the elements and then change them once you have them. And DIDisguise-Element keeps track of its scale in addition to its position and image.

With the changes organized into classes, it's a lot easier to think about each message and what it will do. For some messages, particularly those in the model classes, you already know pretty much how to proceed. For others, you have to learn more about the iOS SDK to implement them. Take a minute and think about how to code each message, and what you think you need to learn in order to do it.

Thinking about what you don't know

Let's consider moving a disguise element. You're storing the point in your model, and you've already used it to position the view's center. You know that to move the element, you have to change x and y, as shown at right.

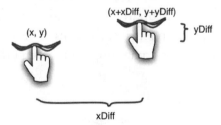

Figure 8.12 To move an element, you need to get a difference in the x and y position.

The only thing you don't know is how to find out what xDiff and yDiff are. To do this, you need to get the initial touch point and track it while it moves. Along the way, you need to update the models and views so the disguise stays under the finger. This is called *recognizing a pan gesture.*

Pinching is similar.

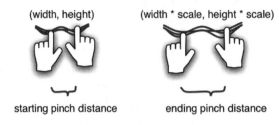

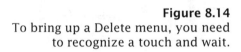

Figure 8.13
To pinch, you need to know
the change in scale.

I CAN'T BELIEVE THAT'S ALL A PINCH IS. IT'S STILL PRETTY COOL!

If you know the scale, you can apply it to the disguise element by multiplying it by the width and height. All you need to learn is how to recognize the pinch gesture.

Popping up the Delete menu involves a few new concepts.

Figure 8.14
To bring up a Delete menu, you need
to recognize a touch and wait.

The first one is recognizing the *hold*, or long press, gesture. But, you probably get the idea that once you learn one gesture, it will be simple to learn the others. The second part is making the pop-up menu, which is something you haven't done.

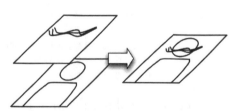

Figure 8.15   To save a photo, you
need to composite the disguises into
one image.

The final thing you need to do is create the composite image. Like the delete, it starts with a menu, but then you need to overlay two UIImage objects into one by drawing the pixels of one onto the other.

This would be hard, but iOS comes with a library called Core

Graphics that can do most of it for you. You need to know where to draw and how to scale, but the actual drawing is a simple message.

With these hints, you might want to see what you can do on your own. The rest of the chapter will take you step by step through the process of making these additions to Disguisey, but it might be fun to figure some of it out. The areas that you know already are the animation and most of the model class updates. The rest will require research.

Using animation to make disguises grow

In chapter 5, you learned that animation on the iPhone is simple. Just start an animation, change properties, and then commit the app. All the actual animation of the in-between states is taken care of for you. The trickiest part is coming up with how to use animations in the first place.

Visualizing the animation

The only part of your user interface that needs an animation is the placement of the disguise element. There aren't that many other transitions, except for tabs (which shouldn't animate) and the image picker (which animates automatically). Here's what you'll do.

To make the mustache grow at the touch point, you want it to start with a small size, then have the height and width change to their final

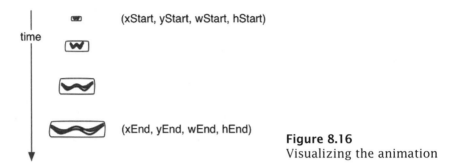

Figure 8.16
Visualizing the animation

values, and finally move the top-left corner of the mustache so the center stays put. The changes are in the `drawDisguiseElement:startingAtPoint:` message, which you'll see next.

Coding the animation

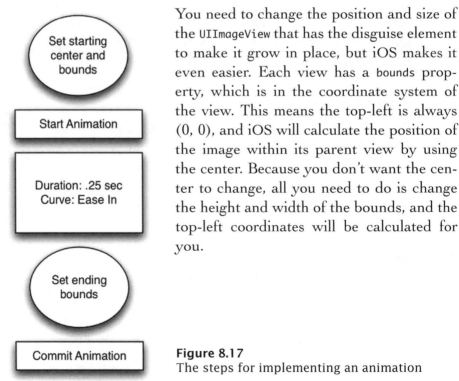

You need to change the position and size of the `UIImageView` that has the disguise element to make it grow in place, but iOS makes it even easier. Each view has a `bounds` property, which is in the coordinate system of the view. This means the top-left is always (0, 0), and iOS will calculate the position of the image within its parent view by using the center. Because you don't want the center to change, all you need to do is change the height and width of the bounds, and the top-left coordinates will be calculated for you.

Figure 8.17
The steps for implementing an animation

Here's how to change `drawDisguseElement:startingAtPoint`.

Listing 8.1   DIFaceViewController.m: new code for
              drawDisguiseElement:startingAtPoint:

```
-(void)drawDisguiseElement:(DIDisguiseElement*)el
        startingAtPoint:(CGPoint)p
{
    UIImageView* imageView =
        [self newDisguise:el.image];

    [faceImage addSubview:imageView];
    imageView.bounds = CGRectZero;
    imageView.center = p;

    [UIView animateWithDuration:.25 delay:0
        options:UIViewAnimationCurveEaseIn animations:^{
        imageView.bounds = CGRectMake(0, 0,
                                    el.image.size.width,
                                    el.image.size.height);
    }
    completion:nil];
}
```

1 START AT ZERO SIZE

END AT IMAGE SIZE **2**

You start by setting the bounds to a rectangle with 0 for x, y, width, and height **1**. Then you put an animation begin and end around the code that sets the bounds to the final value **2**. As you saw before, you can change how the animation looks by setting a few parameters.

IF I CHANGE THE BOUNDS, IT DOESN'T CHANGE THE CENTER.

To get ready for later, move the allocation of the disguise element to its own message:

```
-(UIImageView*) newDisguise:(UIImage*)image
{
    UIImageView* iv = [[UIImageView alloc] initWithImage:image];
    return iv;
}
```

Try it out by building and running the app with Cmd-R. Now, when you touch the face, you get a nice animation instead of the instant placement, which is jarring on the iPhone.

IT'S SIMPLE. ALL YOU NEED TO DO IS GET THE TOUCHESBEGAN METHOD, GRAB THE TWO TOUCH POINTS, AND CALCULATE THE DISTANCE BETWEEN THEM. THEN, WHEN YOU GET A TOUCHESMOVED EVENT, YOU CALCULATE THE NEW DISTANCE AND DIVIDE THAT BY THE DISTANCE YOU CALCULATED EARLIER WHICH YOU STORED SOMEWHERE. GOT IT?

ACTUALLY, YES.

Speaking of touching the face, do you remember how you did that in the last chapter? You learned that if you inherit from `UIImageView`, you can implement touch messages to detect the tap. It's not hard to recognize a tap this way, but imagine what a pain it would be to do something harder, like a pinch. Luckily, you don't have to.

Recognizing touch gestures

A lot of views, like buttons or tables, do all the work for you. They have built-in ways for you to interact with them. You don't need to worry about touches or recognizing gestures. But if you have your own ideas for interaction, you have to do a little more. You could look at every touch and react to it, but some gestures are too complex for that.

There's a set of gestures that are used so often, they are built in—not just to save you time, but also to make sure they acted the same in all apps. If they weren't, you would have a lot of buggy pinch implementations in the App Store.

Picking the right gesture

In the first few versions of iOS, developers had to recognize taps, pinches, pans, and holds. Because these are so common, you now have a whole set of classes to help you. They're organized like this in the iOS SDK.

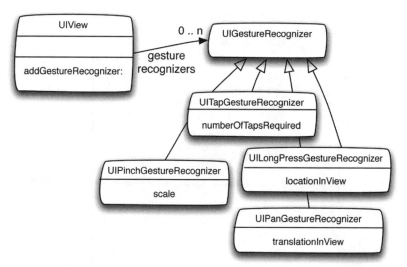

Figure 8.18 Gestures class diagram

HEY! ARE THOSE IS-A
ARROWS? I MISSED THEM

Each view can have a gesture recognizer object attached to it. To detect a tap or a series of taps, use `UITap-GestureRecognizer`. For a hold, use a `UILongPressGesture-Recognizer`. You can probably guess what to use to pinch and pan a view. Each gesture has different properties you use to set it up and get information from when the gesture is recognized.

Use the built-in apps as a guide to what users may expect these gestures to do. For example, use pinch to change the size of things. It might be fun to use them in other ways, but don't do so in a way that confuses the user.

Attaching gesture recognizers

Gestures are so easy to use that you don't need to think about independent touches any more. But because you know views receive these messages, let's see how gestures work.

If a view has a gesture recognizer attached to it, the view will send the recognizer all the touch messages it receives.

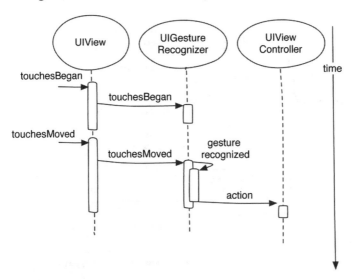

Figure 8.19   Sequence of messages for a recognized gesture

Each gesture class is responsible for analyzing these touches and deciding whether the series of touch events correlates to the kind of gesture it's responsible for detecting. If so, it sends an action message that you set up.

Tap is easy to explain. Here's what it looks like.

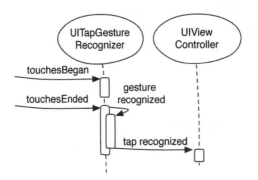

Figure 8.20   Recognizing a tap

When you touch the view, the tap recognizer gets a touchesBegan message. It remembers the location and time, and if you let go at the same point (or close enough) within a certain time window, a tap action is sent to the controller that created the tab recognizer.

All you need to do is create the right recognizer, attach it, and set it up to call an action in your controller. Here's the new code for the new-Disguise message you added.

Listing 8.2   DIFaceViewController.m: attaching gesture recognizers

```
-(UIImageView*) newDisguise:(UIImage*)image
{
    UIImageView* iv = [[UIImageView alloc] initWithImage:image];
    iv.multipleTouchEnabled = YES;
    iv.userInteractionEnabled = YES;

    UIPanGestureRecognizer* move =                          DETECT
        [[UIPanGestureRecognizer alloc]                     MOVES ...
            initWithTarget:self
            action:@selector(onMoveDisguiseElement:)];      ADD THE
    [iv addGestureRecognizer:move];                         RECOGNIZER, ...

    UIPinchGestureRecognizer* pinch =
        [[UIPinchGestureRecognizer alloc]                   ... DETECT
            initWithTarget:self                             PINCHES ...
            action:@selector(onPinchDisguiseElement:)];
    [iv addGestureRecognizer:pinch];

    UILongPressGestureRecognizer *hold =
        [[UILongPressGestureRecognizer alloc]               ... AND HOLDS, TOO
            initWithTarget:self
            action:@selector(onHoldDisguiseElement:)];
    [iv addGestureRecognizer:hold];
                                                            ... AND CALL
    return iv;                                              THIS MESSAGE.
}
```

That's all you need to do to detect these three new gestures on a disguise element. The one thing you haven't seen before is how to connect actions with code instead of with Interface Builder. To do so, you use @selector to turn the name of the message into something you can pass

@SELECTOR LETS YOU PASS A MESSAGE TO A MESSAGE SO IT CAN BE SENT LATER.

as a parameter. The message needs to be defined on the targeted object, self, which is a DIFaceViewController.

> **SELECTOR** A way of making it possible to pass a message to another message so it can be called later.

To finish, you need to implement the three actions. We'll go through each of them next.

Moving a disguise into place

The first gesture you'll implement is moving the disguise element. This gesture is called *panning,* because it's often used to pan around large views. It works like this.

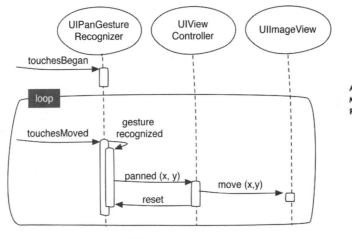

AS LONG AS YOU KEEP MOVING, YOU WILL GET PAN RECOGNIZED MESSAGES.

Figure 8.21 Recognizing a pan gesture

That's all that needs to happen to see the disguises move around, but remember, you have model classes too. Here's a more complete picture of what's going on.

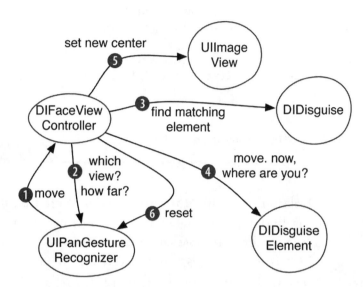

Figure 8.22 Interaction between objects when an element is moved

First the recognizer tells the controller that a move was detected. The controller sends messages to the recognizer to get the view and the amount the user's finger moved. Then the controller sends a message to the Disguise object it holds to get the specific element associated with this view, and tells the element to move by the amount the recognizer gave the controller. Finally, the controller uses the element's position property to set the new center of the disguise image view.

Here are the new messages for DIDisguiseElement:

```
-(void)translateByX:(CGFloat)xDiff y:(CGFloat)yDiff
{
    self.point= CGPointMake(self.point.x + xDiff, self.point.y + yDiff);
}
```

Remember to declare `translateByX` in the header so the view controller can send the message to it.

And here's how you find the matching element in the `DIDisguise` class:

```
-(DIDisguiseElement*)getElementAtPoint:(CGPoint)pt
                        withImage:(UIImage*)image
{
    for (DIDisguiseElement *d in self.elements) {
        if (CGPointEqualToPoint(pt, d.point) && image == d.image) {
            return d;
        }
    }
    NSAssert(false, @"This should never happen");    ◀  SHOULD ALWAYS
    return nil;                                          FIND A MATCH
}
```

TO DECLARE A MESSAGE, USE
THE NAME AND PARAMETERS AND
PUT A SEMICOLON AFTER IT.

Declare this in the `DIDisguise` header. Note that if you can't find a disguise element, that must mean you have a bug somewhere. `NSAssert` will alert you so you can fix it. Of course, it does this by crashing the app, so you want to be sure you find all problems in this area before releasing the app.

That takes care of the models. Now update FaceViewController.m with the following messages to orchestrate a move through the models and views.

Listing 8.3   A move gesture in DIFaceViewController.m

```
- (IBAction)onMoveDisguiseElement:(UIPanGestureRecognizer *)recognizer
{
    if ([recognizer state] == UIGestureRecognizerStateBegan ||
        [recognizer state] == UIGestureRecognizerStateChanged) {

        UIImageView* v = (UIImageView*)recognizer.view;
```

GET VIEW AND ➊
DISTANCE

```
CGPoint translation =
    [recognizer translationInView:[v superview]];

DIDisguiseElement *el =
    [self.disguise getElementAtPoint:v.center          ❷ GET ELEMENT
                          withImage:v.image];
[el translateByX:translation.x y:translation.y];

v.center = el.point;
                                                        ❸ RESET FOR
[recognizer setTranslation:CGPointZero                    NEXT TIME
                          inView:[v superview]];
    }

}
```

To begin, you check to see if this gesture is starting or changing, because you want to ignore its other states. Next ❶ you get the view and pan distance (also known as the *translation*). Then ❷ you get the disguise element from the disguise, move it, and set the view's center. Finally ❸, you tell the recognizer that next time, you just want to know how much you moved from here.

You can run the app, but be careful. You haven't set up the other recognizers, so if they're triggered, the app will crash. Until then, you'll have to be happy that you can use the mustache to cover up bald spots or hide blemishes.

WHAT IS UP WITH
THIS APP?

When you're done, you can move on to pinching, which is, unsurprisingly, very similar.

Figure 8.23
Moving a disguise element
in the simulator

Pinching the DIDisguise to resize it

Your disguises look great if they happen to be just the right size for the face photo you choose. Let's make it possible to resize disguises when they don't fit.

Like moving, pinching has this interaction.

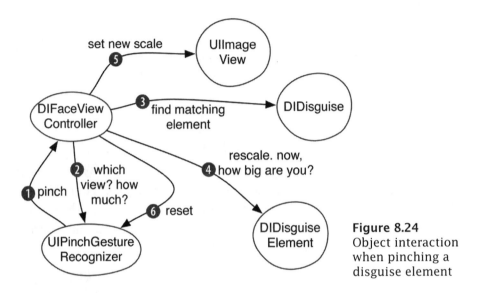

Figure 8.24
Object interaction when pinching a disguise element

So, the code is nearly the same, except that you are changing a scale instead of moving a position. To start, go into the DIDisguise element and add a new CGFloat property called scale. Then set it to 1.0 in the init message.

Add this message to the DisguiseElement module (declare it in the header, too):

```
-(void)scaleBy:(CGFloat)scaleDifference
{
    self.scale = self.scale * scaleDifference;
    if (self.scale < .5 ||
        isnan(self.scale) || isinf(self.scale)) {
```

KEEP SCALE
INBOUNDS

```
        self.scale = .5;
    }

}
```

You do a check to make sure the scale keeps the mustaches big enough to be pinched. The functions isnan() and isinf() will tell you if you're overflowing the numbers, so you can fix that too. If you're curious, remove them later and see what happens.

NAN MEANS NOT A NUMBER. INF MEANS INFINITY. FLOATING-POINT OPERATIONS SOMETIMES RESULT IN THESE.

Now you can implement the gesture in the Face View Controller.

Listing 8.4   DIFaceViewController.m: implementation of pinching

```
- (IBAction)onPinchDisguiseElement:
    (UIPinchGestureRecognizer *)recognizer
{
    if ([recognizer state] == UIGestureRecognizerStateBegan ||
        [recognizer state] == UIGestureRecognizerStateChanged) {

        UIImageView* v = (UIImageView*)recognizer.view;

        CGFloat scaleDifference = recognizer.scale;
        DIDisguiseElement *el =
            [self.disguise getElementAtPoint:v.center
                                   withImage:v.image];
        [el scaleBy:scaleDifference];                      SCALE THE ELEMENT WITH
                                                           AN AFFINE TRANSFORM
        v.transform =
            CGAffineTransformMakeScale(el.scale, el.scale);

        [recognizer setScale:1];
    }
}
```

The transform property of views allows you to change their size, rotation, and position with a matrix called an *affine transform*. You don't need to know the math to use it, though. Just make one from the element's scale, and use it.

AFFINE TRANSFORM An object that represents how to scale, move, and rotate any view in 2D. Affine transforms can be combined to make more complex ones and inverted to reverse the transformation.

Try it with Cmd-R. The simulator can simulate a pinch if you hold down the Option key. Hold down Shift as well to move the pinch points away from the center. Obviously, when you get this over to the device, you can test it more thoroughly.

Recognizing gestures is pretty simple. You could easily implement the hold gesture if you knew how to pop up a menu. We'll cover that next.

Figure 8.25 Pinching in the simulator

Using a menu to remove parts of a disguise

You're going to make mistakes or change your mind about what disguises you want to use, so you need a way to delete them once you've aded them. In iPhone apps, one nice way to interact with a view is to hold it until a menu comes up. It's similar in spirit to the right-click context menus in mouse-driven GUIs.

The object interactions are somewhat different for this case.

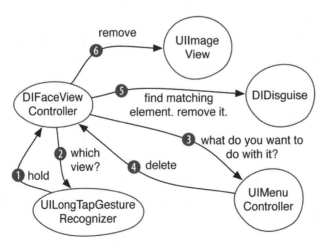

Figure 8.26
Object interactions for deleting an element

THOSE POP-UP MENUS SHOULD
BE SPECIFIC TO THE THING
YOU'RE TOUCHING.

As before, you detect the gesture. This time, you have to pop up a menu to find out what to do. Once the user chooses to delete an element, you can tell the disguise object and then remove the view.

To make pop-up menus, you use the `UIMenuController` class. Creating a menu works like this.

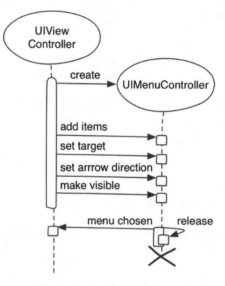

First you create a `UIMenu-Controller`. Then you add items, give the menu a target to point to, and make it visible. Each item has an action message associated with it, so when an item is chosen, the action is sent back to the controller, and the menu is released.

Figure 8.27 The sequence of messages for configuring and using a menu

MENUS ARE LIKE GESTURE
RECOGNIZERS IN THAT YOU
GIVE THEM A MESSAGE TO
CALL LATER.

Let's look at the code. First, let's update the `DIDisguise` model. Here's the implementation, but remember to declare the message in your header:

```
-(void)removeElement:(DIDisguiseElement*)el
{
    [self.elements removeObject:el];
}
```

Now let's recognize that gesture in the Face View Controller.

Listing 8.5   DIFaceViewController.m: recognizing the hold in the controller

```
-(void)addMenu:(NSArray*)items toView:(UIView*)view
    pointingAt:(CGRect)target
{
    [self becomeFirstResponder];

    UIMenuController* mc =                        ① GET MENU
        [UIMenuController sharedMenuController];
    mc.menuItems = items;

                                                 ② TARGET MENU
    [mc setTargetRect: target inView: view];
    if (target.origin.y > view.frame.size.height/2)
        mc.arrowDirection = UIMenuControllerArrowDown;
    else
        mc.arrowDirection = UIMenuControllerArrowUp;

    [mc setMenuVisible: YES animated: YES];
}


- (IBAction)onHoldDisguiseElement:
    (UILongPressGestureRecognizer *)recognizer
{
    if ([recognizer state] == UIGestureRecognizerStateBegan) {
        self.viewToDelete = recognizer.view;        ③ SAVE VIEW
                                                       TO DELETE
        UIMenuItem* miDelete = [[UIMenuItem alloc]
            initWithTitle: @"Delete"
            action:@selector( onDeleteDisguiseElement: )];

        [self addMenu:[NSArray arrayWithObjects: miDelete, nil]
            toView:self.viewToDelete.superview
          pointingAt:self.viewToDelete.frame];
    }
}
```

The first message, addMenu, makes it a little easier to make menus. First you get the menu ① and set its items based on the array you'll make later. Then you point the menu at the thing you'll be affecting ②. If the touch is near the top of the phone, you put the menu below the finger pointing up at it; otherwise, you point down. Finally, you save the view ③ in a new property called viewToDelete. This property is a strong UIImageView*, which you should add to the controller.

FIRSTRESPONDER Onscreen controls can receive shake events and text from the keyboard. When an object becomes the first responder, it's the first object allowed to handle the keyboard and shake notifications.

YOU'RE GOING TO REMEMBER TO SYNTHESIZE IT, RIGHT?

To use this message in the gesture action, you need to create an array of UIMenuItem objects. Even if you have only one, as in this case, you must use an array. Each item has some text to show and an action that you make with @selector as you did before.

You need to implement the onDeleteDisguise action with this code:

```
- (void) onDeleteDisguiseElement: (UIMenuController*) sender
{
    UIImageView* v = (UIImageView*)self.viewToDelete;
    if (v != nil) {
        DIDisguiseElement *el =
            [self.disguise getElementAtPoint:v.center
                                  withImage:v.image];
        [self.disguise removeElement:el];
        [v removeFromSuperview];
        self.viewToDelete = nil;
    }
}
```

If you run a test at this point, you'll see that the app doesn't work. What's going on?

It turns out that you need to let the controller know that it has menus and that deleting is allowed. First, add this message to the Face View Controller:

```
-(BOOL) canBecomeFirstResponder
{
    return YES;
}
```

Now this controller can have menus. When the menu is requested, it asks the controller if the delete action is allowed. Here's how you say yes:

```
-(BOOL) canPerformAction:(SEL)action withSender:(id)sender
{
```

```
    if (action == @selector(onDeleteDisguise:))
        return YES;
    return [super canPerformAction:action withSender:sender];
}
```

Run the app again. Pick a face, add a disguise, and then touch and hold it.

Tap the Delete menu to remove the disguise.

You can now use your elements pretty much however you like, but there's no way to save your work.

Figure 8.28
Deleting an element in the simulator

Saving the disguised face

To finish Disguisey, you need a way to save the final photo so you can access it later or share it with others. What good is making your friends look ridiculous if they don't know about it?

Displaying a Save menu

To implement a save, you could add another button to the Navigation Bar or add a toolbar. Because you've been playing with pop-up menus, let's use one for this, too.

Here's the interaction you'll implement.

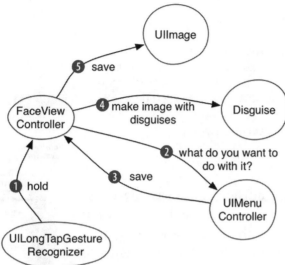

Figure 8.29
Object interactions
when saving a photo

You already know how to do ❶, ❷, and ❸. First, add the following code to the controller's viewDidLoad message to add the recognizer to the face image:

```
UIGestureRecognizer *hold =
    [[UILongPressGestureRecognizer alloc]
      initWithTarget:self
      action:@selector(onHoldFace:)];

[self.faceImage addGestureRecognizer:hold];
```

Don't forget to allow the action by adding this to canPerformAction:

```
if (action == @selector(onSaveFace:))
    return YES;
```

When the hold is recognized, you handle it with this action:

```
- (IBAction)onHoldFace:(UILongPressGestureRecognizer *)recognizer
{
    if ([recognizer state] == UIGestureRecognizerStateBegan) {

        UIMenuItem* miSave =
```

```
        [[UIMenuItem alloc] initWithTitle: @"Save"
           action:@selector( onSaveFace: )];
```

POINT AT WHICH
VIEW WAS TOUCHED

```
    CGPoint point =

       [recognizer locationInView:self.view];
    CGRect targetFrame = CGRectMake(point.x, point.y, 0, 0);

    [self addMenu:[NSArray arrayWithObjects: miSave, nil]
          toView:self.view
       pointingAt:targetFrame];
    }
}
```

If you run the app and hold the face, the menu comes up—but don't tap it yet, unless you want Disguisey to crash. Without the onSaveFace message to call, you're not finished. If you're dying to save, take a screenshot.

TECH SUPPORT.
WHAT'S UP?

YOUR APP CRASHES
EVERY TIME I
TOUCH IT.

DON'T TOUCH IT

Overlaying one image onto another

When the Save menu is tapped, you need to take all the images for each disguise element and somehow draw them onto the face image, so you have one UIImage object at the end. Then you can easily put this image in the Photos app. How easily?

```
- (void) onSaveFace: (UIMenuController*) sender
{
    UIImage* face =
        [self.disguise overlayDisguisesOnFace:[faceImage image]];

    UIImageWriteToSavedPhotosAlbum(face, nil, nil, nil);
}
```

OK, that's nice, but this only works if DIDisguise can overlay disguises. Add this message to Disguise, and don't forget to declare it in Disguise's header:

```
-(UIImage*) overlayDisguisesOnFace:(UIImage *)face
{
    UIImage *newFace = face;
```

```
    for (DIDisguiseElement *d in self.elements) {
        newFace = [d overlayOnFace:newFace];
    }
    return newFace;
}
```

See what you're doing? You're making each model class responsible for its part. DIDisguise is responsible for telling elements that they're supposed to overlay, but elements do the heavy lifting. Here's what's happening.

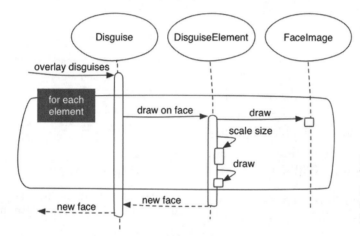

Figure 8.30
The sequence of messages when compositing an image

I ONCE GOT IN TROUBLE FOR PASSING MESSAGES, BUT OBJECTS DO THAT ALL THE TIME.

The controller starts by requesting the overlay from the DIDisguise model class. In turn, it loops through each element in the disguise and sends the element a message to overlay itself. The result makes sure each object encapsulates the behavior that it should be responsible for.

To finish, add the following code to DIDisguiseElement's module file.

Listing 8.6   DIDisguiseElement.m: overlaying a **DIDisguiseElement**'s image on the face

```
-(UIImage*)overlayOnFace:(UIImage *)face
{
    UIGraphicsBeginImageContext(CGSizeMake(face.size.width,
                                            face.size.height));
    [face drawAtPoint: CGPointMake(0,0)];
```

CALCULATE
ELEMENT'S
SIZE ...

```
    CGSize scaledSize =
        CGSizeMake(self.image.size.width * self.scale,
                   self.image.size.height * self.scale);

    CGPoint topLeftPoint =
        CGPointMake(self.point.x - scaledSize.width/2,
                    self.point.y - scaledSize.height/2);

    [self.image drawInRect:CGRectMake(topLeftPoint.x, topLeftPoint.y,
            scaledSize.width, scaledSize.height)];
    UIImage *newFace = UIGraphicsGetImageFromCurrentImageContext();
    UIGraphicsEndImageContext();
    return newFace;
}
```

... AND ITS UPPER-
LEFT CORNER

The only hard part is seeing how to use the center and scale to find the destination rectangle for the disguise. Core Graphics handles resizing and drawing for you. This illustration will help.

scaled width

width

center point

(scaled width) / 2

Figure 8.31 Calculating the new size and position of an element

The dashed box represents the size of the mustache on the screen after you scale it. To find this rectangle's upper-left point, you need to subtract half the scaled width from the center point's x-coordinate, and half the scaled height from the center's y-coordinate.

WOULD HAVE BEEN NICE IF I COULD USE A CENTER AND A SIZE, SINCE THAT'S WHAT I HAD.

But enough of this chit-chat. Let's run it. After you save, tap the home button at the bottom of the simulator, and go to the Photos app to see the saved face. Your enhancements are finished, so go show a friend. Be sure to hide all your doctored photos of their face first.

Moving on from Disguisey

You did a lot to make Disguisey better, and we hope we covered some of the ideas you came up with. Keep playing around with the app and see if you can figure out how to rotate an element, add another menu item to make a mustache wiggle, or add a new tab with jewelry and accessories.

Doing that last one is easy: all you need to do is create another XIB file, connect it to the Disguise View Controller, set it up in the app delegate, and add a new tab bar item for it in Interface Builder. Then, grab some pictures of earrings and add them to the tab. You already know how to do these things.

Later in the book, you'll see how to access the internet so you can come back and send this photo to a friend or post it to a photo-sharing site.

If you have ideas but need some help to get started, don't forget to visit the online forum associated with this book (www.manning.com/franco/).

Working with location and maps

This chapter covers

- Using maps in your views
- Getting the current location
- Showing pins on a map

The iPhone has so many features that many things that used to be separate gadgets can be apps. For most of us, the GPS on the phone is sufficient for our location and direction needs, and we don't need a dedicated GPS device. The next application you'll write, Parkinator, uses this feature to solve an important mobile computing problem: remembering where you parked.

Designing a map application

Let's make the UI for this app just a front and back screen. On the front, you'll see your location and the last place you parked. On the back, you'll take a picture of your car, and when you're finished, the app will flip back and put a pin at your spot.

Sketching Parkinator

Let's make a quick sketch.

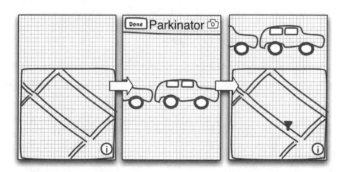

Figure 9.1
Sketch of the front and back screens

See the little *i* in a circle at the bottom? That's how you get to the flip side of the app. You haven't used this kind of navigation before, but lots of apps use it, including the built-in Weather app.

Looking at how it works

This application's behavior is simple. Because you just want to learn about location, maps, and pins, we'll make sure the rest of the app uses things you've seen before.

Here's how you want it to work.

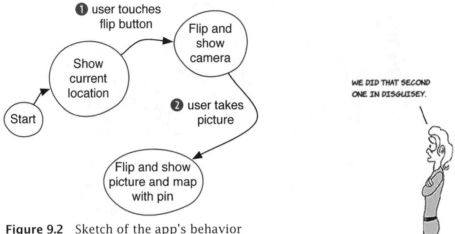

Figure 9.2   Sketch of the app's behavior

When the app comes up, you want to get the current location and show it on the map. When the user touches the *i*, you'll flip the app around. There they can take a picture. Then you'll flip the app around again to show the parking spot picture and a pin on the map.

Designing the models, views, and controllers

It's pretty obvious from the sketches that you have two views (and controllers): one for the front side, which we'll call the main view, and one for the other side, which we'll call the flip-side view.

The main view needs to respond to two things. First, when the *i* is touched, it needs to show the other side of the app. You'll see soon that you get that behavior for free with the template you're going to use. Second, when the user is finished with the flip side, you need to show the parking-spot photo and put a pin on the map. To hold this information, you'll use a model class called PAParkingSpot.

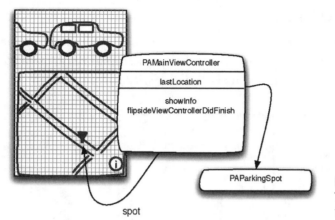

spot

Figure 9.3
The MVC classes for
the front of the app

The flip side is simple as well. It needs to take a picture, show it on the screen, and then let the user say that they're finished.

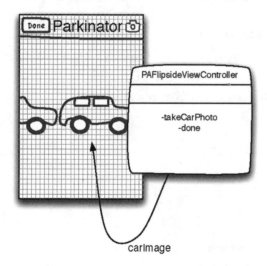

carImage

Figure 9.4   The MVC classes
for the flip side of the app

Most of the hard part of this app involves interacting with the new frameworks you'll incorporate. Other than that, the behavior and the kinds of classes you'll make are similar to the other apps you've built already.

Creating an app with a map

You want the app to use a kind of navigation that you haven't seen yet. It uses a main view to show most of the functionality of the app and a flip-side view to set it up. This is called a *utility application*.

Using the Utility Application template

To get started, go into Xcode and choose File > New > Project from the menu. When you do, you'll see the list of templates: choose Utility Application under the choices for iOS applications.

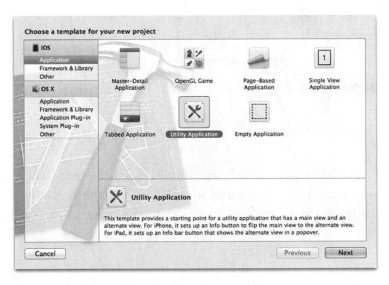

Figure 9.5   The Utility Application template

In the next dialog, name the application `Parkinator`, and click Next.

Figure 9.6   Name the application.

If you run the app in the simulator, you'll see that it has a blank main screen and that it already includes the *i* button that flips to the other side. You've probably seen Map View in the Interface Builder object library when you were building other apps, and you probably already know that you'll use it next. Before you do, however, you need to add the frameworks to your project.

Adding the proper frameworks to your app

WHENEVER YOU NEED EXTRA
FUNCTIONALITY, YOU
MIGHT HAVE TO ADD A
FRAMEWORK TO GET IT.

Because maps and location aren't used in every app on the iPhone, Xcode makes you add them if you're going to use them. To do that, click the main Parkinator node at the top of Project Navigator, and then choose the Parkinator target.

Click the Build Phases tab, and open the Link Binary with Libraries area as shown.

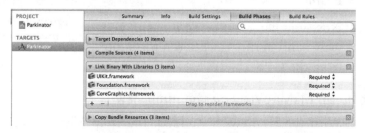

Figure 9.7   The frameworks in the Build Phases screen

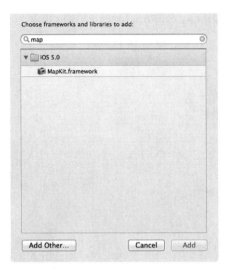

Figure 9.8 The MapKit framework

You need to add two frameworks: MapKit, which draws maps for you, and CoreLocation, which talks to the GPS. To add MapKit, click the + button, and then type map in the search bar.

Choose MapKit.framework, and then click the Add button. Repeat this with CoreLocation.framework.

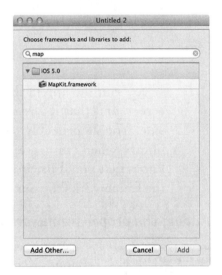

KEEPING EVERYTHING
ORGANIZED MAKES IT EASIER
WHEN THE PROJECT GETS
BIGGER.

Figure 9.9
The CoreLocation framework

Notice that in Project Navigator, these frameworks are in the main group. To make things tidier, drag them into the Frameworks group.

Now you can start using maps in your views and getting location information from the GPS.

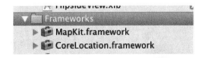

Figure 9.10 The Frameworks group in the project

Placing an MkMapView on the main view

With the frameworks added, the Map View object is like any other object you've put onto views. Let's go add it.

Click PAMainViewController.xib in Project Navigator, and scroll the Object Library until you see the Map View.

Drag it onto the bottom area of your screen, taking up about half the area.

Figure 9.11 The Map View object

Figure 9.12
MkMapView on PAMainViewController.xib

To make sure you can still touch that *i* button, while the Map View is still selected, choose Editor > Arrangement > Send to Back. Doing so puts the map under the button.

I BET SHOWING THE USER LOCATION MEANS IT WILL TALK TO THE GPS.

Finally, go to the Attributes Inspector and select the Shows User Location check box.

Run the application by pressing Cmd-R or clicking the play button at upper-left in Xcode. When you do, you'll see this.

Figure 9.13
Running the map app in the simulator

If you live in the United States and don't need to see any streets on the map, then you can skip the next step. The rest of us would like the map to show the current location.

By default, the simulator acts like you're at Apple headquarters in Cupertino, California. If you slide the map over to California and zoom in, you'll see a blue dot showing that you're there. Once you learn how to test your apps on an actual iPhone, you'll see that the map will show your real location. In the meantime, choose Debug > Location in the simulator and select a new location or even a simulation of movement.

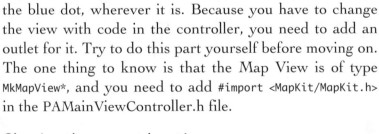

REMEMBER. PUT THE INSTANCE VARIABLE AND IBOUTLET PROPERTY IN THE HEADER. THEN SYNTHESIZE IN THE MODULE.

Right now, you want to get the map view to center around the blue dot, wherever it is. Because you have to change the view with code in the controller, you need to add an outlet for it. Try to do this part yourself before moving on. The one thing to know is that the Map View is of type `MkMapView*`, and you need to add `#import <MapKit/MapKit.h>` in the PAMainViewController.h file.

Showing the current location

You added a lot of outlets in the previous chapters, and this one is no different. Always make sure your view controller knows the type of view you're using: unless it's part of `UIKit`, you need to add an `import` line for it. Put this at the top of PAMainViewController.h:

```
#import <MapKit/MapKit.h>
```

To create the outlet, click PAMainViewController.xib and display the Assistant Editor. Ctrl-drag from the `MKMapView` into the assistant, and call the property `mapView`.

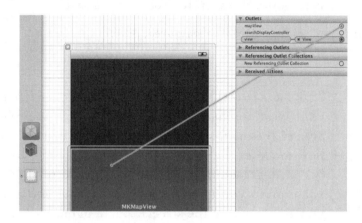

Figure 9.14
Connect the `MKMapView` to PAMainView-Controller.h using the assistant.

The `MkMapView` needs a way to tell you about location changes, and it does that by sending messages to a delegate. You saw this with `UITableView`, which did the same thing. To set it up, click the `MkMapView` and, in its Connections Inspector, drag the delegate outlet to the File's Owner cube icon.

Finally, to make the controller able to receive these messages, go to PAMainViewController.h and change the interface declaration to look like this (adding `MKMapViewDelegate`):

```
@interface PAMainViewController : UIViewController
    <FlipsideViewControllerDelegate, MKMapViewDelegate>
```

Now you can get messages from the Map View in your controller. You want to know whenever the map senses you're at a new location. That's the time to update the map. To handle this, add the following code to PAMainViewController.m.

Listing 9.1   PAMainViewController.m: handling the Map View reporting a location

```
- (void) mapView:(MKMapView *)mapView
    didUpdateUserLocation:(MKUserLocation *)userLocation
{
```

SET ZOOM
LEVEL ❶

```
MKCoordinateSpan span = MKCoordinateSpanMake(.02f, .02f);

self.lastLocation = userLocation.location.coordinate;
MKCoordinateRegion region =
    MKCoordinateRegionMake(self.lastLocation, span);

[self.mapView setRegion:region animated:YES];

}
```

SAVE
LOCATION
❷ FOR LATER

ONE DEGREE OF LATITUDE IS
ABOUT 69 MILES.

A DEGREE OF LONGITUDE IS 69
MILES AT THE EQUATOR BUT GETS
SMALLER AS YOU MOVE TOWARD
THE POLES.

This message will be sent to your controller whenever your location changes. You want to show the relevant area of the map, so the first thing to do is to figure out how much of the map to show ❶. The .02 is the number of degrees of latitude and longitude to show; this value gives you a good overview of the area and lets you get a sense of the streets. Zoom in more by making this number smaller, and zoom out by making it larger.

Later you'll want to place a pin here, so let's save the location in a property ❷. Locations are stored in a CLLocationCoordinate2D. Create this property on your own by putting this line in its proper locations:

```
@property(nonatomic) CLLocationCoordinate2D lastLocation;
```

Run the app, and it should look like this.

Now that you can show where you are, the next step is to let the user take a picture of their parked car. Almost all the code to do this is like the code you used to get a face for Disguisey, so we'll go through it fairly quickly in the next section.

Figure 9.15   The app with the current location

If you're feeling adventurous, try to do it on your own. Set up the app to grab a photo from your photo library, because there is no camera in the simulator. You don't have to worry about hooking up the Info button or the Done button on the flip side, because the Utility Application template did that for you.

Flipping the view to take a picture

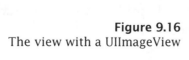

I KNEW THIS LOOKED FAMILIAR.

In order to implement the flip side, you need to be able to take a photo and show it. In Disguisey, you used an image from the Photo Library; the steps and code to use the camera are basically the same. You'll begin by putting a UIImageView on the flip-side view and hooking it up to an outlet.

Adding a UIImageView

After you take the picture, you want to show it on the view, so you need to drag a UIImageView onto the flip-side view. Select PAFlipsideViewController.xib in Project Navigator, and set the UIImageView to take up the view's entire size.

Figure 9.16
The view with a UIImageView

In order to set the image, you have to connect it to an outlet. Here's what PAFlipsideViewController.h needs to look like. Most of this code was written for you by the template, but you have to add the outlet and prepare the interface with the proper delegates for using the image picker to get photos.

Listing 9.2   PAFlipsideViewController.h after adding an outlet

```
#import <UIKit/UIKit.h>

@class PAFlipsideViewController;

@protocol FlipsideViewControllerDelegate
- (void)flipsideViewControllerDidFinish:
    (PAFlipsideViewController *)controller;
@end

@interface PAFlipsideViewController : UIViewController
    <UIImagePickerControllerDelegate,                    ← IMAGE PICKER
                                                           DELEGATES
    UINavigationControllerDelegate>

@property (nonatomic, weak)
    id <FlipsideViewControllerDelegate> delegate;
@property (nonatomic, strong)
    IBOutlet UIImageView *carPhoto;                      ← IMAGE
                                                           PROPERTY
- (IBAction)done:(id)sender;
- (IBAction)takeCarPhoto:(id)sender;                     ← SEND THIS TO
                                                           TAKE PHOTO
@end
```

When you take a photo, the image picker takes over the GUI and sends you messages to let you know what's going on. To do that, it needs you to implement these delegates. Once the photo is taken, you need to update the UIImageView with it, so you declare a property to connect the view to the controller. Later, to make the camera button take a picture, you'll attach the button to the takeCarPhoto action.

To finish this part, select PAFlipsideViewController.xib and connect the UIImageView to the carPhoto outlet.

You added the takeCarPhoto action so you can hook a button up to it, so the next step is to add that button.

Adding a camera button

The iOS SDK gives you some premade icon buttons that are used in the built-in apps and in apps throughout the App Store. Let's add the camera button to the Navigation Bar.

Find the Bar Button Item in the Object Library.

Drag it onto the right side of the Navigation Bar. Then, in the Attributes Inspector, change Identifier to Camera.

Figure 9.17 The Bar Button Item to use for the camera button

Figure 9.18 Change to a camera button.

Doing so changes the look of the button to a standard camera icon.

Figure 9.19
The camera button in the title bar

Connect the camera button to the selector action by dragging its File's Owner.

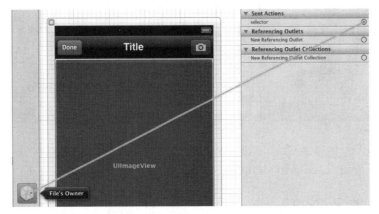

Figure 9.20 Drag the action to the File's Owner

Then, choose the takeCarPhoto action from the list.

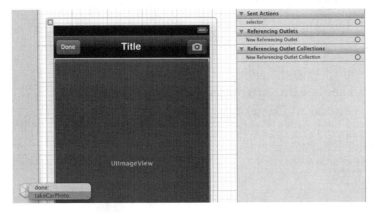

Figure 9.21 Choose takeCarPhoto to connect this action to the button.

Now you need to implement the message to get a photo and put in it the carPhoto UIImageView on the app screen.

Getting a photo

To get photos from the photo library or camera, you use the iOS SDK's UIImagePickerController. Here's what the takeCarPhoto implementation looks like.

Listing 9.3   PAFlipsideViewController.m: takeCarPhoto

```
-(IBAction)takeCarPhoto:(id)sender {

    UIImagePickerController* picker =
        [[UIImagePickerController alloc] init];
    picker.delegate = self;

    if ([UIImagePickerController
        isSourceTypeAvailable:                                    ① CHECK FOR
            UIImagePickerControllerSourceTypeCamera] ) {             CAMERA
        picker.sourceType =
            UIImagePickerControllerSourceTypeCamera;
    }
    else {                                                        ② USE LIBRARY IF
        picker.sourceType =                                          CAMERA UNAVAILABLE
            UIImagePickerControllerSourceTypePhotoLibrary;
    }
    [self presentViewController:picker animated:YES completion:nil];
}
```

OOOH NICE TRICK!

Before trying to use a camera, make sure you have one ①. This helps you in the simulator and also makes sure your code works on any iOS devices without a camera, such as the original iPad. If there's no camera, you show the photo library ②.

Next you have to handle the messages from the image picker. This is exactly like what you did for Disguisey.

Listing 9.4   PAFlipsideViewController.m: handling messages from the picker

```
- (void)releasePicker:(UIImagePickerController*)picker
{
    [picker dismissViewControllerAnimated:YES completion:nil];
}


- (void)imagePickerController:(UIImagePickerController *)picker
    didFinishPickingMediaWithInfo:(NSDictionary *)info
{                                                         ① SET THE
    self.carPhoto.image =                                    IMAGE
        [info objectForKey:UIImagePickerControllerOriginalImage];
    [self releasePicker:picker];
}
```

```
- (void)imagePickerControllerDidCancel:(UIImagePickerController *)picker
{
    [self releasePicker:picker];
}
```

When you get an image, you use the UIImage-View outlet you set up to put it on the screen ❶.

Run the app. The camera button now gets an image from your library.

On a device with a camera, the app will take a new picture instead.

You're almost done. The final step is to get back to the front side of the app, show this picture, and put a pin on the map.

Figure 9.22
Viewing the parking spot in the simulator

Showing the parking spot on the map

The Utility Application template set up a Done button for you that automatically flips the app back to the main view. Because it's likely that the information on the flip side will alter the main-view side, the template set up a message that it will send to the main view when the user clicks Done. Look in PAMainViewController.m and see if you can guess which message you'll alter to update the image.

Using the flipped view's image

Before you can handle the message that you've flipped back, you have to put a UIImageView onto the main view. Click PAMainViewController.xib, and drag on an ImageView.

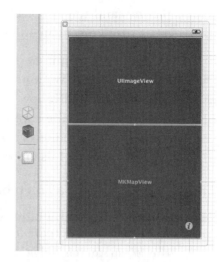

Figure 9.23 Putting a UIImageView onto PAMainViewController.xib

DON'T FORGET TO ATTACH THEM IN INTERFACE BUILDER.

Of course, because you want the controller to update this view, you need an outlet for it. Add one called carPhoto by making a property in your header.

When you've done that, edit the flipsideViewControllerDidFinish: that the template created for you so it looks like the following listing.

Listing 9.5 PAMainViewController.m: flipsideViewControllerDidFinish

```
- (void)flipsideViewControllerDidFinish:
    (FlipsideViewController *)controller {

    self.carImage.image = controller.carPhoto.image;    GET IMAGE
                                                         FROM FLIP SIDE

    [self dismissModalViewControllerAnimated:YES];
}
```

Run the app, click the info button, choose a picture, and touch the Done button to see the image used on the main view.

If you stick a pin here, you're done. Then, when you start walking away from your car, the blue dot will follow you, but a pin will be left behind to make sure you can find your car later. You'll make a model class called PAParkingSpot and use it to hold the location.

Creating a map annotation model

In order to put a pin on a map, MapKit requires you to create a class that implements the MKAnnotation delegate and has a property called coordinate that holds the location of the pin. Because you want a model class anyway, you'll make it conform to what the Map View

Figure 9.24 After choosing a picture in the simulator

wants. To begin, right-click the Classes group in Project Navigator and choose New File. Then, in the next dialog, choose Objective-C Class under Cocoa Touch in the iOS section.

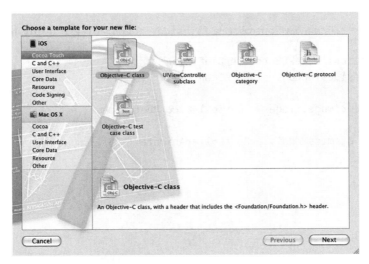

Figure 9.25 Creating a new class

Like most model classes, you're going make this one inherit from NSObject. But to also conform to the MKAnnotation delegate, use NSObject<MKAnnotation>.

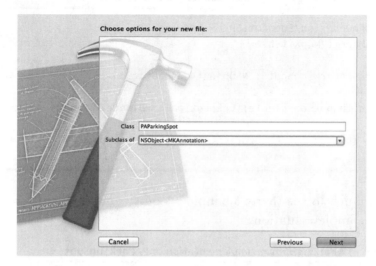

Figure 9.26   Make the class able to be a map annotation.

Save it in the main group.

Figure 9.27   Save the class in the main group.

Finally, you need to add an `init` and the `coordinate` property. Here's the header.

Listing 9.6   PAParkingSpot.h: interface for **PAParkingSpot**

```
#import <Foundation/Foundation.h>
#import <MapKit/MapKit.h>

@interface PAParkingSpot : NSObject<MKAnnotation>

-(id)initWithSpotCoordinate:(CLLocationCoordinate2D)spot;

@property (nonatomic) CLLocationCoordinate2D coordinate;

@end
```

Nothing much to see there: a simple property and an `init` to set it up. Here's the implementation.

Listing 9.7   PAParkingSpot.m: implementation of **PAParkingSpot**

```
#import "PAParkingSpot.h"

@implementation PAParkingSpot

-(id)initWithSpotCoordinate:(CLLocationCoordinate2D)spot
{
    self = [super init];
    if (self != nil) {
        self.coordinate = spot;
    }
    return self;
}

@end
```

EASIEST MODEL
CLASS EVER!

It doesn't get much simpler than that.

All you have to do now is to create a `PAParkingSpot` object and add it to the map. Remember, you want to do that once the main view is flipped back, so you need to add a little more code to the message where you set the `UIImageView` to the car photo.

Adding the pin to the map

When the view flips back, you already know `flipsideViewController-DidFinish` will be sent, because that's where you set up the main view's image from the flip side. Now you want to create a `PAParkingSpot` object, hold onto it in a property, and add it to the map.

The first step is to add a `PAParkingSpot*` property called `spot`. Add the property yourself, and then update this message to use it.

Listing 9.8   PAMainViewController.m: creating a **PAParkingSpot** object

```
- (void)flipsideViewControllerDidFinish:
        (PAFlipsideViewController *)controller {

    self.carPhoto.image = controller.carPhoto.image;

    self.spot = [[PAParkingSpot alloc]              ❶ INIT FROM
                    initWithSpotCoordinate:self.lastLocation];    LASTLOCATION
    [self.mapView addAnnotation:self.spot];

    [self dismissViewControllerAnimated:YES completion:nil];
}
```

ADD PIN ❷

A PIN IS ONE TYPE OF ANNOTATION. THERE ARE OTHER THINGS YOU COULD PUT ON A MAP. OF COURSE.

You saved the last location that you received from the map, so now you can use it to init the `PAParkingSpot` ❶. Then you add it to the map view ❷.

The map knows it has the pin, but it doesn't know what you want the pin to look like yet. To find that out, it sends the controller a message if the pin is on the screen; you have to implement it to set what kind of annotation to use and what color it should be.

Showing the pin

The final step is to implement the message to provide the viewing properties of any annotation. Viewing annotation properties is similar to viewing table elements, in that messages sent to request viewing properties are only generated for pins that are in view.

Listing 9.9 PAMainViewController.m: viewing the pin

```
-(MKAnnotationView*)mapView:(MKMapView *)mView                    ❶ IS IT ASKING
        viewForAnnotation:(id<MKAnnotation>)annotation               ABOUT THE SPOT?
{
    MKPinAnnotationView *pin = nil;
    if (annotation == self.spot) {                               ❷ REUSE AN
        pin = (MKPinAnnotationView*)[self.mapView                    OLD PIN
            dequeueReusableAnnotationViewWithIdentifier:@"spot"];

        if (pin == nil) {
            pin = [[MKPinAnnotationView alloc]                   ❸ MAKE A PIN IF
                    initWithAnnotation:self.spot                    YOU NEED TO
                    reuseIdentifier:@"spot"];
            pin.pinColor = MKPinAnnotationColorGreen;
        }
    }
    return pin;
}
```

This message is sent for every annotation on the map, including the current location. First you need to check to see if the message is asking about your parking spot ❶. If it is, then you want to reuse old pins that you saved under the name spot ❷. If you haven't saved a pin yet, then you make one ❸ and set its color to green.

Run the app, and mark a parking spot with the flip side to see the new pin.

You see that there are two annotations on the map. The green pin represents the parking spot, and the glowing blue dot is your current location. If you were on a device, you could start moving, and the blue dot would follow you. The green pin would remain behind to let you know where you parked.

Figure 9.28 Viewing the pin in the simulator

Making the data in Parkinator useful to others

That's a simple utility app with a map and a pin. You could use this basic idea for all kinds of location-based apps. You've used it to track parking spots, but you could tag your favorite outdoor art, track birds on a nature walk, or remember the antique store where you saw that cool lamp. This is the first step toward building a check-in–style app like FourSquare.

But let's say you're successful at getting millions of users to use Parkinator. If so, each user collects some valuable data about where there have historically been parking spots and which spots have recently been vacated. In the next chapter, you'll use some simple mechanisms to collect that data on the internet and use it in your app to find a place to park.

10

Accessing the internet

This chapter covers

- *Showing web pages in your user interface*
- *Posting updates to Twitter*
- *Getting and processing information from the web*

One of the most amazing things about the iPhone is that it's always connected to the internet. For some users, that means they can check their email while speeding down the highway. For you, it means your app can display web pages, download data, and share information with the world. You'll build Parkinator into an application that allows you to share and discover available parking spaces using the internet. You'll also create a web page to display a nicely formatted help page to help the user master these new features.

Overview of an internet-enabled Parkinator

In this chapter, you'll extend Parkinator to advertise the location of available parking spaces via Twitter. You'll also be able to use Parkinator to search for free spaces posted by others. Because Twitter support is built into iOS, reading and writing Twitter messages is a convenient way to share information. As an app becomes more complex, it's a good idea to provide the user with help. You'll create a help page for Parkinator using HTML, the language used to create web pages. HTML is an easy way to create and display nicely formatted text in iOS.

Updating the main view

You're adding three new features to the application, and users will need access to them. A common way to expose multiple features is to place multiple buttons in a toolbar at the bottom of the screen. At right is a quick sketch of the main view with a toolbar containing new buttons for viewing help, tweeting a spot, and searching Twitter, and the original button for going to the camera view.

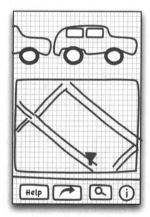

Figure 10.1 Sketch of the toolbar at the bottom of the screen

Tweeting an empty parking spot

You're adding new functionality to Parkinator. Because the rest of the app is unchanged, you'll limit this discussion to the new features. Users will share the location of available spaces as longitude and latitude via Twitter. iOS makes it easy to send messages (tweets) via Twitter: after you compose a tweet, iOS handles posting it to Twitter automatically. App tweets will begin with the string #Parkinator. This tag will make the tweets easy to identify and allows you to share information via Twitter without having to build your own website.

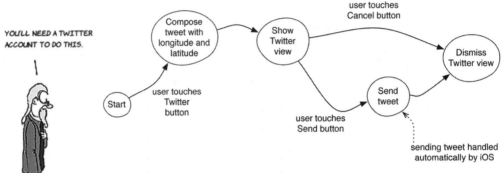

YOU'LL NEED A TWITTER ACCOUNT TO DO THIS.

Figure 10.2   Tweeting an empty spot behavior

Getting a list of open spaces

To find available spaces posted by other Parkinator users, you'll search for recent tweets with the #Parkinator tag. Once you receive a list of tweets with this tag, you'll iterate over the list. For each tweet, you'll read the latitude and longitude in the tweet and add a pin in the map.

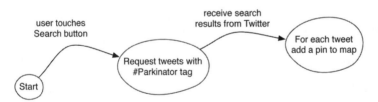

Figure 10.3   Getting open spaces behavior

Using HTML for Help

In iOS, you can display web pages or HTML files in an app using a UIWebView. The UIWebView renders the page exactly like Mobile Safari except that the page is displayed in your app in a view that you created. The web pages can include formatted text and images, and they're a perfect way to

Figure 10.4   Sketch of the Help view

lay out and render help information to the user. You'll create a UIWeb-View to display help to the users of Parkinator when they press the Help button.

Adding buttons on a toolbar

Let's edit Parkinator's MainView.xib file in Xcode to add the toolbar and buttons to the bottom of the main view. Once the UI elements are in place, you'll add the code that allows the user to get help, tweet, and search.

Creating a toolbar

The first step in creating a toolbar is to open the Parkinator project and click MainView.xib in Project Navigator. Before you add your toolbar, you need to make room for it. Drag the bottom of MKMapview up to make it smaller. Don't worry about its exact size at the moment; you can adjust it later. Also move the *i* button up so it's easier to grab.

Now that there is room, find the Toolbar object in the Object Library.

Figure 10.5
The Toolbar object

Drag a toolbar onto the bottom of the main view. Resize the MKMapview so it meets the top of the toolbar. Also place the *i* button inside the toolbar.

SOMETIMES YOU NEED TO TEMPORARILY MOVE INTERFACE ELEMENTS AROUND TO MAKE EDITS.

Figure 10.6   Toolbar added to Mainview.xib

Adding buttons for send, search, and help

With the toolbar in place, you can add buttons to view help, to send tweets, and to search tweets. Because you want one button per feature, you'll add two more Bar Button Items in addition to the item that was automatically added by Xcode and which you'll rename later.

From the Object Library, drag two Bar Button Items into the left side of the toolbar.

Figure 10.7 Bar Button Item object

Figure 10.8 Bar Button Items added to the toolbar

You'll now change the buttons to visually represent their function. To make the leftmost button say *Help*, double-click the word to highlight the text and then type `Help`.

For the Tweet button, you'll use the action icon, which looks like an arrow. Click once on the second button to select it, and in the Attributes Inspector, choose Action from the Identifier drop-down menu.

USE ACTION ICONS FOR
COMMANDS THAT DO
SOMETHING WITH THE
DATA ON THE SCREEN.

Figure 10.9
Setting Identifier to Action

To make your Search button look like a magnifying glass, do the same thing you did for the Tweet button, but instead of choosing Action for the Identifier, choose Search.

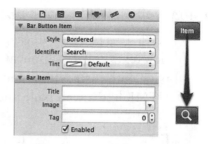

Improving the toolbar layout

Currently, all four buttons are bunched together in the left part of the toolbar. For most apps, you

Figure 10.10 Setting Identifier to Search

would like to evenly space the buttons. It looks better, and it makes it easier for the user to press the buttons. Buttons in the toolbar can be evenly spaced using the Flexible Space Bar Button Item found in the Object Library.

Figure 10.11
The Flexible Space Bar Button Item

Drag a flexible space between each pair of buttons.

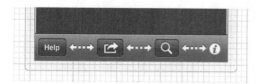

Figure 10.12 Flexible spaces added between buttons

Using web views in your app

UIWebViews provide an easy an convenient way to display web pages and rich text. For this application you'll use this iOS feature to create a help page with instructions for using the app. The page will be formatted in HTML like a web page and loaded into the web view.

Making the Help view

To display a UIWebView, you need to create a view and a view controller. Like most views in iOS, you'll create a view using a XIB file and a View-Controller for the XIB. Select File > New > File, and then select the UIViewController Subclass template.

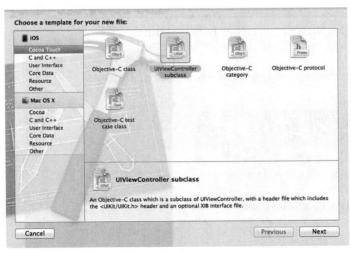

Figure 10.13   Creating a new UIViewController subclass

For the controller's title, enter `PAHelpViewController`. Make sure With XIB for User Interface is selected.

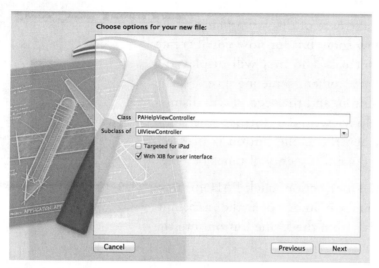

Figure 10.14 Creating `PAHelpViewController` and the XIB file

Setting up the Help view

As in the sketch, you'll add a Navigation Bar, display Help at the top of the view, and provide a Done button. Then you'll add a `UIWebView` to display the help.

THE WEBVIEW IS ALMOST EXACTLY WHAT SAFARI USES, SO YOU CAN DO A LOT WITH IT.

Click PAHelpViewController.xib. From the Object Library, drag a Navigation Bar to the top of the view. Double-click the Navigation Bar title, and type `Help`. Add a Bar Button Item to the left of the Navigation Bar. As you did with the toolbar items, double-click the word *item* and type `Done`.

Next you'll add the web view to your Help view to display the help information.

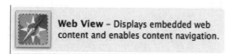

Web View – Displays embedded web content and enables content navigation.

Figure 10.15 Web View object

From the Object Library, drag the UIWeb-View into the space remaining below the Navigation Bar.

You'll take care of displaying help in the web view soon, but for now you'll create two IBActions. The first will display the Help view when someone presses the Help button, and the second will dismiss the Help view and return to the main view when the Done button is pressed. You've done this plenty of times before.

Figure 10.16 Help view with the web view and Navigation Bar

For the Done action, click PAHelpView-Controller.xib and open the assistant. Ctrl-drag from the Done button into the assistant.

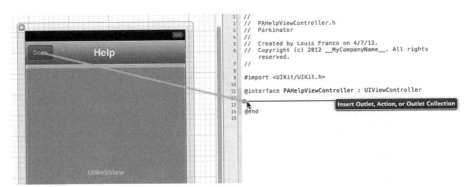

Figure 10.17 Ctrl-drag the Done button to PAHelpViewController.h in the assistant.

Select Action for the Connection type, and call the message onDone.

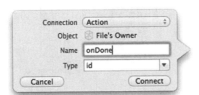

Figure 10.18 Name the action onDone.

Open PAHelpViewController.m, and fill in the implementation of onDone to make the method dismiss the view:

```
-(IBAction)onDone:(id)sender
{
    [self dismissViewControllerAnimated:YES completion:nil];
}
```

Finally, you need to create an IBAction to display the new view when the user presses the Help button. This process is almost identical to what you just did for the Done button. Open PAMainViewController.xib, select the Help button, and Ctrl-drag from the button into PAMainViewController.h in the assistant. (Make sure you have the Help button selected and not the whole toolbar.)

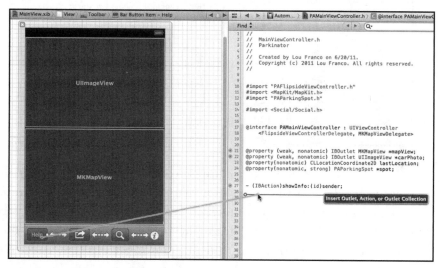

Figure 10.19 Ctrl-drag from the Help button.

Call the action showHelp.

Figure 10.20 Name the action showHelp.

Then fill in the message's definition in PAMainViewController.m so it looks like this:

```
- (IBAction)showHelp:(id)sender
{
    PAHelpViewController *help =
      [[PAHelpViewController alloc]
        initWithNibName:@"PAHelpViewController"
        bundle:nil];
    [self presentViewController:help animated:YES completion:nil];
}
```

Making an HTML resource

At the moment, if you run the app and press Help, you get a blank web view with Help in the navigation bar and a Done button. Before you can use the web view, you need to create a web view outlet property. Open PAHelpViewController.xib in Interface Builder, and show the assistant. Ctrl-drag from the UIWebView into PAHelpViewController.h.

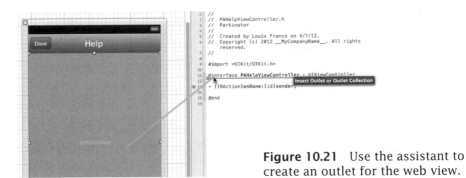

Figure 10.21   Use the assistant to create an outlet for the web view.

Call the property `helpView`.

Now, if you wanted to display a web page (any web page) in the web view, you could change `PAHelpViewController`'s `viewDidLoad` definition to this:

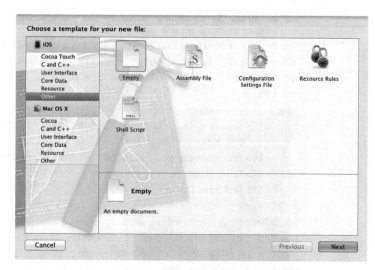

Figure 10.22   Naming the outlet

```
- (void)viewDidLoad
{
    [self.helpView
      loadRequest:[NSURLRequest
        requestWithURL:[NSURL URLWithString:
          @"http://www.manning.com/"]]];
}
```

You would replace http://www.manning.com/ with you help web page URL. But in this case you don't plan to change the web page, and it doesn't make sense to require an internet connection just to view help. Fortunately, iOS allows you to create an HTML resource that is a web page saved on the phone as part of your app.

To create an HTML resource for the help page, choose File > New > New File. In the left column, under iOS, choose Other. Create an Empty file.

RESOURCES ARE FILES
THAT COME WITH YOUR APP,
LIKE IMAGES.

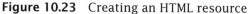

Figure 10.23   Creating an HTML resource

Call the file help.html, and save it in Parkinator's project folder.

HTML provides a simple way to create formatted text in iOS. The topic of formatting HTML could be its own book, but here are the basics. An HTML file is a plain text file. Styled text is surrounded by tags: an opening tag, surrounded by angled brackets, < >; and a closing tag that looks like the opening tag but that also has a forward slash,/.

THE WEB VIEW CAN SHOW ANYTHING THAT SAFARI CAN. SO YOU CAN USE HTML5, INCLUDING EMBEDDING VIDEO IF YOU WANT.

For example, <h1>Parkinator Help </h1> creates a top level (level 1) heading, whereas <h2>Remembering where you parked</h2> creates a second-level heading (which is usually formatted slightly smaller than the first level). Individual paragraphs are surrounded by <p> and </p> tags, and numbered lists can be created by surrounding list items <li></li> with the ordered list tags <ol> and </ol>. For more information about HTML, see www.w3schools.com/html/default.asp.

To create your HTML resource, add the following text to help.html.

Listing 10.1   help.html

```
<html>
    <style>body {font: 10pt Helvetica  }</style>
<body>
<h1>Parkinator Help</h1>
    <h2>Remembering where you parked</h2>
    <p>Parkinator lets you take a picture to remember where you parked.
    When you do, it also automatically gets the current location from
    your phone's GPS and places a pin on a map beneath the picture. To
    do this:
    <ol>
        <li>Tap the information button (the i) on the bottom right of
            the homescreen</li>
        <li>Tap the camera icon on the next screen</li>
        <li>Take a picture</li>
        <li>Tap the Done button</li>
    </ol></p>
    <h2>Tweeting that your spot is open</h2>
    <p>Tap the action button (2nd button from the left).  Tweeting your
    spot will only work if you have entered a valid Twitter username and
    password into the iOS Twitter settings.</p>
```

```
<h2>Viewing available spots</h2>
<p>Tap the seach button (2nd button from the right).  Free spaces
near your location will appear as pins on the map.</p>
</body>
</html>
```

When viewed in your app, it looks like the figure at right.

When you set up the IBAction that created the web view, you used http://manning.com as a stand-in for your help page. Now you need to display help.html instead of the external web page. To do that, you create a new URL that refers to the HTML file that is stored in your application bundle rather than a web page on the internet. Then you tell the web view to load the new URL:

Figure 10.24 help.html formatted by the Help web view

```
- (void)viewDidLoad
{
    [super viewDidLoad];
```

GET PATH TO
HELP.HTML →
```
    NSString *helpPath =
        [[NSBundle mainBundle]
            pathForResource:@"help" ofType:@"html"];
    NSURL *url =
        [NSURL fileURLWithPath:helpPath];
```
← CREATE URL
FOR HELP.HTML

```
    [self.helpView
        loadRequest:[NSURLRequest
            requestWithURL:url]];
}
```
← LOAD HELP.HTML
INTO WEB VIEW

Integrating with Twitter

THIS IS WHERE YOU
NEED A TWITTER
ACCOUNT.

Twitter is a popular social network. It's particularly good at quickly sharing small bits of information publicly in the form of 140-character messages nicknamed *tweets*. Twitter also facilitates searching existing tweets. iOS 6.0 makes it easy for developers to use social networks, including

Twitter and Facebook, in their apps. You'll use Twitter in Parkinator to tweet the location of free spaces and to locate available spaces tweeted by others.

Looking at iOS support for Twitter

iOS provides system-wide support for Twitter, Facebook, and the Chinese social network Sina Weibo. For these networks, users can go to iOS Settings and provide their usernames and passwords or even create accounts. In order to test Parkinator, you'll need to log in to Twitter.

Figure10.25
iOS settings

In Settings, click Twitter, and enter your Twitter username and password. If you don't have a Twitter account, you can click Create New Account at the bottom of the screen.

Figure 10.26   Twitter account settings

Once a Twitter username and password are provided, any app can send tweets without asking the user to log in. This is a convenience for the user and greatly simplifies the developer's task by allowing you to send a tweet using the SLComposeViewController class without worrying about account management.

`SLComposeViewController` displays a Tweet sheet, which has a text field for composing text and Send and Cancel buttons. It's the standard view for sending tweets.

To use Twitter in Parkinator, you need to add the Social framework to your project target. Adding the Social framework is similar to how you added the MapKit framework in the last chapter. Click Parkinator in Project Navigator, and then select the Parkinator target. Click the Summary tab, and scroll down to the Linked Frameworks and Libraries section. Click the + button, and scroll down to find Social.framework (or start typing `Social` into the text field to filter the list).

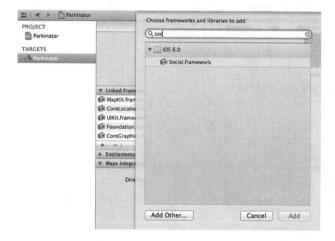

Figure 10.27 Adding the Social framework to Parkinator

After you add the Social framework to the project, you must also import the Social library. In PAMainViewController.h, add `#import <Social/Social.h>` to the `import` statements.

Composing and sending a tweet

The `TWTweetComposeViewController` class provides all the functionality you need to send a tweet. You'll use this class to send a tweet when the user presses the action button you added to the main view.

First add an `IBAction` to PAMainViewController.h that will be called when the user presses the action button:

```
- (IBAction)tweetLocation:(id)sender;
```

The `tweetLocation` method uses `SLComposeViewController`'s class method `isAvailableForServiceType` to confirm that the device can send tweets. Then you construct a string that has the #Parkinator tag and the phone's latitude and longitude. Each tweet should look something like `#Parkinator 37.787505 -122.403359`. You'll create a `SLComposeView-Controller` and then initialize its text to your string. You'll present the tweet view; and when you're done, you'll dismiss the controller.

In PAMainViewController.m, add the following:

```
- (IBAction)tweetLocation:(id)sender {
    if([SLComposeViewController
        isAvailableForServiceType:SLServiceTypeTwitter]) {
        NSString *tweetText =
        [NSString stringWithFormat:@"#Parkinator %F %F",
         self.lastLocation.latitude,
         self.lastLocation.longitude];
        SLComposeViewController *tweetComposeViewController =
        [SLComposeViewController
         composeViewControllerForServiceType:SLServiceTypeTwitter];
        [tweetComposeViewController setInitialText:tweetText];
        [self presentViewController:tweetComposeViewController
                           animated:YES completion:nil];
        tweetComposeViewController.completionHandler =
        ^(SLComposeViewControllerResult result)  {
            [self dismissViewControllerAnimated:YES completion:nil];
        };
    }
}
```

Annotations: CHECK FOR TWITTER ACCOUNT → `isAvailableForServiceType:SLServiceTypeTwitter`; CREATE STRING → `[NSString stringWithFormat:@"#Parkinator %F %F",`; CREATE VIEW → `SLComposeViewController *tweetComposeViewController =`; SET INITIAL TEXT → `[tweetComposeViewController setInitialText:tweetText];`; PRESENT VIEW → `[self presentViewController:tweetComposeViewController`; DISMISS VIEW → `tweetComposeViewController.completionHandler =`

Finally, connect the Tweet button in the toolbar to the `tweetLocation` action. The process is the same as it was for the Help button. Use the assistant to Ctrl-drag from the Send button to the action (or, if you want some variety, use the Connection Inspector to drag the selector to the File's Owner and choose `tweetLocation` from the action list).

By the way, you may have noticed that none of the Social framework classes say anything about Twitter. That's because they work the same way for all three networks. Just change `SLServiceTypeTwitter` to `SLServiceTypeFacebook`, and you can post status updates to Facebook. Use `SLServiceTypeSinaWeibo` to post to that service. Three networks for the price of one. Social.framework FTW!

Searching Twitter

Once you give users a way to tweet parking spots for other users, you also need to provide a way to search for spaces. Twitter allows you to search existing tweets via a URL. The following URL

```
http://search.twitter.com/search.json?q=
  Parkinator&amp;result_type=recent&amp;rpp=10
```

asks for the 10 most recent tweets with the #Parkinator tag. If you type this URL into a web browser, you'll see something like this.

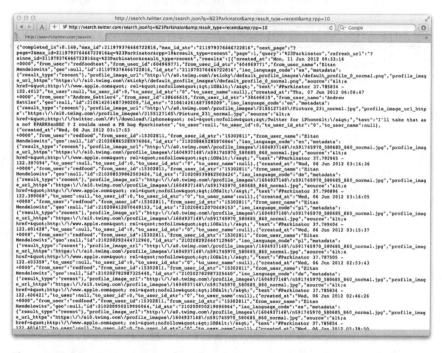

Figure 10.28 Twitter search in browser

Don't panic! These tweets are returned in a data format called JSON, and you'll see in a moment that iOS has methods to interpret them.

The following code constructs the twitter request and then handles the resulting JSON data, parses the returned tweets, and displays their location on the map. Add this to PAMainViewController.h:

```
@property(nonatomic, strong) NSMutableArray *freeSpaces;
- (IBAction)searchTwitter:(id)sender;
- (void) updatePins;
- (void) parseTweet:(NSString*) tweet;
```

To PAMainViewController.m, add the following definition.

Listing 10.2   PAMainViewController.m: additions for Twitter search

```
- (IBAction)searchTwitter:(id)sender {
    SLRequest *twRequest =                                          ← CONSTRUCT SEARCH REQUEST
    [SLRequest requestForServiceType:SLServiceTypeTwitter
        requestMethod:SLRequestMethodGET
            URL:[NSURL URLWithString:
                @"http://search.twitter.com/search.json?"
                "q=%23Parkinator&result_type=recent&rpp=10"]
                    parameters:nil];

    [twRequest performRequestWithHandler:                           ← SEND REQUEST TO TWITTER
     ^(NSData *responseData, NSHTTPURLResponse *response,
       NSError *error) {

        if ([response statusCode] == 200) {                        ← CODE 200 MEANS OK
            [self.mapView removeAnnotations:self.freeSpaces];
            [self.freeSpaces removeAllObjects];                    ← CLEAR OLD RESULTS
            NSError *jsonError = nil;
            NSDictionary *results =                                ← CONVERT JSON TO OBJECTIVE-C
            [NSJSONSerialization
              JSONObjectWithData:responseData
              options:0
              error:&jsonError];
            NSArray *tweets = [results valueForKey:@"results"];
            for(id tweet in tweets) {
                NSString *tweetText = [tweet valueForKey:@"text"];
                [self parseTweet:tweetText];                       ← PARSE EACH TWEET
            }
            [self performSelectorOnMainThread:@selector(updatePins)
                              withObject:nil
                            waitUntilDone:NO];
```

```
        }
    }];

}
```

WE'RE LUCKY THAT JSON IS SO POPULAR THAT IOS CAN HELP YOU PARSE IT.

The `NSJSONSerialization` class turns the JSON data into an `NSDictionary`. The dictionary contains a lot of information about the query that you don't care about—for example, how long the search took to execute on Twitter's servers. The tweets themselves are stored with the key results and are returned as a `NSArray` by the call `[results valueForKey:@"results"]`.

The data for each individual tweet in the `NSArray` is stored in an `NSDictionary`. The dictionaries have fields for the author, date, and so on. You're interested in the content of the tweet, which is stored in the text field and is returned as an `NSString` by `[tweet valueForKey:@"text"]`.

Once you finally get the text of an individual tweet, you call `parseTweet` to parse the tweet and add a map pin.

Parsing individual tweets

As we mentioned earlier, each individual tweet generated by Parkinator should look like `#Parkinator 37.785834 -122.406417`. In other words, it should consist of the #Parkinator tag followed by a space, a floating-point number, a space, and then another floating-point number. The following code splits the tweet wherever there is a space and puts the pieces into an `NSArray`.

Listing 10.3   PAMainViewController.m: additions for Twitter search

```
- (void)parseTweet:(NSString*) tweet {
    NSArray *parsedText =                                        SPLIT ON
        [tweet componentsSeparatedByString:@" "];               SPACES
    if([parsedText count] == 3) {                        ❶  CHECK FOR
        if([@"#Parkinator" isEqual:                              3 PARTS
            [parsedText objectAtIndex:0]]) {
PARSE           double latitude =
LATITUDE AND        [[parsedText objectAtIndex:1] doubleValue];
LONGITUDE  ❷
```

```
                        double longitude =
                          [[parsedText objectAtIndex:2] doubleValue];
                        if((latitude != 0) && (longitude != 0)) {
IF VALID,         ❸        CLLocationCoordinate2D freeSpacelocation;
CREATE SPOT                freeSpacelocation.latitude = latitude;
                           freeSpacelocation.longitude = longitude;
                           PAParkingSpot *freeSpace =
                             [[PAParkingSpot alloc]
                               initWithSpotCoordinate:freeSpacelocation];
                           [self.freeSpaces addObject:freeSpace];
ADD SPOT          ❹      }
TO ARRAY               }
                     }
                   }
```

If there are three pieces in the tweet (as there should be) ❶, then the code checks to see if the first is #Parkinator and the next two are valid doubles. If there are two doubles, the code uses them as the latitude and longitude ❷ to create a new PAParkingSpot ❸, which it adds to the array freeSpaces ❹.

Displaying locations in the Map View

When you perform a Twitter search request, the results are returned in a different execution thread. Each thread is like a separate program running along side the main program. The results are returned by Twitter in their own thread. You need to add the pins to the map in the app's main thread because this is also the Map View's thread. This is why you put the spots into the freeSpaces array and it's also why you have

```
[self performSelectorOnMainThread:@selector(updatePins)
                       withObject:nil
                    waitUntilDone:NO];
```

at the end of the handler. This causes updatePins to be called in the main
program thread. updatePins then adds the annotations to the Map View,
just like you did when you wanted to display your current location.
Finally, you update the mapView:viewForAnnotation method to add free
spot pins to the Map View. The new code is almost identical to the earlier code for marking a parking spot.

Listing 10.4   Dropping pins for free spaces

```
-(MKAnnotationView*)mapView:(MKMapView *)mView
        viewForAnnotation:(id<MKAnnotation>)annotation
{
    MKPinAnnotationView *pin = nil;                          OLD CODE
    if (annotation == self.spot) {                          UNCHANGED
        pin = (MKPinAnnotationView*)[self.mapView
            dequeueReusableAnnotationViewWithIdentifier:@"spot"];

        if (pin == nil) {
            pin = [[MKPinAnnotationView alloc]
                    initWithAnnotation:self.spot
                    reuseIdentifier:@"spot"];
            pin.pinColor = MKPinAnnotationColorGreen;
        }
    } else if ([self.freeSpaces containsObject:annotation]) {
        pin = (MKPinAnnotationView*)               REUSE
          [self.mapView                            OLD PINS
            dequeueReusableAnnotationViewWithIdentifier:@"freeSpot"];
        if(pin == nil) {
            pin=[[MKPinAnnotationView alloc]                CREATE IF
                initWithAnnotation:annotation              NEEDED
                reuseIdentifier:@"freeSpot"];
            pin.pinColor = MKPinAnnotationColorRed;
        }                                          DIFFERENT
                                                   COLOR                ANIMATE
        [pin setAnimatesDrop:YES];                          THE PIN DROPS

    }
    return pin;
}
```

What's next

You have learned some great stuff. You can write apps that use the camera, GPS, maps, and even the internet! You're now able to load web pages and display formatted text using `UIWebViews`. You also know how to send tweets using iOS's built-in Twitter support and search Twitter using special URLs. You're ready for the next level. In chapter 11, you'll learn how to evaluate and optimize the performance of your app, after which you'll finally be ready to submit apps to the App store.

Part 3

Going from Xcode to the App Store

This part of the book will help you move the apps you've created on your Mac onto your device for testing and then into the App Store for sale. You'll learn how to

- ○ Join Apple's developer program
- ○ Get certificates from Apple so you can create device and App Store builds
- ○ Test your application on your device
- ○ Debug your application
- ○ Install apps, distribute them, and offer them in the App Store

In chapter 11, you'll learn what to do when something in your app goes wrong. By the end of the chapter you'll be able to locate bugs and optimize your app's code.

Chapter 12 explains how to run your app on an iPhone. You'll also learn how to distribute your app to users and, finally, submit your app for sale in the Apple App Store.

11

Debugging and optimizing your application

This chapter covers

- *Debugging applications without tools*
- *Using breakpoints and stepping through your code*
- *Watching variables*
- *Optimizing the performance of an app*

You've written some great-looking apps that work well, but what happens when things don't go so smoothly? Sometimes a newly written app may behave unexpectedly or even crash. These problems are caused by programming errors often called *bugs*, and even the most experienced programmers make them.

I GET THESE ALL THE TIME.

Because bugs aren't automatically detected by Xcode, they can be more difficult to find and fix, but don't worry. Fortunately, there are tools and techniques you can use to fix bugs: a process called *debugging*. And, like a mechanic tuning up a car, there are even things you can do to make a bug-free app faster and more efficient—this is called *optimization*. In this chapter, you'll learn how to debug and optimize your code to make sure your app runs as smoothly as possible.

Debugging without tools

Xcode has a wonderful debugger, which we'll cover later in the chapter. But first: patience, grasshopper. A number of coding tricks allow you to test for bugs without using the debugger. Once upon a time, this was the only way to debug a program, and these techniques are still useful today—particularly when a bug is intermittent and hard to reproduce.

Intentionally introducing a bug

In order to learn about debugging, you need a bug. Let's take a walk down memory lane and introduce a bug to the trusty old flashcard app. Open FCCard.m, and find the line in initWithQuestion that chooses a random slot for the correct answer. Change the 3 to a 4. When you're done, the line should look like this:

```
int randomAnswerSlot = arc4random()%4;
```

INTENTIONAL BUG

The original code correctly picked a 0, 1, or 2 to randomly assign the question's answer to one of three buttons. With this bug, the number 3 may also be chosen. If the random-number generator picks a 3, the program will try to place the answer in a button that doesn't exist. This will cause the program to crash. Occasionally, because it's random, the program won't choose a 3 for any question and will run correctly; but most of the time the program will crash.

IF WE RANDOMLY GET A 3. WE'LL CRASH.

You're now going to learn about debugging by pretending you don't know about the new bug. Take a nice long look at a neuralyzer and forget the bug ever existed.

USER FRIENDLY by Illiad

Logging messages

Finding bugs is sometimes like detective work. You need to look for clues. When you run the FlashCards app, it loads correctly. It only crashes when you press the Show States or Show Capitals button. And, if you get lucky, the app doesn't crash and runs fine. From these facts, you can deduce that the bug is located somewhere in showCards. (Remember, you forgot what the problem is.) Fortunately, you can use NSLog to find where the crash happens.

IN MY DAY, WE CALLED THIS "PRINTF DEBUGGING."

NSLog prints strings to a special window in Xcode called the *console*. Add the statement NSLog(@"Shall you play a game?"); to the program, and you'll see the *log message* "Shall you play a game?" appear in the console when the app reaches the NSLog call in the program. You can use this log to see if and when a particular section of code is ever run.

To locate a crash, you can call NSLog at the beginning and end of a section of code. If you see only one of the two expected messages in the console, you know that the bug is somewhere between the two calls to NSLog. Because you have a pretty good idea that this bug is located after one of the Show buttons

is pressed, start by putting NSLog statements at the beginning and end of
allocStateCards in FCAnswerKey.m:

```
-(NSMutableArray*) allocStateCards
{                                                        LOG METHOD'S
    NSLog(@"start allocStateCards");           ←⎯        START
    NSMutableArray *cards = [[NSMutableArray alloc] initWithObjects:
     [[FCCard alloc]
       initWithQuestion:@"Alabama"
       answer: @"Montgomery"
       wrongAnswer1:@"Birmingham"
       wrongAnswer2:@"Mobile"],
     [[FCCard alloc]
       initWithQuestion:@"New York"
       answer: @"Albany"
       wrongAnswer1:@"New York City"
       wrongAnswer2:@"Buffalo"],
     [[FCCard alloc]
       initWithQuestion:@"New Jersey"
       answer: @"Trenton"
       wrongAnswer1:@"Camden"
       wrongAnswer2:@"Newark"],
     nil ];                                              LOG METHOD'S
    NSLog(@"end allocStateCards");             ←⎯        END
    return cards;
}
```

Although you can use any string you want in the log statements, you
use @"start allocStateCards" and @"end allocStateCards" to make the
messages easy to recognize in the console. It's important that the last
call to NSLog is *before* the return statement. If the NSLog was placed after
return, it would never be called. You can also place NSLog statements at
the beginning and end of allocCapitalCards if you want.

Figure 11.1   The debug area
expander

Run your app. When it crashes, Xcode
should make the debug area with the
NSLog messages visible automatically. If
it's not visible, you can expand it manually by clicking the expand icon at
lower-left in the Xcode window.

Here is what the console window looks like after the crash.

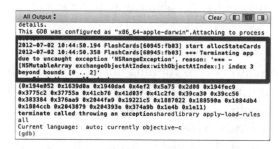

Figure 11.2 The Xcode debug console with NSLog and error messages

Notice that there is a line that reads start allocStateCards but not one that says end allocStateCards. This confirms your suspicion that the bug is located somewhere in alloc-StateCards (or one of the methods it invokes). Also notice the error message printed out after the log message. It tells you that the error is caused by a call to exchangeObjectAt-Index:withObjectAtIndex: with a value that is out of bounds. This gives you another clue that you'll explore in the next section.

Using assertions

The log statements confirmed that the bug is somewhere in allocState-Cards. You also got a bonus clue from the console that said you're trying to call an NSMutableArray's exchangeObjectAtIndex:withObjectAtIndex: with a value that is out of bounds. The only place you use this method

is in `initWithQuestion` in FCCard.m when you try to modify answers. To confirm that this is the cause of the problems, you'll use another debugging technique called an *assertion*.

Assertions allow you to test a value or condition in your code. If the condition is true, your program keeps running normally. But if the condition is false, a statement is printed to the debug console and an exception is thrown, which usually causes the program to stop executing. For example, if you write `NSAssert(foo = 10, @"foo doesn't equal 10")`, your program will run fine if the variable `foo` is `10` but will stop and print "`foo doesn't equal 10`" to the console if `foo` has any other value. An assertion is like a centurion guarding a gate who asks a question and only lets those with the correct answer pass. Because the assertion allows you to send messages to the console only when there is a problem, it's useful with bugs that occur infrequently.

You suspect the problem is in `initWithQuestion`, and you know there should be only three buttons in `answers`, so create an assertion in `init-WithQuestion` that won't let `exchangeObjectAtIndex` be called with a value greater than 2.

Listing 11.1   FCCard.m: adding `NSAssert` to `initWithQuestion`

```
int randomAnswerSlot = arc4random() % 4;
NSAssert(randomAnswerSlot < 3,                                 ASSERT
                   @"slot is greater than 3!");                ADDED
[self.answers exchangeObjectAtIndex:0
withObjectAtIndex:randomAnswerSlot];
self.correctAnswer = randomAnswerSlot;
```

Now, when you run the app, you see in the console an assertion failure that says '`randomAnswerSlot is greater than 3!`'. You can use `NSAsserts` to guarantee that different parts of your program are working the way you think they should be. If an assertion fails, your program stops running and you've found the problem.

Now that you've identified the bug, let's fix it by changing the 4 back into a 3. You should be able to run the app without it crashing and without the `NSAssert` printing a message in the console. Congratulations on finding and fixing your bug!

Popping up dialogs

Sometimes you can't use the simulator or Xcode to debug a program. This is particularly true for apps that use any of the devices' sensors. Suppose you have an app that uses GPS data and only crashes when you're moving. Although you could try to walk around town balancing your iPhone and a laptop in your hands like a deranged juggler, it's much easier to use the techniques introduced in this section.

IT WOULD BE A PAIN TO HAVE TO MODIFY THE UI TO FIND BUGS.

We'll talk about deploying an app to a real device in the next chapter, so try to be patient for now. (We know it's hard to wait!) One way to make an app give you feedback is to set the text field of a label. You already know how to do this; you did it in chapter 3. The downside of this approach is that you have to modify a view to display a message. Depending on your app, this may required modifying multiple views and XIBs.

Another option is to pop up a dialog box with the message, value, or condition you want to monitor. The advantage of this approach is that it doesn't require modifying any of your existing views. To demonstrate this technique, you'll add a pop-up alert to allocCardsFromInfo so you can confirm that it's successfully completing without having to look at the log messages in the console. To create a pop-up, add the following code to the end of allocCardsFromInfo in FCAnswerKey.m. As you did with NSLog, make sure you add these statements before the return statement.

Listing 11.2   FCAnswerKey.m: adding Alert

```
UIAlertView* alert =
    [[UIAlertView alloc]
        initWithTitle:@"Debug Alert"
            message:[NSString
                stringWithFormat:@"allocStateCards completed"]
            delegate:nil
            cancelButtonTitle:@"Dismiss"
            otherButtonTitles:nil];
[alert show];
```

Figure 11.3 An alert box giving debugging information.

Now when you run the app you'll see a dialog box after the cards are created.

You can use alerts like `log` statements or combine them with `if` statements to behave like assertions. With alerts, you don't even need Xcode to debug a program, which will be especially handy when you start running your app on a real iPhone.

Although it's sometimes necessary to debug a program without any tools, Xcode's debugger is usually more convenient. And now that you know how to debug an app without any tools, you'll appreciate the power and flexibility provided by the debugger all the more.

Debugging with Xcode

In the last section, you used logging statements, assertions, and alert boxes to debug your program. Although these techniques are effective, they have the disadvantage of requiring you to modify your code. The Xcode debugger allows you to debug without modifying a line of code. Using the debugger, you can watch variables as they're changed and step through the program line by line as it's executing. The debugger makes you a superhero with the ability to stop time using breakpoints. The variable watcher gives you X-ray vision with the ability to peer into your program's inner workings.

Setting breakpoints

Breakpoints allow you to pause a program so you can examine variables. If a program isn't working as expected, it's useful to make sure the variables have the values you expect. Breakpoints are like giant stop signs that tell Xcode to stop executing and wait. To set a breakpoint, click the gutter to the left of the code, and Xcode will mark the line with a dark-blue

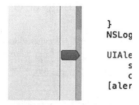

Figure 11.4 An enabled breakpoint

arrow. This arrow informs you that Xcode will pause before this line is executed. Clicking an existing arrow toggles individual breakpoints on and off. Disabled breakpoints are translucent.

Try placing a breakpoint next to the line that creates the alert you added in the last section, and then run your app. When Xcode stops at the breakpoint, it accentuates the point of execution by highlighting the relevant line.

```
                          answer:cardInfo[i][1]
                          wrongAnswer1:cardInfo[i][2]
                          wrongAnswer2:cardInfo[i][3]] ];
    }
    NSLog(@"end allocCardsFromInfo");

    UIAlertView* alert = [[UIAlertView alloc]
                          initWithTitle:@"Debug Alert"
                          message:[NSString stringWithFormat:@"allocCardsFromInfo completed successfully"]
                          delegate:nil
                          cancelButtonTitle:@"Dismiss" otherButtonTitles:nil];        Thread 1: Stopped at breakpoint 1
    [alert show];

    return cards;

    -(NSMutableArray*) allocStateCards
    {
```

Figure 11.5 Highlighted line showing execution stopped at a breakpoint

When you're writing a complicated program, it's sometime hard to tell if a particular line of code is being executed. Breakpoints are one way to check on a section of code. You can place as many breakpoints as you want. If the debugger doesn't stop on your breakpoint, it means that line isn't being run.

Stepping through code

Just like pressing a Play button to play a paused song, your can press the debugger's Continue button to resume running an app paused by a breakpoint. When you press Continue, the program continues running until another breakpoint. The Continue button is the first of four debugger controls found above the variable view.

Figure 11.6 The four debugger control buttons: Continue, Step Over, Step Into, and Step Out

In addition to allowing your program to continue running after a breakpoint, you can use the debugger to execute code one line at a time. Stepping through the code lets you observe the effects of each line as it executes. Step Over and Step Into are located next to the Continue button. If the current line doesn't send an object a message, both buttons tell the debugger to execute the current line and advance to the next. But if the current line sends a message, Step Over tells the debugger to send the message and advance to the next line of code after the message is handled.

IF I WANT TO SEE WHAT THE MESSAGE WILL ACTUALLY DO, I NEED TO STEP INTO IT.

Similarly, if the current line of code sends a message, Step Into tells the debugger to move inside the invoked method so you can see its inner workings. Once inside the method, you can step through its execution or step out of the method and return to the line after the initial message was sent.

Watching variables

When Xcode stops on a breakpoint, it makes the debug area visible. On the right, you see the console in which you viewed the NSLog statements, and to its left you see the Variables View. The Variables View allows you to observe variables to confirm that they have their expected value.

As its name implies, the Variables View lets you see the value of variables. You can click the small arrow to the left of an object to look at

Figure 11.7 Variables View

variables contained within the object. Amazingly, you can even double-click a value and type to assign a new value to a variable. Let's say you're debugging the FlashCards app, and you notice that 3 was chosen as the random number. You can manually change that 3 to a valid number and see how the program runs with that change.

At the top of the Variables View is a pull-down menu that offers these choices: Auto, Local Variables, All Variables, Registers, Globals, and Statistics. Auto displays the variables that are relevant to the current line in the debugger and will usually be the most useful.

WATCHING VARIABLES AS YOU STEP IS EASIER THAN HAVING TO LOG EVERYTHING.

Breaking when something happens

Sometimes you need to set a breakpoint in a frequently called method or a loop, but you don't want your program to stop every time execution reaches the breakpoint. Xcode allows you to set a breakpoint that pauses the program only under certain conditions.

To create a conditional breakpoint, set a breakpoint as you normally would by clicking the gutter. Then right-click (or Ctrl-click) the blue arrow and enter an expression in the Condition text field. If the expression is true when the program reaches the breakpoint, the program will pause, and you can then step through the code or use the Variables View. If the condition evaluates to false, the program will keep running. You can also tell the debugger how many times the breakpoint should be ignored.

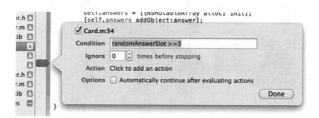

Figure 11.8 Setting a conditional breakpoint

It isn't enough just to write a program that doesn't crash. An app should be responsive and efficient. Xcode provides a number of tools called *instruments* that help to make apps run as smoothly as possible.

Speeding up your app

Now that your app doesn't crash, you can use Xcode to give it a tune-up. Profiling your code helps you write applications that run faster and use less memory. A good tune-up is the difference between an app that works and one that runs Fast and Furious.

Profiling your code

Xcode provides a number of instruments to profile your code. Profiling allows you to measure things like how long individual methods take to execute and how much memory the program is using. You can use profiling to find and fix inefficiencies in the code. To profile your code, choose Profile from the Product menu in Xcode's menu bar. Doing so opens a window in which you can choose an individual profiling tool.

Figure 11.9
The Profile window

Clicking an instrument displays its description in the lower pane. The Profile button in the lower-right corner runs the selected profiler.

Finding bottlenecks

If your application is running slowly, the *Time Profiler* can help you figure out why. The Time Profiler samples your code every millisecond while the app is running and records what is executing. After you're done profiling the program, the Time Profiler presents its data so you can figure out which methods are taking the most time and know where to focus you optimization efforts.

The code you've written so far works pretty well, so, as you did with the bug, you'll intentionally introduce some inefficient code. Open FCViewController.m, and add the following to the beginning of show-Cards:

```
NSMutableArray *uselessArray = [[NSMutableArray alloc] init];
for(int i = 0; i < 10000; i++) {
    [uselessArray addObject:[NSNumber numberWithInt:i]];
}

for(int i = 0; i < 10000; i++) {
    [uselessArray removeObject:[NSNumber numberWithInt:i]];
}
```

THIS IS CALLED A SPEED-UP LOOP. WHEN YOUR BOSS ASKS YOU TO MAKE THE PROGRAM FASTER, REDUCE THE LOOP COUNT.

Now try running the app in the simulator. You'll notice a delay after you press Show States and Show Capitals: your program is needlessly adding and removing numbers from a mutable array.

Let's pretend you didn't know the cause of the delay and wanted to find the culprit. Open the Profile window, select the Time Profiler, and click the Profile button. Doing so opens a new Instruments window and launches the app in the simulator. Run through the game a couple of times. As you run the app, you'll notice some activity in the other window. Quit the simulator or press the Stop button (the second button from the left on the toolbar) to stop profiling, and look at the Time Profiler.

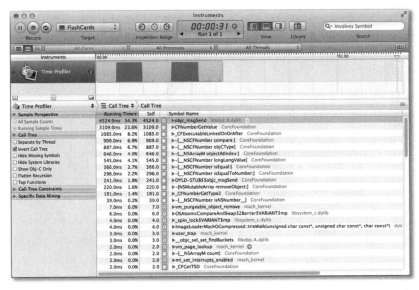

Figure 11.10 The Time Profiler

Toward the top of the window is a rectangle containing a graph. This graph shows you CPU utilization. Below that, you should see a Call Tree listing all the functions and methods used in your program, along with their running time in milliseconds and as a percentage of total running time. Make sure Invert Call Tree is selected in the Cell Tree settings at left in the windows.

I'D LOVE TO INVERT THIS CALL AND ASK THEM FOR SUPPORT.

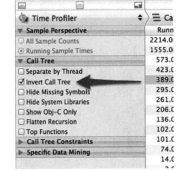

Figure 11.11 Select the Invert Call Tree check box.

Whoa! There's a lot of information in that call stack. Finding a performance bottleneck is like looking for a needle in a haystack. Fortunately, you can do a number of things to reduce the size of the haystack and quickly zero in on the problem.

The first thing you can do is tell Xcode to only display timing information for the slice of time when you're experiencing a slowdown. If you look at the CPU utilization graph, you'll notice a spike in usage that corresponds to each time you started playing the game.

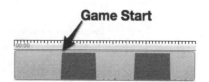

Figure 11.12 Spike in CPU usage at the start of the game

You can limit your search to this spike by clicking and dragging the mouse across the spike while holding down the Option key. As the CPU usage graph is selected, the Call Tree below is filtered to show only methods and functions from the highlighted time slice.

Next you can make the Call Tree easier to read by having Xcode display only the information that is most likely to be relevant. In the Call Tree settings menu at left, in addition to Invert Call Tree, select Hide System Libraries and Show Obj-C Only. This will limit what is displayed to only methods you've written.

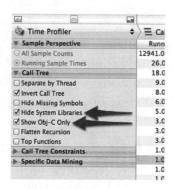

THIS WORKS AS LONG AS THE PROBLEM IS IN YOUR CODE. WHICH IT USUALLY IS.

Figure 11.13
Choose Hide System Libraries and Show Obj-C Only.

The result should look much more manageable. Now you should see a handful of methods, most of which you've implemented. Because they're sorted by running time, the most likely performance problem will be at the top of the list. In this case, it's [FCViewController show-Cards:]. Double-click [FCViewController showCards:] to see a detail view of the method. Highlighted in red is the costliest line of code: in this case, [uselessArray removeObject:[NSNumber numberWithInt:i]];.

```
44
45   NSMutableArray *uselessArray = [[NSMutableArray alloc] init];
46   for(int i = 0; i < 10000; i++) {
47       [uselessArray addObject:[NSNumber numberWithInt:i];      ⓘ 0.1%
48   }
49   for(int i = 0; i < 10000; i++) {
50       [uselessArray removeObject:[NSNumber numberWithInt:i]];   ⓘ 99.9%
51   }
52
```

Figure 11.14
Time Profiler
detail view

Here you can clearly see that the one line removing objects from use-lessArray is taking 99.9% of the running time. For comparison, let's replace the costly second for loop with the single line [use-lessArray removeAllObjects];. Calling removeAllObjects removes everything in uselessArray just as your loop did, only more efficiently. Now try running the code; even without the profiler, you can tell that the program is more responsive. Using the Time Profiler, you can see that show-Cards: is no longer the costliest method and is running significantly faster. Leave the for loops in your code, because you'll examine their memory usage in the next section.

IT'S STILL USELESS, BUT AT LEAST IT'S FAST.

Optimizing memory usage

Computers use *memory* to store running programs and their data. iPhones and iPads have much less memory than traditional computers, so iOS app developers should be especially careful to use memory efficiently. To profile memory usage, Xcode provides the Allocations instrument.

Allocations

Figure 11.15
Allocations

ARC CAN'T RELEASE MEMORY IF YOU DON'T STOP REFERRING TO IT.

There are potentially two types of memory problems: short-term memory allocations and long-term *memory leaks*. A memory leak is caused by allocated memory not becoming deallocated after it's needed. Due to the introduction of Automated Reference Counting (ARC) memory to iOS, leaks are less common, but they can still happen. A memory leak will cause your program to use more and more memory over time, which will eventually cause iOS to terminate the app.

To check your app's memory usage, open the Profile window and double-click the Allocations icon. You'll see a window similar to the one opened by the Time Profiler. Before you click Show States or Show Capitals, click the Mark Heap button to the

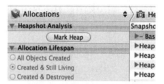

Figure 11.16 Allocations

left of the Instruments window. The *heap* is the pool of memory used by your app.

Play the game at least five times, and click Mark Heap before you press Start Again. Mark Heap tells the iOS record-profiling data so you can refer to it later. Playing the game five times will let you see how your app performs over time. Each time you click Mark Heap, you'll see a new heapshot appear in the Snapshot column.

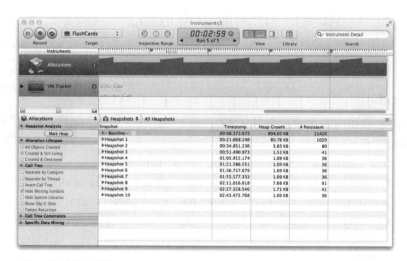

Figure 11.17 The Allocations window

The most important column to look at for the heapshots is Heap Growth. Heap growth measures how much additional memory each heapshot is using. In a perfect world, the number would be 0, meaning your program doesn't need extra memory to run. Notice that after the first few runs of the game, the heap growth value is usually close to 1. This is good, because it means the program's memory footprint is barely growing. Even better, if you expand one of the heapshots by clicking the small triangle, you'll see that the two biggest contributors to the heap growth are related to CardResult. Some memory growth here makes sense because the app is supposed to store the results of games. If the heap growth was consistently a big number, it would mean your program was constantly eating memory and that you'd need to find the cause if you wanted your program to run smoothly.

At the top of the window is a graph representing the app's total memory usage. Notice the sawtooth pattern that results from the for loops adding numbers to and removing them from an array.

Figure 11.18   Memory usage graph

Keeping an eye on total memory utilization can help you diagnose and avoid short-term memory spikes.

What's next

You've skillfully squashed a bug that caused your app to crash, by using log statements, assertions, and alert boxes. You now know how to use the debugger to step through a program's operations, and you found performance bottlenecks and monitored memory usage. Your app is finally ready to leave the simulator and run on a real iPhone.

12

Building for the device and the App Store

This chapter covers

- Installing your app on an iPhone
- Distributing an app to others for testing
- Submitting your app to the App Store

Running your app on a device

This is exciting! You've written a polished program that runs efficiently and is free of bugs. But although the simulator is great, it's no substitute for using your program on an actual phone. For example, there are some things like the GPS that you can't test well in the simulator. This chapter will explain how to install your app on your phone and distribute it to others for testing. It will also lead you to the Holy Grail: submitting your app to the Apple App Store.

Getting developer certificates

USER FRIENDLY by Illiad

HEY SID, MY IOS PROGRAMMING BOOK HAS CARTOON CHARACTERS. AND ONE OF THEM LOOKS LIKE YOU.

THAT'S NOT WEIRD. I HAVE ONE OF THOSE CLASSIC LOOKS.

RATTLE RATTLE RAPTAP

COPYRIGHT © 2001 ILLIAD HTTP://WWW.USERFRIENDLY.ORG/

RIIIIIGHT ...

ON ANOTHER TOPIC, I'M ABOUT TO UPLOAD MY APP TO THE APP STORE, AND I NEED HELP CONNECTING OUR BANK ACCOUNT.

DON'T CHANGE THE SUBJECT. I'M THE GUY WITH THE HAMMERS, NOT THE CHECKBOOK

The first step in installing your app on an actual device is getting a developer certificate. *Developer certificates* are encrypted files that act like IDs. They allow Apple, Xcode, and iOS devices to know that you are who you say you are and that your program was written by you. To test your app on the simulator, you only need a free Apple developer account; but in order to install your app on an iPhone, you'll need to join the *iOS Developer Program* to get a developer certificate. Membership in the program is $99 and can be purchased through Apple's website: https://developer.apple.com/programs/ios/. You may have to wait up to two days for an activation email from Apple.

$99 IS NOT A PROBLEM BECAUSE MY APP IS GOING TO MAKE MILLIONS!

After activating your developer account, you need to take a series of steps to install your developer certificate. These steps are all designed to verify your identity with Apple. It sounds like an Abbott and Costello routine, but you'll download and install an intermediate certificate to generate a certificate request so you can download and install your developer certificate which is needed to install a provisioning profile certificate.

The first step in this crazy sequence is to log on to the iOS Dev Center (https://developer.apple.com/devcenter/ios) and go to the iOS Provisioning Portal. In the portal, click Certificate and then download the WWDR Intermediate Certificate. Once it's downloaded, double-click the WWDR certificate file to install it in your Keychain.

Figure 12.1 Download certificates from the iOS Provisioning Portal.

The next step is to create a certificate signing request. If it isn't already open, launch Keychain Access, found in the Applications > Utilities folder on your Mac.

Keychain Access   **Figure 12.2** Keychain Access, found in the Utilities folder

In Keychain Access, go to Keychain Access > Preferences, and select the Certificates tab. Set both options to Off.

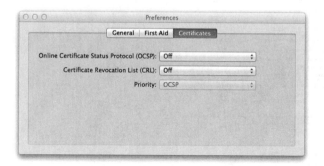

Figure 12.3
Keychain Access
Certificates Preferences

Next, select Keychain Access > Certificate Assistant > Request a Certificate from a Certificate Authority. Enter your email address and name exactly as you did when you signed up for the developer program. Leave the CA Email Address field blank, select Saved to Disk, and select Let Me Specify Key Pair Information.

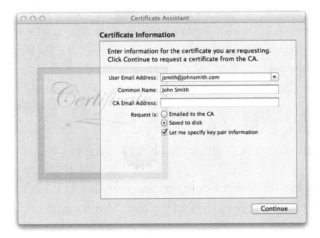

Figure 12.4
Creating a certificate request

Click the Continue button, and save the certificate to your desktop. When prompted for Key Pair Information, choose a key size of 2048 bits and the RSA encryption algorithm.

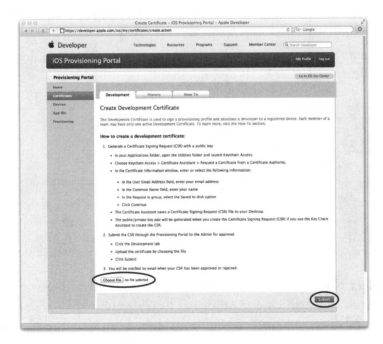

Figure 12.5
Submitting a certificate request

Finally, return to the Certificate section of the portal and click the Request Certificate button. The page that loads is a bit confusing. It looks like nothing more than instructions for what you just did. But if you look carefully at the bottom of the page, there are two easy-to-overlook buttons. Click Choose File, and select the certificate signing request you created and saved with Keychain Access. Next, click Submit, and the certificate request will appear in the portal with a status of Pending Approval.

THERE SURE ARE A LOT OF STEPS TO THIS.

You're halfway there. As an individual developer, you should receive an email notifying you that a certificate request requires your approval. But you don't have to wait for the email to arrive in your inbox—just reload the page in your web browser, and click the Approve button. Download the certificate, and double-click the certificate file to add it to your keychain. If Keychain Access gives you an error message, something like Error: 100013, try quitting the program and double-clicking the .cer file while Keychain Access is closed. It will work the second time.

You downloaded the intermediate certificate so you could upload the certificate request so you could download the developer certificate. Who's on first, What is on second, and I Don't Know is on third. The bases are loaded, and you're ready to begin provisioning.

Provisioning your device

Provisioning you device is a fancy way of saying "getting your phone ready to install your apps." When you provision, you create a profile that tells Xcode which test phones are allowed to run your apps. Like installing the developer certificate, a number of steps are involved to provision a phone. Fortunately, the iOS Provisioning Portal provides a Provisioning Assistant to help you through the task. Click Home, just above the Certificates link. Then click the Launch Assistant button at the bottom of the screen.

Figure 12.6 The Development Provisioning Assistant

Click Continue, choose Create a New App ID, and click Continue again.

Figure 12.7 Choosing an App ID

Choose a name for the provisioning profile that has meaning to you. It doesn't have to be the same as the name of your project. Click Continue, select Assign a New Apple Device, and click Continue again.

When the assistant asks for a Device Description, enter a name for your phone that you'll recognize, like My iPhone.

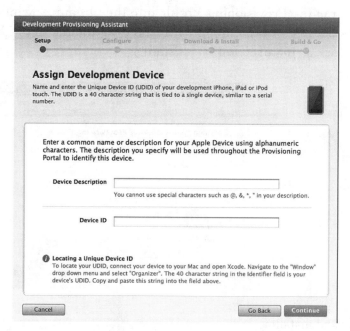

Figure 12.8
Choosing a Device Description

The assistant also asks you to enter your phone's Unique Device ID (UDID). This isn't your phone's serial number. You can look up the UDID through Xcode. To do so, connect your iPhone to your computer, and launch Xcode. Go to Window > Organizer, and click the Devices tab. Your phone should appear at left in the window, under Devices. Right-click (or Ctrl-click) the phone, and select Copy Device Identifier.

Figure 12.9 Getting your phone's UDID

Return to the Provisioning Assistant, click in the Device ID text field, and select Edit > Paste to paste in your phone's UDID. Click Continue, and then click it again in the next window. Give your profile a description, and click Generate. Click Continue, and then download the newly generated provisioning profile to your Mac. Double-click the file, and the profile will appear in the Xcode Organizer. (Warning: The assistant tells you to drag the Provisioning Profile into the Organizer window in Xcode. This doesn't work, although you can drag the file to the Xcode icon in the dock as pictured in the assistant.)

THANKS FOR POINTING THAT OUT. I WOULD HAVE BEEN DRAGGING IT THERE FOR HOURS.

Figure 12.10
Downloading and installing your provisioning profile

Installing your program

Now that you've downloaded and
installed your developer certificate and
a provisioning profile, you have everything you need to place your program
on your phone. With your iPhone connected to the computer, all you have to
do is open your project and select your
iPhone as the build target.

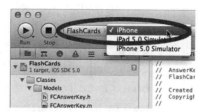

Figure 12.11 Selecting your
iPhone

Now, when you run your program, Xcode will install and launch the
app on the iPhone instead of the simulator. Be patient: depending on
the size of the program, it may take a while to load. But once it does,
your app is installed on your phone! When the phone is connected to
your computer, you can run the program on the
phone from Xcode and use the debugger just as
you did with the simulator. Even better, you can
disconnect your phone from the computer, and the
application will remain installed. The provisioning
profile is good for a year. For one year, your app
will work just like an app from the App Store.
When the year is over, the app will need to be rein-
stalled if you want to continue using it.

COME BACK A YEAR FROM NOW
FOR YOUR UPGRADE.

Distributing to testers who don't have Xcode

Question: What is better than installing your app on your iPhone?
Answer: Installing your app on your friends' iPhones! It's important to
thoroughly test your app before you submit it to the App Store. This
means other people, who aren't developers, need to use the program
too. Apple allows you to install your app on other peoples devices using
a method called *ad hoc distribution*.

In order for your app to run on testers' phones, it must be compiled
with a provisioning profile that contains their UDID. If your testers
don't have Xcode, they can also use iTunes to discover their UDID.
Here's how. Launch iTunes, and connect the iPhone. Select the

iPhone in the Devices list at left. If it isn't already selected, click the Summary tab at the top of the window. Click the iPhone's serial number, and the UDID will become visible. Now choose Edit > Copy or press Cmd-C. Doing so copies the UDID to the clipboard even though it didn't appear to be selected. Have your testers follow these steps to look up their UDIDs in iTunes and then send you the UDIDs via email.

IT'S LONG, SO MAKE SURE YOU EXPLAIN TO YOUR TESTER THAT IT CAN BE COPIED WITH CMD-C.

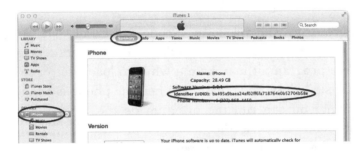

Figure 12.12
Getting the UDID from iTunes

Return to the iOS Provisioning Portal, and click Devices. For each iPhone on which you want to install your app, click Add Devices, and enter a name and the phone's UDID. You can add multiple devices by clicking the + button before you click Submit, but be sure to click Submit when you're finished.

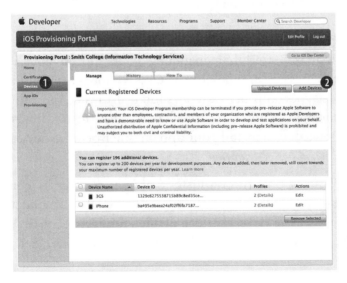

Figure 12.13
Adding devices to the Provisioning Portal

Click Provisioning, and click the New Profile button. Choose a profile name (Ad Hoc sounds good), make sure your name is selected in the Certificates section, select an App ID (it can be the same one you used before), and select the phones to which you wish to distribute your program. Hint: you can click Select All if you want to distribute the app to all the UDIDs you already entered. Click Submit, and you'll see your new Provisioning Profile with a pending status. Refresh your browser, and click Download to download your profile. Double-click the downloaded profile to install it in Xcode.

Figure 12.14   Download the Ad Hoc provisioning profile

Return to Xcode, select your project, and select the project name under Targets. Scroll down to the Entitlements section. *Entitlements* are an app's way of requesting permission to do certain things. By default, Xcode requests extra entitlements that you don't need. Removing these entitlements makes it easier to distribute your program. To remove the extra entitlements, select Enable Entitlements, but click the minus signs to remove iCloud Containers and Keychain Access Groups. Also delete the text in the iCloud Key-Value Store text field.

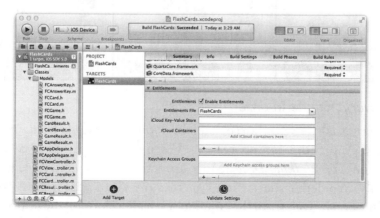

Figure 12.15
Entitlements
settings

The next step is to compile an archive that you can distribute to your testers. Select iOS Device as your target using the Scheme menu next to Xcode's Run and Stop buttons, and then choose Product > Archive. Your program will compile, and the Archive tab of the Organizer window will open. Select your program, and click the Share button. Choose iOS App Store Package (.ipa), and make sure the Ad Hoc provisioning profile is selected. Click Next, and save your IPA file.

Your app can now be distributed to any of the phones listed in the provisioning profile. Send your testers the IPA file you just saved. Have each tester launch iTunes and connect their iPhone to their computer. They should then drag the IPA file into iTunes. That's it! The tester can then sync their iPhone, and your app will be installed on it.

Submitting your app to the App Store

Congratulations! You've finally done it. You've written a great program, debugged it in the simulator, and distributed it to testers, and now you're ready to submit the program to the App Store. This is the moment you've been waiting for, the big kahuna. You just need to get all your ducks in a row for the App Store.

Making sure everything is in order

The internet is rife with horror stories about great apps being rejected from the App Store for no reason. Fortunately, real life is a lot less scary than *The Walking Dead*. Most apps that are rejected are refused for easily avoided issues. First, make sure your app is bug free. It shouldn't crash, freeze, or have memory leaks. Any of these problems will result in rejection—and you learned how to fix all of them in the last chapter. Your program shouldn't have any partially implemented functionality. For example, don't have grayed-out buttons that pop up a Coming Soon message in an alert box.

Finally, don't run afoul of any Apple rules outlined in the App Store review guidelines. To view the guidelines, log in to your dev account and visit http://mng.bz/s9bT. Most of these guidelines are common sense, but there are some hidden nuggets that are worth discovering. For example, if your application needs the internet. Although it may seem tedious, reading the guidelines will save you time in the long run.

You need to check a number of details related to your project's configuration before submitting the app to the App Store. Examine the iOS Application Target settings, and make sure they're correct. To do so, select your project in the Project Navigator and click the project name under Targets.

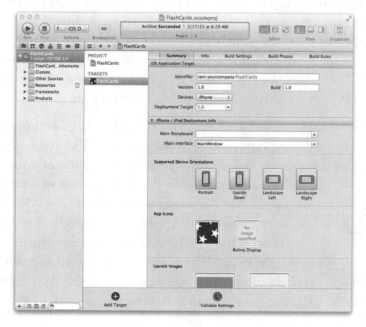

Figure 12.16
Target settings

Set the Identifier. It can be any unique string, but if you have your own internet domain, the convention is to use your address in reverse DNS format starting with com: for example, com.yourDomain.yourApp. Pay special attention to the Version Number. Apple will reject apps with version numbers less than 1.0. If your app is already in the App Store, the version number must exceed the number already in the store.

Apps submitted to the App Store are required to have icons and launch images. If you didn't do so already, add them to your app as outlined in chapter 5. Be sure to set Supported Device Orientations if your app can be rotated.

Creating your App Store application record

The App Store requires the developer to submit a number of items before an app will be considered for approval. These are the images and text that appear on your app's page in the store. It's helpful to gather the necessary files before beginning the application process. In addition to the icons included in your application, you'll need a 1024 x 1024 pixel app icon and screenshots. The easiest way to create screenshots is with the simulator. While your app is running, select File > Save Screen Shot. Apple requires screenshots to be of retinal resolution. If the status bar is visible in your application, it should be cropped out of the screenshots. Screenshots should be 640 x 920, or 640 x 960 if the app covers the status bar. You're allowed to submit images in a variety of image formats, but PNGs are probably the best option.

PNGS DON'T LOSE QUALITY LIKE JPEGS DO. YOU WANT YOUR SCREENSHOTS TO LOOK PERFECT.

In addition to the graphics, you'll need to have an application name, a description, and a list of comma-delimited keywords. The description should reflect the functionality of your application and not reference the names of competing apps. The description can be up to 4,000 characters long, but Apple recommends descriptions shorter than 600 characters. The keywords should be accurate. Violating these guidelines in an attempt at search-engine optimization is grounds for an App Store rejection. The App Store will also ask for a URL for product information and a customer-support email, so it's good to have a public email address and at least one web page ready (even if it's just a blog).

I COULD EVEN SET IT TO MY TUMBLR.

The first time you try to submit an app, you'll be asked for a company name. This company name will appear in the App Store. It doesn't have to be an actual corporation, but choose the name wisely: *this company name will be used for all your apps, and once you choose a company name, you can't change it.*

Take some time to polish the icons, screenshots, app name, and description. These are the elements that make a first impression. In addition, once your app is approved, they can't be changed without submitting a new application version; so take a breath and get these things right.

Submitting your app to the App Store

Now that you have everything you need, you're ready to submit your app to the App Store. Submissions are handled through iTunes Connect (http://itunesconnect.apple.com). Log in to iTunes Connect with your developer ID and password. If you plan to charge for your app, go to the Contracts, Tax, and Banking section and request, read, and submit the requisite contracts. You'll also have to add tax, bank, and contact information (even if the contact info is the same as your developer account).

YOU NEED TO USE A BANK THAT
CAN ACCEPT WIRE TRANSFERS.

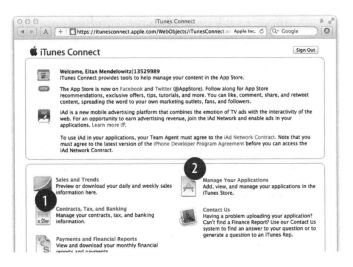

Figure 12.17
iTunes Connect
Contract section

Click Manage Your Applications and then Add New Application. If this is your first time adding an app, you're asked for your company name.

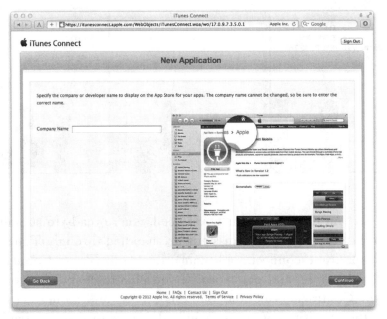

Figure 12.18   Pick a company name.

Click Continue, and then enter the language, the app name, and a SKU number. The SKU number is a code that Apple will use to report sales to you. Despite the fact that it's called a number, you can pick anything you want for the SKU, including letters. You may want to use an abbreviated app name with the version number. Also select the Bundle ID you're using to provision your app.

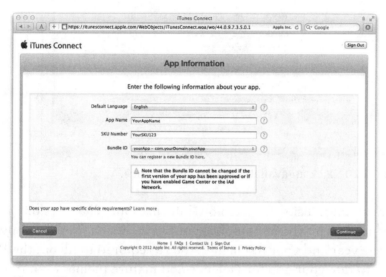

Figure 12.19 Name your app.

After you name your app, you need to pick an availability date. This is the date your app will appear in the App Store once it's approved.

I NEED TO TIME THIS WITH THE SUPER BOWL COMMERCIAL WE'RE BUYING.

Approval usually takes only a week, but if your app happens to be approved after the availability date, then the app will appear in the App Store immediately upon approval. Many developers like to time app availability with publicity. To maintain control, they pick an availability date more than a year in the future; then, when the app is approved, they choose a real availability date.

Apple requires that you choose your app's price in a fixed tier. You can choose from 88 pricing tiers with prices between free and $999.00. Click View Pricing Matrix to see how the different tiers correspond to actual app prices. Unlike much of the app information, which can only be changed when you submit a new version to the store, the price can be changed at will.

Figure 12.20   Pick an availability date and a price.

The next page asks for version information. The version number should match the version number you set in Xcode. For the copyright, enter the year and your full name. You're required to fill out the Rating section to rate your app for violence and mature themes even if the app contains nothing remotely suggestive.

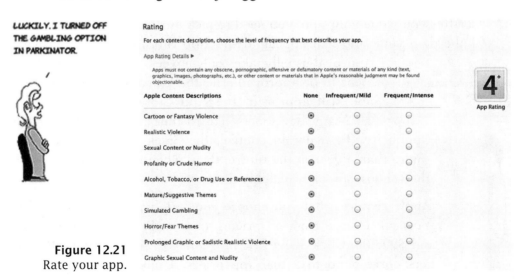

LUCKILY, I TURNED OFF THE GAMBLING OPTION IN PARKINATOR.

Figure 12.21
Rate your app.

Now you can use the materials you gathered in the last section. Enter the description, keywords, email address, and URL. Upload your icon and screenshots. When you're finished, be sure to click the Save button at lower right. Phew! You're ready to upload the app.

Click View Details under your app icon.

Then, in the upper-right corner of the next window, click Ready to Upload Binary, and answer when you're asked whether your application uses encryption (which is related to the USA export restrictions). Click Continue.

Versions

Figure 12.22
Click View
Details.

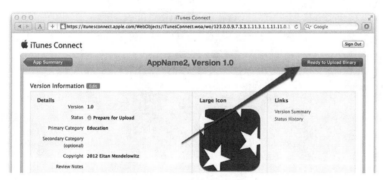

Figure 12.23   Click Ready to Upload Binary

The actual uploading of your app is done though Xcode and not through the iTunes Connect website. Return to Xcode, and open your project. Choose iOS Device as the target.

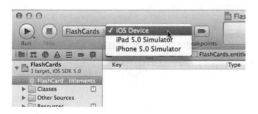

Figure 12.24   Set the target.

Edit the active compilation scheme by clicking the project name and choosing Edit Scheme.

Figure 12.25
Edit the compilation scheme.

Change Build Configuration to Release.

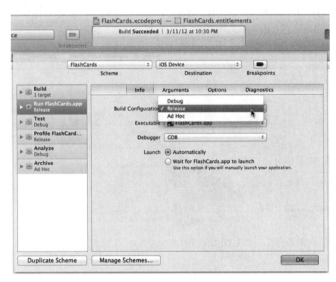

Figure 12.26   Change Build Configuration to Release.

Choose Product > Archive. Xcode will build a release version of your application, and it should automatically open the Archives tab of the Organizer. If not already selected, select the archive you just built and click Validate. If your app validates without any errors — drumroll please — click Submit.

WE'RE SO CLOSE ...

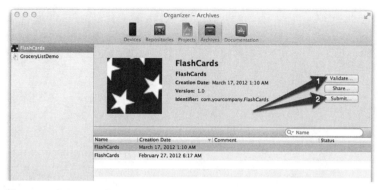

Figure 12.27   Submit your app.

Now comes the hardest part of the process: waiting for approval. Assuming all goes well, Apple should approve your app in under a week.

Congratulations!

You've installed your app on your phone and distributed it to friends and testers using ad-hoc distribution. You have an iTunes Connect account, and you know how to place apps in the iTunes App Store. It was a long haul, but you did it! You're officially a full-fledged iOS developer.

Online resources for iOS app developers

Frameworks and libraries

Here is a list of useful iOS libraries to add functionality to your app:

- *Cocos2d*—www.cocos2d-iphone.org/. A framework for creating 2D games on iOS.
- *Three20*—http://three20.info/. Originally created for the Facebook app. A collection of useful GUI controls.
- *Tapku*—https://github.com/devinross/tapkulibrary. A collection of useful components, such as CoverFlow.
- *ASIHTTPRequest*—https://github.com/pokeb/asi-http-request. Makes interacting with web servers much easier than the functionality included in Objective-C.
- *ShareKit*—http://getsharekit.com/. Provides ways of sharing with many more services than are in iOS.
- *Core Plot*—http://code.google.com/p/core-plot/. Provides comprehensive support for 2D graphs.
- *CrashKit*—https://github.com/kaler/CrashKit. Lets you catch crashes and have the user send a detailed report directly to your servers.

Design resources

These sites provide backgrounds, icons, and other inspiration for your app's graphic design:

- *Nathan Barry's 25 Free iOS Design Resources*—http://nathanbarry.com/25-free-ios-design-resources/. A comprehensive list of places to get icons, PSDs, game art, and textures.

- *Dribbble's iPhone feed*—http://dribbble.com/tags/iphone. Dribbble is like Twitter for designers. Go there to be inspired.
- *99 Designs*—http://99Designs.com. Not free, but a good way to get a professional icon on a budget. You sponsor a contest and award the prize to the designer whose icon you want to use.
- *The Noun Project*—http://thenounproject.com/. A collection of free black-and-white vector icons for a huge variety of situations. They aim to cover every noun.

App sketching

Sketching your app with these utilities will make your life a little easier:

- *Keynote Kung-Fu*—http://keynotekungfu.com/. iOS templates for Keynote.
- *AppCooker*—www.appcooker.com/. Full-featured app-mocking iPad app.
- *iMockups*—www.endloop.ca/imockups/. Another iPad app focused on mocking. Somewhat less expensive than AppCooker.
- *Balsamiq Mockups*—www.balsamiq.com/. High-quality desktop and web-based mockup software.
- *Printable templates*—http://mng.bz/URA4. If you want to use a pen and paper, these printable templates from Speckyboy Design Magazine will make it easier.

Simulating, deployment, and other tools

The built-in support for simulating, deployment, and developing in Xcode is good enough to start, but you'll want to check out these tools as you do more:

- *iSimulate*—www.vimov.com/isimulate/. Use your iPhone to provide accelerometer, GPS, and multitouch events to the simulator.
- *Accelerometer-simulator*—http://code.google.com/p/accelerometer-simulator/. Open source solution for getting accelerometer events from the device to the simulator.
- *TestFlight*—https://testflightapp.com/. The easiest way to deploy apps to non-developer beta testers. Makes ad-hoc deployment a breeze.
- *UDID Sender*—http://mng.bz/60yC. Free iOS app to send the UDID of a device via email. Necessary for ad-hoc deployment to the device for testing.
- *PonyDebugger*—http://mng.bz/O1ej. Tool to see your app's network traffic and Core Data from your desktop browser.

Index

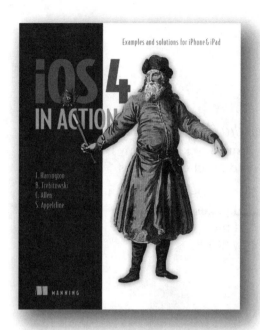

iOS4 in Action
Examples and Solutions for iPhone & iPad

by Jocelyn Harrington
    Brandon Trebitowski
    Christopher Allen
    and Shannon Appelcline

ISBN: 978-1-617290-01-5
504 pages
$44.99
June 2011

iOS in Practice
by **Bear Cahill**

ISBN: 978-1-617291-26-5
304 pages
$44.99
November 2012

For ordering information go to www.manning.com

MORE TITLES FROM MANNING

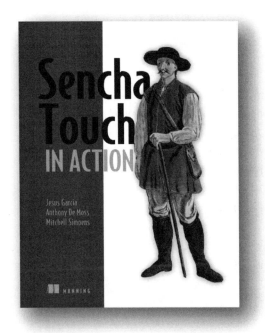

Sencha Touch in Action
by Jesus Garcia, Anthony De Moss,
 and Mitchell Simoens

ISBN: 978-1-617290-37-4
320 pages
$44.99
July 2013

50 Android Hacks
by Carlos Sessa

ISBN: 978-1-617290-56-5
216 pages
$34.99
June 2013

For ordering information go to www.manning.com

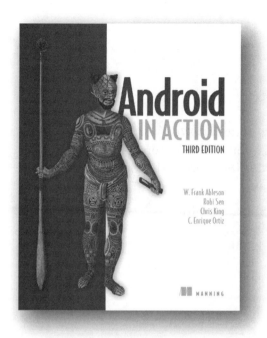

Android in Action, Third Edition
by W. Frank Ableson, Robi Sen,
　Chris King and C. Enrique Ortiz

　ISBN: 978-1-617290-50-3
　664 pages
　$49.99
　November 2011

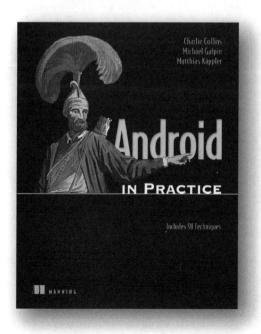

Android in Practice
by Charlie Collins, Michael D. Galpin,
　and Matthias Kaeppler

　ISBN: 978-1-935182-92-4
　648 pages
　$49.99
　September 2011

For ordering information go to www.manning.com

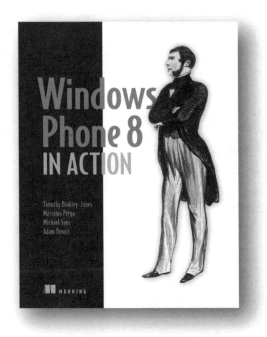
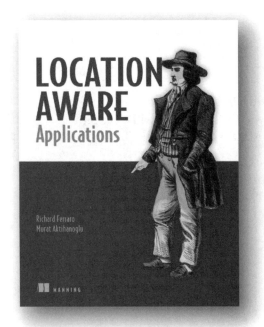